ARCHBISHOP RIORDAN HIGH SCHOOL

T0016068

DATE DUE

GAYLORD

PRINTED IN U.S.A.

★ OLD HICKORY ★

Andrew

Jackson
AND THE
AMERICAN PEOPLE

ALBERT MARRIN

DUTTON CHILDREN'S BOOKS ★ NEW YORK

200626

The publisher wishes to thank those institutions and individuals who granted permission to reproduce works and for their kind cooperation in the realization of this book.

PHOTO CREDITS: Pages 17, 23, 33, 39, 54, 85, 87, 95, 108, 127, 133, 147, 152, 189, 206, 231, 232, courtesy of the author; pages 19, 20, 21, 29, 31, 46, 49, 57, 67, 75, 78, 80, 84, 98, 100, 101, 103, 112, 115-124, 128, 130, 138, 145, 148, 153, 155, 157, 161, 162, 169, 173, 175-177, 180, 182, 184, 191, 193-195, 198, 203, 205, 208, 216, 220, 224, 225, 227, 228, 230, 236, 240-243, courtesy of the Library of Congress; pages 63, 65, 69, courtesy of The Hermitage: Home of President Andrew Jackson, Nashville, TN; page 93, courtesy of the Smithsonian Institution; page 150, courtesy of the Metropolitan Museum of Art, Gift of I. N. Phelps Stokes, Edward S. Hawes, Alice Mary Hawes, and Marion Augusta Hawes, 1937. (37.14.34); pages 164, 217, courtesy of the White House; pages 188, 245, courtesy of the National Portrait Gallery; page 229, courtesy of Boston Athenaeum; page 244, courtesy of George Eastman House.

Library of Congress Cataloging-in-Publication Data

Marrin, Albert.
Old Hickory : Andrew Jackson and the American people / by Albert Marrin.—1st ed.
p. cm.
Includes bibliographical references (p.   ) and index.
ISBN 0-525-47293-2
1. Jackson, Andrew, 1767-1845—Juvenile literature. 2. Presidents—United States—Biography—Juvenile literature. [1. Jackson, Andrew, 1767-1845. 2. Presidents.] I. Title.
E382.M37 2004
973.5'6'092—dc22
2003028299

Published in the United States by Dutton Children's Books,
a division of Penguin Young Readers Group
345 Hudson Street, New York, New York 10014
www.penguin.com

Maps and book design by Richard Amari

Manufactured in China   ★   First Edition
2 4 6 8 10 9 7 5 3 1

For Jeffrey Odel and Howard Eggers: keepers of the vision

CONTENTS

Andrew Jackson was eight feet tall.
His arm was a hickory limb and a maul.
His sword was so long he dragged it on the ground.
His every friend was an equal. Every foe was a hound.

Andrew Jackson was a Democrat,
Defying kings in his old cocked hat. . . .
He licked the British at Noo Orleans;
Beat them out of their elegant jeans. . . .

Yes,
Yes,
Yes!
By the Eternal!
Old Andrew Jackson!

—Vachel Lindsay, "The Statue of Old Andrew Jackson," 1918

OLD HICKORY

PROLOGUE

UP FROM THE PEBBLES

Himself! The great God absolute! The center [of] our divine equality . . . Bear me out in it, thou great democratic God! . . . Thou who didst pick up Andrew Jackson from the pebbles; who didst hurl him upon a war-horse; who didst thunder him higher than a throne! . . . Bear me out in it, O God!

—HERMAN MELVILLE, *MOBY-DICK,* 1851

Sometime in the 1850s, James Parton, America's first best-selling author of biographies, boarded a southbound train in New York City. A few years earlier, in 1845, Andrew Jackson, seventh president of the United States, had died at The Hermitage, his plantation near Nashville, Tennessee. To gather material for his planned, three-volume *Life of Andrew Jackson* (still a vital source for historians), Parton interviewed people who had known his subject as a youngster.

In Salisbury, North Carolina, Parton met a lady who said she had been acquainted with Jackson when he studied law there more than seventy years before. She recalled her amazement at learning how, in 1824, he had won nomination for president of the United States. "What!" she exclaimed. "Jackson up for President. *Jackson? Andrew* Jackson? The Jackson that used to live in Salisbury? Why, when he was here, he was such a rake that my husband would not bring him into the house! . . . Well, if Andrew Jackson can be president, anybody can!"[1]

Perhaps she told Parton the truth. Perhaps not. It does not matter; the *idea* hit the mark. For if a person like Andrew Jackson could reach for the highest office in the land, and do so without violence, America was truly a marvel among nations.

Americans saw Jackson as unique, a person who *always* stirred strong emotions in others. There was nothing "neutral" or "low-key" about him. He was a hard, relentless man who never shirked a quarrel; you might hate him or love him, but you could never ignore him. He forced you to notice him, like a tornado or an earthquake.

Opponents called Jackson "brute," "tyrant," and "dictator." When Jackson died, Philip Hone, a wealthy New York merchant, wrote in his diary: "Now, to my thinking, the country has greater cause to mourn on the day of his birth than on that of his decease. This iron-willed man has done more mischief than any man alive." An iron will he surely had. Soon after his death, the story goes, a visitor asked a Hermitage slave if he thought the master had gone to heaven. After a moment's thought, the man replied, "If General Jackson wants to go to heaven, who's to stop him?"[2]

That same iron will sometimes made him seem reckless and headstrong. He had a ruthless quality that at times led him to push the bounds of legality, and even go beyond them. General Jackson violated treaties which the U.S. government made with foreign countries as if they did not apply to him. President Jackson appeared ready to wreck the nation's financial system in his "war" against the Bank of the United States. Yet he also promised to hang anyone who threatened secession; that is, leading their state out of the Union because they disagreed with its laws. For these actions, fellow Americans both reviled and applauded him.

Jackson was a complicated man, a man of many contrasts and qualities that still amaze and puzzle us. Perhaps that is part of why he is so interesting. Yes, he could be a holy terror. Quick to anger and slow to forgiveness, he was stubborn, arrogant, moody, and sharp-tongued. When Jackson lashed out, his foes were not merely mistaken "opponents." They were "degraded," "cowardly," "traitorous," "unchristian wretches" who lied through "polluted lips." A bully, he hated anyone who crossed him. When Jackson hated, it was with a fury that consumed his entire being. He never forgot an "insult," always seeking what he called "retributive justice"—revenge. When he spoke of punishing a foe "unto death," one had to take him seriously. Of all our presidents, only he and Theodore Roosevelt killed another man with his own hand; he in an illegal pistol duel, and Roosevelt in battle during the Spanish-American War.

Yet Jackson could also be charming and tender, courteous and generous— qualities that inspired fierce loyalty. A boy soldier during the American Revolution, he became the only president to have been a prisoner of war—at the ripe old age of thirteen! A man of legendary courage, he never fled danger.

Jackson craved affection and amply repaid it, particularly from children and women. Although so much of his story concerns war and politics, his relationship with his wife is also a love story. Perhaps theirs was the greatest romance in American history, for it is true, not the figment of some writer's imagination. Few men ever loved a woman more than Jackson loved Rachel, his wife of thirty-eight years. Rachel was everything to him, and everyone knew it. Her death soon after his victory in the presidential election of 1828 left him devastated. He spent the rest of his life mourning "the dear one's" loss. No day passed without him thinking about Rachel and, yes, weeping for her.

Should anyone offer a prize for our worst-educated president, Jackson would win it easily. In their education, the political leaders of his day—John Quincy Adams, Henry Clay, Daniel Webster, John C. Calhoun, Martin Van Buren—towered over him. Unlike them, Jackson knew little and cared less about literature, art, science, philosophy, or music. Still, he was no fool—far from it. Jackson combined keen intelligence with native wit and a "gut" feeling about people and situations. That feeling seldom led him astray. It often allowed him to grasp the essence of a problem before others, more learned than he, could express it in words.

Jackson captured the nation's imagination as nobody had since George Washington, or would again until Abraham Lincoln. He first came to national attention as a victorious general who inspired admiration and gratitude. A citizen would have to have been a hermit not to know the details of his defeat of the British at New Orleans in 1815. Thus the nicknames "Old Hickory," because of his toughness, "the General," or simply "the Hero." These stuck with him after he moved into the White House, making him the first president to carry a nickname there.

Old Hickory's name and image appeared everywhere, on nearly every kind of object imaginable. Some found this too much to bear. An indignant reader voiced his irritation in a letter to the editor of an Ohio newspaper:

Sir, a man can't get shaved without feeling his presence or his razor or his box. No barber conceives his shop sufficiently decorated to receive customers without this resemblance of his chieftain. . . . We have Jackson hats, and Jackson coats, and Jackson jackets, and Jackson trousers, and Jackson boots, and Jackson slippers. From our public squares to the country taverns, from the Hall of State to our modest homes, all is Jackson, Jackson, Jackson. Why, sir, a man can't enter into the retirement of his bedchamber, but he may see his head, his services, and maybe now, sir, his . . . wounds displayed on the curtains of his windows, or his couch.[3]

Jackson's name and ideas—about slavery, Native Americans, the power of the presidency—defined an earlier era in American history. He so dominated his times that, when he left office in 1837, a newspaper, the Chicago *Democrat*, made a prediction. In years to come, it said, those now too young to take part in public affairs would boast, "I was born in the Age of Jackson." We still call the three decades after 1815 "the Age of Jackson." One of our greatest modern historians, Arthur Schlesinger Jr., took this as the title of his famous book on the Jacksonian era.[4]

Jackson understood ordinary people better than any politician of the time. He himself started out ordinary. Deep down, he felt what they felt, knew what they wanted, how they looked at life. He never lost the "common touch," the ability to relate to even the most humble person. One day, for example, the presidential carriage halted at the door of a roadside tavern in Maryland. Jackson went inside by himself, sat by the fireplace, and began puffing on his long-stemmed pipe. The Hero seemed so plain, so human, that passengers from a stagecoach pulled up chairs and began to chat with him. Jackson "shook hands with us, politely enquiring concerning our health," one reported. Just then, an Irish immigrant, a farm laborer, came in. The man wore tattered clothes, tracking up the floor with his muddy boots. He had drunk too much whiskey, and it showed.

"Gineral," said he, "folks say you are a plaguey proud fellow, but I do not see as you are."

The passengers snickered at the crude fellow. Not the president of the United States. "It is like a great many other things folks say of me, there is no truth in it," Jackson replied in a respectful tone.

Moments later, the stagecoach driver tooted his trumpet, calling passengers to board at once or stay behind. As they hurried from the tavern, they saw the two men deep in conversation. The laborer had taken a seat and was leaning across the table, speaking to the president face-to-face, as an equal. It was, a passenger recalled, "a striking picture of *democracy.*"[5]

The first president to be born in a log cabin, Jackson came into the world poor. Whatever he achieved, he did on his own, against long odds. For countless Americans, his life gave vivid proof that ordinary men could become self-made men, breaking with the past and grasping life's rewards just as he had done. Like him, they believed every *white* man should have a fair chance in life. Jackson's life demonstrated how with brains, work, grit, and the right to use them, average Americans could better themselves. Abraham Lincoln would call it "the right to rise."

Every white man! Like most white Americans of his day, Jackson saw the world through the prism of racial prejudice. If the belief that one group or race is inferior to another is racism, then Jackson was a racist, although that term did not exist in the early nineteenth century. Old Hickory believed that, when it came to Native Americans and African-Americans, whites were superior in their morality, intelligence, and ability. Thus, to him, these "inferiors" were not entitled to the same rights as whites. Nor did he believe women, whatever their color, were on an equal footing with men. Although Jackson worshiped his wife, and always defended women, he believed they belonged in their "proper sphere." A woman should stay at home, raising children and being her man's best "helpmate."

Jackson rose to power at a time of dramatic change in the fledgling United States. The industrial revolution had begun to transform America from a land of farms and villages into a land of factories and cities. Steamboats and railroads moved people and things farther, faster, and more cheaply than ever before. Nearly all white men had gained the right to vote. Waves of settlers flooded into the Western territories, soon to become states, drawn by a burning desire to better their lives.

As always, there is more than one side to an issue, more than one way of seeing things, of justifying actions. Whites usually considered Western lands theirs for the taking, part of an inevitable "march of progress," a "Manifest Destiny" ordained by God. To them, the Native Americans, the current inhabitants of those lands, were "barbarous," "savage," "heathen"; that is, people who did not see the world as the newcomers did, or make the "best" use of the land by farming. True, many tribes raised corn (maize) and rice; mostly, however, they had a mixed economy, combining agriculture with hunting and gathering wild plants. For them, land was not a "commodity," not merely something to use up and abandon, as whites often did. The land was sacred in itself, "the mother that nourishes us all." So were the other living beings, animals and plants, that shared the land with humans. And the coming of the whites threatened not only tribal homelands. Native Americans saw a brutal invasion that threatened to destroy a good life, a holy life, a life worth preserving—and fighting for—at any cost. The result was war and cruelty in which each party believed it had perfect justice on its side. When Native Americans were finally driven away, cotton plantations worked by enslaved black people often rose on their former lands. Similarly, for these victims, "progress" meant shattered families, degradation, and exploitation.

Change is seldom smooth or easy. In the Age of Jackson, as in our own time, big changes raised big questions. Could America, or any nation for that matter, survive democratic rule? History offered no encouragement here; the democracies of ancient Greece and Rome had all ended in corruption, civil war, and dictatorship.

Should government aid or resist the new economic forces? If so, how and by how much?

What rights, if any, did Native Americans have to the lands they had inhabited for countless generations before Europeans "discovered" the New World? Could "superior" whites forcibly remove them in the name of "civilization"?

What about black people? Was it right or wrong to enslave them? If wrong, how should slavery be ended, and at what cost?

What price "progress"?

Jackson had strong convictions about these and other questions. Many Americans disapproved of his answers; many, including historians, still do. Yet all agreed that he never shied away from difficulty. Even political enemies respected his sincerity. Of these, Massachusetts senator Daniel Webster paid him the supreme tribute. "General Jackson," said Webster, "is an honest and upright man. He does what he thinks is right, and does it with all his might." Unfortunately, what he thought right might cost innocent people dearly.

In the long run, we can only judge good intentions by their results. Jackson's decision to remove Native Americans from their homes in the South created untold suffering for Indian tribes and thus became a blot on the honor of the United States.[6]

Some historians have described Jackson as "the first modern President in American history, the first to conceive himself as the head of a democracy." Jackson was a democrat in the true sense of the word. He believed in what the ancient Greeks called the *demos,* the people, with all his heart. He had total faith in the goodness and wisdom of free people, whatever their wealth, occupation, social position, or education. To him, the people's will was absolute, and the majority always right.[7]

Jackson influenced the development of the presidency in key ways. Those who held office before him had a narrow view of their place in our system of government. They believed Congress, the legislative branch of our government, should make laws and the president, the executive branch, enforce them, provided the laws squared with the Constitution. Jackson disagreed. Seeing himself not only as head of state, but as leader of the whole nation, he vastly increased the power of the presidency. Since the whole people elected the president, Jackson demanded to be a partner in lawmaking with Congress. Not only must the president enforce the laws, as the Founding Fathers intended, but, Jackson insisted, he must also have a leading role in shaping them. So it is today.

Jackson's vision of presidential power led him to become a creator of the Democratic Party, today the world's oldest existing political party. Its two greatest twentieth-century presidents took him as their model of courage and determination. In November 1934, in the depths of the Great Depression, with 10 million Americans jobless, Franklin D. Roosevelt visited The Hermitage. FDR had undergone stinging attacks over the New Deal, his policies for rebuilding the economy, as Jackson had a century earlier. FDR identified with his predecessor, finding in him a source of personal strength. Upon leaving the mansion, he said: "The more I learn about old Andy Jackson, the more I love him." FDR saw himself as the modern Andrew Jackson, fighting for the people against the special interests that wanted to use the government for their own benefit. Of Jackson, Roosevelt said:

An overwhelming proportion of the material power of the Nation was arrayed against him. The great media for the dissemination of information and the molding of public opinion fought him. Haughty and sterile intellectualism opposed him. Musty reaction disapproved him. Hollow and outworn traditionalism shook a trembling finger at him. It seemed sometimes that all were against him—all but the people of the United States. . . . History so often repeats itself.

When FDR died, he was succeeded by Vice President Harry S. Truman, another Jackson admirer. Nicknamed "Give-'em-Hell Harry," Truman saw something of his own grit and determination in the seventh president. A prized possession was a small bronze statue of Jackson on horseback.[8] Truman called Jackson "my favorite president," because "he knew what was right for the country and for the average man and woman, and he went to work to try to accomplish what was right even when his action wasn't very popular."[9]

Above all, Jackson held that the United States must always be united—one nation, indivisible. In the 1830s, many Southerners opposed his idea, claiming that a state could disobey a federal law, even leave the United States, if it so decided. Because Jackson backed his belief in the inviolability and necessity of union with the threat of military force, they backed down. His actions chained the monster of "secession" for nearly three decades. When it finally broke loose and eleven states seceded to form the Confederacy, he had lain in his grave for nearly fifteen years. Yet in that terrible autumn of 1860, before Abraham Lincoln won the presidency, countless Americans looked back to Old Hickory. Some wrote him in on their ballots, hoping that, by magic or miracle, he might rise from the dead to avert the approaching Civil War.

I

A RAW LAD

I was but a raw lad then, but I did my best.
—ANDREW JACKSON

In the last years of his life, Jackson would sit for hours on the patio of his mansion. If there were guests, as there often were, he let his mind drift back across the busy years. Old people like to reminisce.

He was proud of having achieved so much, not through formal education, but through "the college of hard knocks," as we might say today. Jackson had learned about life from living it, not from books. His path had never been smooth, the going never easy. Yet he had thrived on hardship because it tested him, forcing him to overcome each obstacle as it came along. "I have been tossed upon the waves of fortune from youthood [sic]," he wrote to a man who asked his advice about a personal matter. "I have experienced prosperity and adversity. It was this that gave me knowledge of human nature, it was this that forced into action all the energies of my mind, and ultimately caused me to progress through life as I have done."[1]

The former president knew his family's history well. In 1765, Andrew Jackson Sr., a poor man, and his wife, Elizabeth Hutchinson, a poor man's daughter, sailed from Northern Ireland. As the green hills faded into the haze, they and their sons, Hugh, age three, and Robert, age two, caught their last glimpse of the old country. It would be two years before their son Andrew Jackson came into the world.

Like so many others before them, the Jacksons sought a better life in America. We do not know the details of their voyage. Yet, like all eighteenth-century voyages, theirs must have been difficult at best, an ordeal at worst. Venturing onto the broad Atlantic in a wooden vessel was not for cowards. Ocean crossings took from six weeks to five months, depending on luck and weather. If the wind was not just right, a ship could be blown off course repeatedly; lack of wind left it becalmed, unable to move. Pirates prowled the sea-lanes; a captain reported they boarded his ship, stole everything of value, and "abused several women." Desperate men, pirates knew they lived every moment as if a hangman were following them. Capture always meant a painful, final journey "up a long ladder and down a short rope."[2]

Even a routine voyage was a struggle to stay alive. Overcrowded, filthy ships swarmed with vermin: rats, lice, fleas, cockroaches. Landlubbers, people unfamiliar with ships, suffered from seasickness, described as a "malady next only to death." With food scarce and disease abundant, many passengers died. Gottlieb Mittelberger, a German who made the voyage a few years before the Jacksons, left a chilling account of his experiences.

> During the journey the ship is full of pitiful signs of distress—smells, fumes, horrors, vomiting, various kinds of sea sickness, fever, dysentery, headaches, heat, constipation, boils, scurvy, cancer, mouth-rot, and similar afflictions, all of them caused by the age and the highly-salted state of the food, especially the meat, as well as the very bad and filthy water. . . . In the course of . . . a storm at sea many people whimper, sigh, and cry out pitifully for home. . . . Children between the ages of one to seven seldom survive the sea voyage; and parents must often watch their offspring suffer miserably, die, and be thrown into the ocean, from want, hunger, thirst, and the like. I myself, alas, saw such a pitiful fate overtake thirty-two children aboard our vessel, all of whom were finally thrown into the sea. . . . The glimpse of land revives the passengers, especially those who are half-dead of illness.[3]

Most likely, the Jacksons landed at Charleston, South Carolina, a bustling seaport that served all the Southern colonies. Charleston was a jump-off point for immigrants bound for the backcountry, or frontier, west of the Blue Ridge Mountains. Elizabeth, or "Betty," as everyone called her, had five older married sisters whose families had crossed those mountains a year or two earlier. Now the Jacksons joined them in the Waxhaw settlement, a narrow strip of land straddling the border of South and North Carolina. It took its name from the Waxhaw Indians, the native inhabitants of that area. By the time the Jacksons arrived, European diseases had wiped out nearly all the Waxhaws. The few survivors lived with the neighboring Catawba tribe.

Andrew Sr. purchased a small parcel of land at Twelve Mile Creek, on the North Carolina side of the border. He built a log cabin, cleared the trees off a few acres of land, and "put in" a corn crop. It was backbreaking work, and it probably killed him. In February 1767, he may have strained himself lifting a log. Whatever the reason, he took to his bed and soon died in agony. While Betty, pregnant with their third child, arranged for the funeral, relatives kept the "death watch." Following ancient tradition, they set the body on a table, then sat with it through the night—to scare off ghosts and goblins. The burial in the Waxhaw churchyard was a somber affair, made even more so when the body slid out of the wagon on the way. The driver and his helpers had gotten drunk "to keep out the cold." Realizing what had happened only when they reached the open grave, they rushed back to recover the body.[4]

Unable to work the farm by herself, the widow went to the home of her sister Jane Crawford. A partial invalid, Jane lived with her husband, James, and eight children on a farm in nearby South Carolina. There, on March 15, 1767, Betty gave birth to a son, naming him Andrew after his father and Saint Andrew, the patron saint of Scotland. When Jane died soon afterward, her husband asked his sister-in-law to move in and take charge of the household. Most likely, Betty was about thirty years of age. She never remarried.

Betty cared for the daily needs of thirteen people, including herself. Both physically strong and strong-minded, she was a no-nonsense person who expected to have her way. An enslaved black woman called Aunt Phyllis described her as a stout person with deep blue eyes and flaming red hair, "a very good woman, and very much respected." Always active, she spent every spare moment knitting or spinning. If she was like most other backcountry women, she also tended the livestock, even slaughtered cattle. The sight of a seemingly frail woman felling a cow with an ax blow to the head, then butchering it, amazed travelers. Betty was the most important person in little Andrew's life. No one else influenced him more than his mother. However, she was not the only influence.[5]

Every person's life is shaped by two powerful forces. We each carry the physical and mental traits inherited genetically from our parents. Yet these are only nature's raw materials; by themselves they do not make a person. Our biological heritage constantly interacts with our immediate environment, our experiences, past and present, and what social scientists call "culture." This term refers to a society's entire way of life—its ideas, beliefs, values, customs—forged over long periods of time. To understand Andrew Jackson, we must see him in relation to the culture that helped shape him. It was a special culture, one unlike any other brought by immigrants to the American backcountry.

Andrew's ancestors originally came not from Ireland, but from the lowlands of Scotland, an area bordered by England to the south. Lowlanders barely scraped by in their endless struggle to raise crops on "thin"—low-grade—land. Even the nobility, called chieftains or lairds, lived in near poverty. Worse, no day passed without the fear of violent death. Brutal cattle thieves called rustlers roamed the lowlands in large gangs. Since its kings had little power, Scotland was a country without law; lairds organized the farmers living on their lands into armies to fight one another whenever they pleased. Yet nothing compared to the English armies that invaded Scotland. For centuries, they terrorized the lowlands, burning farms, killing farmers, and kidnapping their women.

Such violence shaped the Lowlanders' view of the world. Where life is a daily battle, fighting ability becomes the main virtue. Courage was the hallmark of the Lowland man. A man stood up for his "natural rights," for if he did not, he would lose them. These included the right to be left alone by distant rulers, the right to have low or no taxes, and the right to defend one's rights by deadly force. The Lowlander believed in the "law of revenge"; that is, "an eye for an eye and a tooth for a tooth." Experience taught that an enemy would leave a Lowlander alone only if faced with a swift, bloody vengeance. Weakness encouraged attacks.[6]

Custom expected the Lowlander to be "touchy," quick to take offense, so as not to be thought cowardly. "Lord, grant that I may always be right," went the saying, "for Thou knowest I am hard to turn." For such people, disagreement was not an honest difference of opinion. No, it was a lack of trust, an insult—a challenge to fight. One's loyalty was to the family and the chief; the king came a very distant last. Families protected their members in their daily lives. Should an outsider attack a family member, the family took revenge on that person or any of his relatives they could catch. In this way, deadly feuds passed down through the generations.[7]

Chiefs were supposed to practice "goodlordship." A good lord won his followers' allegiance by fighting for them. Lowlanders took as their model Sir William Wallace, Scotland's greatest hero. As a youth, an uncle—a priest—taught him that life without liberty is meaningless:

> My son, I tell thee truly,
> No gift is like to libertie;
> Then never live in slaverie.

After slaughtering an invading English army in 1297, Wallace was captured, tortured, his body cut into quarters, and his head stuck on a pole set on London Bridge, a typical punishment in the Middle Ages.

Scotland and England became unified in the same decade as the founding of Jamestown, Virginia (1607), the first permanent English settlement in America. After that, King James I invited Lowland families to cross the Irish Sea to Ulster; that is, to the seven counties of Northern Ireland. These Scottish people belonged to the Presbyterian Church; most native Irish were Roman Catholics. Since England occupied Ireland by force, the newcomers, called Scotch Irish, were meant to help them keep the Catholics in line. Having brought their fighting ways with them, the Scotch Irish harassed their neighbors without mercy. Within a century, however, they also became victims of oppression. English lawmakers raised their taxes and prevented the sale of their farm products abroad. English landlords raised their rent sky-high. The Scotch Irish, for their part, despised everything English.

By the early 1700s, they began to turn toward America. Britain's colonies there seemed like heaven to them, a divine gift. "God has open'd a Door for [our] Deliverance," an immigrant wrote home, adding "this is a bonny country, and aw Things grows here that I ever did see grow in Ereland." America, another wrote, "is a good poor mans country where there are noe oppressions of any kind whatsoever." So began the great migration. Between 1718 and 1775, at least 150,000 Scotch Irish crossed the Atlantic. Most headed for the backcountry of the Carolinas, Pennsylvania, and Virginia. Land was cheap or free there, beyond the reach of government officials greedy for power.[8]

Immigrants had to become "seasoned"; that is, adapt their bodies and minds to their new surroundings. Seasoning proved difficult, because everything was on a larger, unfamiliar, scale. For instance, distances. Villages in the old country were usually a few miles apart—at most a few hours' walk. In the backcountry, you might travel for days without seeing another human being. Accustomed to cool weather, even in summer, newcomers had to get used to heat. "Carolina is in spring a paradise, in summer a hell" one reported.[9]

Forests of pine and hickory, oak and chestnut, maple and walnut, covered the land. "The country," a traveler wrote in the 1780s, "must be imagined as a continuous measureless forest, an ocean of trees." Passing through a forest a decade later, a British officer reported his astonishment at the "universal gloomy shade, rendered dismal by the intermixing branches of the lofty trees, which overspread the whole country [so that] the sun never shines." Branches grew so close together that, people said half-jokingly, a squirrel could leap through the treetops for a thousand miles without having to touch the ground.[10]

Creatures roamed the land and filled the sky in numbers that today seem unbelievable. Flocks of wild turkey paraded through the forests, along with herds of deer. Brown and grizzly bears grabbed anything they could eat and used their claws to tear open the nests of honeybees. Yet nothing compared to the passenger pigeons. Although the last one died in a zoo in 1914, passenger pigeons, much larger than today's common city pigeons, once existed in vast flocks, their fluttering wings sounding like the crackling of fire among dry leaves. When a flock landed, thick branches snapped like twigs. Naturalist John James Audubon described a flock he saw near Louisville, Kentucky, in 1813: "The air was literally filled with Pigeons; the light of noonday was obscured as by an eclipse; the dung fell in spots, not unlike melting flakes of snow." This was just one of scores of flocks he saw that day![11]

Immigrants brought old-country ways of speaking to the backcountry. "Scotch-Irish speech" sounded nothing like the English spoken in New England, Pennsylvania, or Virginia. Like their Lowland ancestors, backcountry people had their own pronunciation. For example, they said *whar* for where, *thar* for there, *critter* for creature, *far* for fire, and *eetcht* for itch. Their unique vocabulary included words like *hippin* (a baby's diaper), *bumfuzzled* (confused), and *honey,* a term of affection. They spoke an earthy dialect, which New Englanders found offensive. Small children, for example, they called "little shits" as a term of endearment. A grandmother, bursting with pride, would coo to an infant, "Ain't you a cute little shit." Often the names they gave backcountry places tell us something about their way of life: *Whiskey Springs, Hangover Creek, Need More, Bloodrun Creek, Breakneck Gap, Lousy Creek, Worry, Big Trouble, Killquick.*[12]

The Scotch Irish introduced the log cabin. French Canadians, the Dutch in New York, and the Germans in Pennsylvania did not build such homes. *Cabin* in Scotland and Ireland meant a tiny house of stone or hardened mud with a straw roof. In America, backcountry people built cabins of logs, the most abundant raw material. Cabins had a standard size: sixteen to seventeen feet in length and twenty-one feet wide, with a wooden roof, front and rear doors (for easy escape), and a stone chimney. Windows were of brown paper dipped in hog fat to let in some light. A log cabin had just one room, in which the family and visitors slept. Tight space meant no privacy. "They sleep altogether in one common room . . . [so] nakedness is counted for nothing," a traveler wrote. If the family lacked even a bed, everyone "pigged lovingly together" on the earthen floor.[13]

A log cabin surrounded by girdled trees. Girdling was a favorite way of killing trees in order to clear the land for planting. The picture is a detail from an 1822 watercolor by John Halkett.

Relatives usually left Northern Ireland in family groups, or within a short time of one another, as the Jacksons did. On the frontier, Scotch-Irish people lived not only as a single household of father, mother, and children but as extended families. An extended family included all members related by blood or marriage: grandparents, parents, brothers, sisters, uncles, aunts, cousins, nephews, nieces. "They called each other cousin, and the old people uncle and aunt," a traveler wrote, "meeting together very often." As in Scotland and Ireland, a large family lent support and protection in a dangerous world.[14]

A wedding brought family and neighbors together from miles around. While the women prepared a feast, the men drank whiskey. Each raised the bottle in his right fist and cried: "Here's to the bride, thumping luck and big children!" Luck *meant* big healthy children, and lots of them, too. A typical family had between seven and ten children. The more children a couple had, the more hands there were to do farm chores. Marriage was not only a joining of two families, but a military alliance for common defense. Backcountry children knew physical work, hardship, and danger as realities of daily life. It is hard to imagine a child reaching adolescence without having seen babies born and old folks die, people hurt and animals slaughtered.[15]

Size mattered. Many backcountry families thought a big girl old enough to become a wife by the age of twelve. When a boy got big enough to hold a gun, a family member gave him shooting lessons. "Every man was a soldier," a traveler reported, "and from early in the spring, till late in the fall, was almost continually in arms. Their work was often carried on in parties, each one of whom had his [gun] and everything else belonging to his war dress." War dress included a dagger or a tomahawk, which youngsters learned to throw with deadly effect.[16]

Backcountry men prided themselves on their skill with muskets and rifles. The musket was the standard military firearm. Five feet in length, it weighed eleven pounds and fired a one-ounce lead ball, called a bullet. An inaccurate, short-range weapon, it lent itself to use by large bodies of soldiers firing together at the same target. Although the rifle took longer to load, its extra-long barrel, with spiral grooves (riflings) cut into its inner surface, allowed its bullet to outreach a musket's by a hundred yards. Boys learned to handle a rifle at an early age. "I'll tell you," a farmer told a British officer, "I have got a boy at home that will toss up an apple and shoot out all the seeds as it's coming down." Betty Jackson's boy was an excellent shot, too. Able to put a bullet into the bull's-eye of a target at the first try by the age of twelve, he could then send two more into the same hole.[17]

Parents expected their sons to fight. "The rearing of male children in the back settlements," says David Hackett Fischer, an authority on early American history, was meant "to foster fierce pride, stubborn independence, and a warrior courage in the young." From an early age, boys were encouraged to show anger, to act out verbally and physically. Like their fathers, growing boys should be sensitive to "insults"—that is, any word or deed that hurt their honor. This was not merely a personal matter. Youngsters who let others shame them invited trouble, thus endangering the entire family. Parents, a visitor noted, took outbursts of anger and rudeness as signs of "spirit and smartness" in their sons. No wonder that, years later as an adult, Andrew wrote a friend, "My reputation is dearer to me than life."[18]

A frontier brawl. Backcountry men might stage vicious fights if they felt their "honor" threatened. From Davy Crockett's Almanac *for 1841.*

Grown men taught by example. Frontier fights usually began with a challenge. A man would ask whether his rival wanted to "fight fair" or "rough-and-tumble." If he chose the second, the aim was to disfigure the other fellow for life. Rough-and-tumble had one rule: there were no rules. Anything went—punching, kicking, head butting, nose biting, ear chewing, tongue pulling.

Eye gouging was in a class by itself. Fighters sharpened their fingernails and grew them extra long, like curved sickles, hardening them over a candle flame. About the year 1793, Charles William Janson, an English traveler, witnessed a typical "gouging match" in the Georgia backcountry. A crowd surrounded two men locked in battle. "We found the combatants," Janson recalled, "fast clinched by the hair, and their thumbs endeavoring to force a passage into each other's eyes; while several of the bystanders were betting on the first eye to be turned out of its socket. . . .

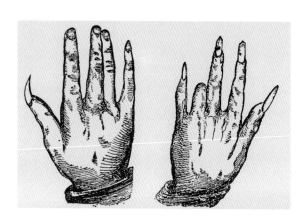

Some frontier brawlers grew their fingernails extra long, then hardened them over a candle, the better to gouge out an opponent's eyes. From Davy Crockett's Almanac for 1841.

At length they fell to the ground, and in an instant the uppermost sprung up with his antagonist's eye in his hand!!! The savage crowd applauded, while, sick with horror, we galloped away from the infernal scene."[19]

Nearly everything backcountry people needed they made themselves, trading only a few hard-to-get items like guns from traveling merchants. Waking at daybreak, families dressed in clothes of homespun cloth; they had no underwear because only those who could afford it had such "luxuries" in those days. All shoes, for frontier farmers and rich townspeople alike, were identical; wear shaped a shoe to the foot, whether left or right. Breakfast consisted of boiled cornmeal, called "mush," or hot corn bread. Most families had no chickens, and therefore no eggs. Buttermilk washed down meals; Scotch-Irish people disliked tea, describing it as "only slops." Visitors described backcountry cooking as "exceedingly filthy." After a meal, one reported, the lady of the house washed her feet in the cooking pot. As women liked to say, "The mair dirt the less hurt."[20] Apparently they believed dirt protected against sickness.

Settlers saw the natural world in brutally practical terms. Unlike Native

Frontier America, 1793, as depicted in a Plan of an American New Cleared Farm *.*

Americans, they did not think of forests as sacred places demanding respect and admiration. Nor did they appreciate a forest's beauty. To them, the only good tree was a dead tree. The forest was an enemy, concealing fierce animals and fiercer people. Forests prevented farmers from getting a living. Before a single seed went into the ground, the trees had to go. Charles Weld, an English traveler, noted their "unconquerable aversion to trees," adding that "war to extermination against the forest is the settler's rule." Benjamin Franklin shared this attitude. "By clearing America of Woods," he wrote, settlers were "Scouring our Planet" of useless things that stood in the way of progress.[21]

Felling trees by ax was dangerous, exhausting work. Whenever possible, settlers "girdled" trees by peeling a wide ring of bark from the trunk, close to the ground. This prevented the sap from rising, killing the tree and causing the withered branches to drop off. With the shade gone, the settler planted corn and wheat in the clearing. After a few years, he easily chopped down the rotting tree trunks and burned them in huge bonfires. Fires consumed living trees, too. The forest fires that swept both backcountry and long-settled areas amazed European visitors. One could hardly go anywhere east of the Mississippi River without seeing forest fires. Frances Trollope, an English lady who traveled in frontier Ohio in the 1830s, found them depressing. "The lurid glare of a burning forest was almost constantly visible after sunset, and when the wind so willed, the smoke arising from it floated in heavy vapor over our heads. [Nothing] could prevent its heavy horror wearying the spirits." Started by lightning or settlers, fires burned until they ran out of fuel or reached a natural barrier, like a river. If flames spared their farms, settlers were happy; it saved them the trouble of clearing the land themselves. Better yet, the ashes enriched the soil.[22]

Sickness and accident were dreadful enemies. Settlers were forever suffering cuts, strains, and broken bones. Diseases unknown in Europe took a heavy toll. If malaria, a disease carried by mosquitoes, did not kill outright, it tormented its victims with recurring bouts of fever, chills, and sweating. Nobody survived the "milk sick," carried by cows that had grazed on the poisonous white snakeroot plant. As the poison took effect, cows trembled violently, dying within three days. It took a week—a week of agony—for a healthy person to die after drinking the poisoned milk. Abraham Lincoln's mother died of milk sick.

Without doctors, settlers became their own physicians. Sometimes they borrowed herbal remedies from the Indians. Mostly, though, they relied on old-world superstitions. Since they lacked knowledge of the true causes of disease, these superstitions gave them the feeling that they had at least some control over their fate. Typical backcountry remedies included:

> A piece of rope by which a person has been hanged will cure epilepsy by its touch.
> The blood of a bat will cure baldness.
> For rheumatism, apply split-open frogs to the feet.
> To reduce a swollen leg, kill a cat and apply its intestines while still warm.
> To cure sore eyes, kiss a redhead.
> The brain of a screech owl, eaten raw, cures headaches.
> To take away freckles, wash your face in cobweb dew.[23]

Backcountry folks were honest, and expected honesty in others. Honesty made sense. No one, however strong or clever, could survive by their efforts

As a boy, Andrew Jackson lived with his Crawford cousins on a farm located about a mile from Waxhaw Creek in South Carolina.

alone. Helping others in need was an insurance policy, because someday you might need help. White travelers knew they could get a meal and a floor to sleep on, free of charge, in any cabin they stopped at. Those who violated their trust paid dearly. Stealing brought severe punishment. A strong farmer carried it out in public, as a warning to others, with a flexible hickory stick. The stick struck the culprit's bare back. "In a little time," a traveler wrote of one thief, "the whole of his shoulders had the appearance of a mass of blood. . . . " Murderers "danced in the air," hung by a rope dangling from a tree limb.[24]

Andrew Jackson grew up in this rough-and-tumble world. He shared the farm chores with his Crawford cousins, and a sleeping place with a brother or another male relative. Sleeping together made the best use of scarce space. It also made it easy to share all sorts of nasty things, like germs and parasites.

This may explain why Andrew got the "big itch." The slave Phyllis explained: "There is two itches, the big itch and the little itch; the little itch ain't nothing to the big itch; the big itch breaks out all over you, and do frighten a body powerful." Most likely, it was scabies, a contagious disease carried by mites, tiny insectlike creatures that burrow under the skin. Scabies drove victims frantic, making them scratch their skin raw. The only treatment was a paste made of an evil-smelling plant called pokeweed. The paste, Phyllis added, "will make you think hell ain't a mile away, but it sure does cure the itch." Andrew got rid of the big itch, but the cure left him exhausted. He also "slobbered," dribbled saliva from his mouth. This may have been due to a mild form of epilepsy, which he outgrew.[25]

Andrew attended an "academy," a glorified one-room schoolhouse where he learned to read, write, and do simple arithmetic. No scholar, he preferred running around with his friends to reading. Even so, he could read by the age of five, and at eight wrote "a neat, legible hand," a neighbor recalled. His spelling was crude, to put it mildly. For example, he wrote *vissit* for visit, *Urope* for Europe, and *devil-ope-ment* for development. Andrew wrote as he spoke; even as an adult, he might spell the same word three different ways in the same letter. Yet faulty spelling never bothered him. "It's a damn poor mind," he would say, "that can think of only one way to spell a word." He also held certain old-fashioned ideas. A family member told a White House aide, "the General did not believe the World was round."[26]

Andrew went in for competitive sports, favored in the backcountry, as in Scotland and Ireland, because they prepared one for battle. He excelled in running, jumping, and "wrasslin'"—wrestling. Wrestling suited the youngster's character best. He had a rock-hard stubbornness, a determination never to let anyone get the best of him. If he found himself in a tight spot, he gritted his teeth and refused to quit, no matter what happened. "I could throw him three times out of four," a boyhood friend recalled late in life, "but he would never *stay throwed*. He . . . never *would* give up."[27]

A gambler even as a young boy, Andrew enjoyed games of chance. Although we do not know if he ever bet on gouging matches, he often attended dogfights and cockfights, so-called sports in which animals tore each other to bits as onlookers cast their bets.[28] The earliest paper we have in his handwriting is a recipe for feeding a cock to get him into a fighting mood; it included pickled beef cut fine, served three times a day. As if born to the saddle, Andrew had a marvelous "feel" for horses. The powerful animals seemed to sense that this child was master. "Young Jackson *loved* a horse," noted James Parton in his biography of Jackson. "From early boyhood to extreme old age he was the master and friend of horses. He was one of those who must own a horse, if they do not a house, or an acre or a coat." Before entering his teens, he rode, trained, and bet on racehorses. Farmers trusted his "horse sense," asking him to appraise animals before buying them.

Fearless when it came to making decisions, Andrew had total confidence in his ability and judgment. Throughout his life, he would say: "I take the responsibility." Outgoing and loyal, he made friends easily, because he *was* a friend. A boyhood friend recalled him as "singularly tender" toward younger boys, who knew they could always turn to him for protection against bullies. He would speak up for them, even fight for them, provided they accepted his leadership without question. If not, watch out![29]

Andrew could also be overbearing and quarrelsome—a bully. James Parton said he had "a Scotch-Irish anger." So he did. Anything might set off his hair-trigger temper. At such times, rage seemed to grip his entire being. His face turned scarlet, the veins in his neck stood out, and his body trembled. The youngster swore a blue streak, sprinkling his sentences with loud "God damns" and other, coarser, expressions. Nor did he have any humor about himself; he never would. Once, some boys handed him a musket they had loaded with a double charge of gunpowder. When he pulled the trigger, the recoil knocked him on his backside. The boys enjoyed the sight, if only for a moment. An eye-witness told James Parton that Andrew sprang up, fists clenched and eyes blazing, shouting, "By God, if one of you laughs, I'll kill him!" Nobody laughed. You laughed with Andrew Jackson, never at him.[30]

Like other backcountry mothers, Betty encouraged her sons' violent be-havior. She demanded they "be men." In her view, men were tough. Men stood up for their rights. Men always faced danger without flinching. One day, five-year-old Andrew came to her in tears. Why? She did not want to know. "Stop that, Andrew," she ordered. "Don't let me see you cry again! Girls were made to cry; not boys!"

"Well, then, mother, what are boys made for?"

"To fight!" she answered.[31]

Eight years later, an eighteen-year-old beat Andrew up. His uncle James Crawford wanted to haul the offender before a magistrate. Betty would hear nothing of it. Her son might be too young and too small to fight back—now. "No, sir!" she snapped. "No son of mine shall ever appear as a complaining witness in a case of assault and battery. If he gets hold of a fellow too big for him, let him wait till he grows up some and then try it again." Betty raised her son never, ever, to forget a wrong. An unavenged wrong, she held, would en-courage future wrongs.[32]

Andrew often challenged others in the fiercest language, but did not always follow through. Lifelong friends understood that he tried to make his anger, though genuine, serve him rather than rule him. In other words, he was aggressive, not foolhardy. "No man," one friend said, "knew better than Andrew Jackson when to get into a passion and when not." His outbursts were for effect—usually. He understood that threats of violence, if convincing enough, might scare off opponents, thus avoiding fights. Similarly, loud swearing might rattle an opponent, making him do what Andrew wanted without coming to blows. Yet, if he felt he had to fight, he would suddenly cut loose with a devastating attack to gain the upper hand.[33]

Nobody ever doubted his willingness to fight Great Britain. In this, he was deadly serious. So, in 1780, at the age thirteen, he enlisted in his first war, America's Revolutionary War against the mother country.

Chinese people still use an ancient curse. To those whom they dislike and wish bad luck, they say: "May you live in interesting times." By interesting times, they mean times of trouble—times of war, famine, and disease. Had Andrew known this curse, he would probably have agreed that he had been born into *most* interesting times.

The Jacksons left Northern Ireland at the end of one troubled time and the start of another. Two years before they sailed, in 1763, the Seven Years' War had ended in Europe. English colonists called this war, which was also fought in America, the French and Indian War, because French soldiers and Native Americans joined forces to block the advance of the English inland. Under its new king, George III, Britain won the war after many hard-fought battles. To ensure peace in America, Britain made France sign a treaty surrendering Canada. France also gave Louisiana, its other possession on the North American mainland, to its ally Spain in return for its wartime help.

Victory had cost Britain dearly in lives and treasures. Now taxpayers demanded that the colonies help pay for both the last war and the cost of their future defense. In reply, lawmakers raised the colonists' taxes. It did not matter that Americans complained they had no representatives in Parliament, the British legislature. "Full-blooded Englishmen" saw Americans as losers, people who could not make it in the mother country. They believed Americans were unfit to govern themselves and must do as their "betters" dictated. Such notions did not go down well in the colonies. When the Jacksons landed, colonists were already shouting, "No taxation without representation." Slowly, at first, the seeds of another war were sprouting. We know it as the Revolutionary War.[34]

Few Waxhaw people had anything good to say about Britain. They may not have read history in books, but their folk tradition contained countless stories of English oppression. Like other Scotch-Irish parents, Betty drilled those stories into her sons' heads. At night, with flaming logs casting shadows on the cabin walls, she made them shiver with fear and anger. She described the arrogant, oppressive nobility back in Ireland. She knew from personal experience how greedy landlords, mostly Englishmen owning vast Irish estates, squeezed every penny in rent from farmers desperate to feed their families. Hero worship reinforced her stories, at least for Andrew. He relished tales of the old-time Scottish chieftains, and none more than those about William Wallace. During his White House years, he advised young men to take Wallace as a role model, as he had. "In him we find a stubborn virtue . . . always ready to brave any danger for the relief of his country or his friend."[35]

Throughout Andrew's childhood, news of the growing crisis between the colonies and Great Britain filtered into the backcountry by newspaper and hearsay. Back east, the colonies seethed with rebellion. In 1770, word came of the Boston Massacre, in which British troops fired on a crowd taunting them with curses and stones. In 1773, during the Boston Tea Party, men disguised as Indians boarded British ships and threw their cargo overboard in protest against the tea tax. Britain then cut off Boston's trade until it paid for the tea, throwing thousands out of work. In reply, the Waxhaws joined other frontier communities in sending corn and cattle to feed Boston's hungry. On April 19, 1775, protest became armed conflict as patriots fought British troops at the Battle of Lexington in Massachusetts. Two months later, they slaughtered His Majesty's troops at Bunker Hill outside Boston, then retreated when their ammunition ran out.

Legend says that some unlettered Waxhaw people selected Betty's youngest son as their "public reader." Late in the summer of 1776, a printed copy of a document dated July 4 arrived from the East. Few, if any, Waxhaw people knew the name of its author: Thomas Jefferson, a Virginian. Anyhow, nine-year-old Andrew stood on a tree stump and read the document aloud, in a squeaky voice, without "stopping to spell out the words." Perhaps he was the first to read the Declaration of Independence to these frontier folk. The story could be true. It would be appropriate if it *were* true. Yet we have no proof that it is.[36]

Although the war was still far away from the Waxhaws, its men began to prepare—just in case. Militia units practiced marching and shooting. Militiamen were part-time soldiers. Since it had always been expensive to keep a large army in the colonies, each colony saw to its own defense. The law required that a man between the age of sixteen and sixty-five own a gun and spend a few days each year at military drill. After winning its independence, the new nation continued the militia tradition. Fearing a large professional army, it relied upon citizen soldiers for its defense.

Although Andrew was too young to join the South Carolina militia, Betty encouraged him to attend the drills. He did so, gladly. One day, while cutting weeds with a scythe, he burst out, "Oh, if I were a man, how I would sweep down the British with my grass blade!" His chance came soon enough.[37]

From the beginning, the war raged almost entirely in the North: in the colonies of Massachusetts, New York, New Jersey, Pennsylvania. By 1779, however, fighting there came to a standstill. Although George Washington had forced the British to withdraw to its stronghold, New York City, neither side seemed able to give the knockout blow. Finally, Britain decided to open a new front in the South. Although thinly settled, with few large towns, the South provided corn and hogs to help feed Washington's troops; its tobacco and rice paid for war supplies bought from foreign nations. Cutting off these supplies would cripple the patriot cause, the British high command believed. Better yet, Tories, colonists loyal to Britain, lived in the South. Given the right leadership, they might play a key role in the war.

In May 1780, British reinforcements captured Charleston, South Carolina, and its 5,500 defenders. From there, Colonel Banastre Tarleton led the British cavalry and the Loyal Legion, a Tory unit, deep inland, burning farms and terrorizing civilians. Tarleton invaded the Waxhaws, routing a patriot force in a slashing raid. The Americans raised a white surrender flag and put their weapons down. Tarleton ignored the flag. For fifteen minutes, the Loyal

During the Revolutionary War, British cavalry units led by Colonel "Bloody Ban" Tarleton and his Tory allies ravaged the Waxhaws, butchering both civilians and rebel fighters.

Legion literally cut helpless men to pieces, lopping off heads and arms with their swords. Where the dead and wounded had fallen one on top of the other, Tories used bayonets as pitchforks, throwing off the topmost bodies to reach those beneath. By the time they finished, 113 Americans lay dead and 150 wounded. Backcountry people gave the colonel a nickname: "Bloody Ban."[38]

Local women tended the survivors in the Waxhaw meetinghouse, used as a makeshift hospital. The women spread straw on the floor to soak up blood, placing the wounded on the hard wooden benches. Without a doctor, they could only bandage the men's injuries and give them whiskey to dull the pain a little.

Andrew joined his mother as she tended the wounded. "None of the men had less than three or four, and some as many as thirteen gashes on them," he recalled sixty years later. Those visits left a profound impression on the youngster, deepening his respect for Betty as nothing else could. In old age, he described her as "gentle as a dove and brave as a lioness." His devotion to her would extend to all women—at least to all white women. As biographer James Parton noted, Andrew "imbibed a reverence for the character of woman"—that is, consideration for women's feelings and "good names," or moral reputations. He would not tolerate a man's insulting, let alone striking, a woman. Anyone who did so in his presence regretted it.[39]

Hugh Jackson, age seventeen, joined the patriot forces. When he died of heatstroke after a skirmish, his brothers took his place. Robert was fifteen, Andrew thirteen. Enlisting in a militia unit led by Colonel William R. Davie, a Waxhaw man, they served as mounted messengers. Colonel Davie liked the brothers, especially Andrew, whom he saw as a bold youngster willing to take risks. As a reward, he gave him a fine pistol. While Andrew never shot anybody with it, it would cost a Tory his life.

A wave of terror swept over the Southern backcountry. "The whole country is one continued scene of blood and slaughter," General Nathanael Greene wrote to George Washington. Tories slaughtered patriot prisoners, even raped and murdered their women. Patriots retaliated with horrors the Jacksons and Crawfords knew firsthand. Cousin Betty Crawford had married Martin McGary, a patriot soldier. When he came home on leave, he found his wife's freshly dug grave. She had died of fright in a Tory raid; her newborn baby survived her by a day. McGary, filled with a thirst for vengeance, hunted and killed more than twenty Tories. "But," Andrew recalled, "he was never a happy man afterwards."[40]

The Jackson brothers fought in no battles, but had several close calls. One day, at dawn, Andrew stood guard at a farmhouse where a patriot officer had spent the night. As the sun rose, he saw enemy troops getting into position for an attack. He fired his pistol, alerting the men inside the house. Moments later, his unit all bolted into the forest, leaving the enemy behind. Another time, none other than Bloody Ban Tarleton rode within a hundred yards of Andrew's hiding place. "I could have shot him," he said years later, "but he had no rifle. On the morning of April 9, 1781, the brothers' luck ran out. They became prisoners in a British cavalry raid.[41]

The officer in charge, a blowhard of a lieutenant eager to show his authority, ordered Andrew to clean his boots. Andrew couldn't abide it. He ordered! This Englishman ordered! Given Andrew's temper, his refusal was probably neither soft-spoken nor polite. We can imagine him standing with the boldness so respected by Scotch-Irish people, squaring his shoulders and looking the officer straight in the eyes.

"Sir," said Andrew, "I am a prisoner of war, and claim to be treated as such."

The lieutenant raised his sword and swung it with all his might. Andrew saw the blade moving toward his neck. Instinctively, he raised his arm to push it aside. It sliced his left hand to the bone and, continuing onward, opened a gash in his forehead. He would carry the scars to the grave. Next, the lieutenant made the same demand of Robert. Here came another refusal. Embarrassed in front of his men by two boys, the officer gave Robert an even deeper cut in the forehead.[42]

As seen in The Brave Boy of the Waxhaws, *a Currier & Ives print dated 1876, young Andrew Jackson defies a British officer and is cut with the bully's sword.*

That afternoon, soldiers marched the wounded boys and other prisoners forty miles to a jail at Camden, South Carolina. The prisoners trudged along without a morsel of food or a drop of water. Should anyone try to scoop up water from the streams they crossed, a bayonet jab kept him moving. Tories stole their shoes and jackets; Andrew lost his prize pistol. Reaching Camden, they found the jail a hellhole, its main room a large overcrowded cell reeking of human filth, sweat, and vomit. There were no medicines or blankets. Nobody treated the boys' wounds, and they became infected. Yet that was the least of their worries.

Smallpox, an extremely contagious disease (caused by a virus we now know), raged in the jail. Until it was eliminated in the twentieth century, this dreaded disease, nicknamed the "Speckled Monster," killed millions throughout the world each year. Victims developed a high fever, followed by pimples that became blisters, broke open, oozed pus, and finally formed scabs. The scabs covered the body, particularly the face, often leaving survivors blind and disfigured by deep "pits" or scars. Terrified, the brothers lay on dirty straw mats, amid horribly disfigured men. "I frequently heard them groaning in the agonies of death," Andrew would recall, "and no regard was paid to them."[43]

Before long, the brothers also came down with smallpox. Luckily, Betty had learned of their capture. She came to Camden to beg for their release because of their youth and arrived just as American and British officers arranged an exchange of wounded prisoners. Released to Betty's custody, they headed back to the Waxhaws. Borrowing two horses from a farmer she knew, she rode one and put Robert, the sickest, on the other. Andrew walked behind the horses barefoot, without a jacket, every muscle in his body aching. Heavy rains drenched them, turning the trail into a river of mud. Wet and miserable, Andrew shook with fever.

Robert died two days after reaching home. Andrew battled smallpox for several weeks, then gradually recovered. He must have had a "mild" case, since it left no marks on his face. "When it left me," he recalled, "I was a skeleton—not quite six feet long and a little over six inches thick!" Anyhow, by getting smallpox and surviving it, he gained a lifelong immunity to the disease. While recovering, he learned that patriots had captured a Tory, and someone recognized the pistol he carried. It was Andrew's. The Tory's unit

While visiting American prisoners of war, such as these aboard a British prison ship in the harbor of Charleston, South Carolina, Betty Jackson contracted typhus and died.

had murdered several people, including women. So the patriots "hanged him forthwith," and sent the weapon back to its owner.[44]

As Andrew recovered, Betty and two other women left to nurse American war prisoners. The British used several old ships anchored in Charleston Harbor as floating prisons. Hundreds of captured patriots, including Waxhaw men, lived aboard them in conditions worse than even Camden jail. After one of her visits, typhus, a disease carried by infected lice, struck Betty down. She died in October 1781, shortly after George Washington trapped a British army in Yorktown, Virginia, forcing it to surrender. As the defeated troops marched out to hand over their weapons, regimental bands played a nonsense tune called "The World Turned Upside Down." It had—for King George. That defeat convinced His Majesty's government to sue the colonies for peace.

Nobody knows where Betty Jackson is buried. Andrew never had a chance to say good-bye to her. All he had of her was a bundle of clothes her companions brought back—and his memories.

"I felt utterly alone," he said.[45]

II

MAKING HIS OWN WAY

Andrew, if I should not see you again I wish you to remember . . . [that] in this world you will have to make your own way. To do that you must have friends. You can make friends by being honest, and you can keep them by being steadfast. . . . No one will respect you more than you esteem yourself. . . . Sustain your manhood always. . . . Never wound the feelings of others. Never brook wanton outrage upon your own feelings. . . . Defend your honor.
—BETTY JACKSON'S LAST WORDS TO HER SON, 1781

A war does not end when the shooting stops and the ink dries on a peace treaty. Wars are such shattering events that, for years afterward, they continue to wound survivors in ways that they may not realize or can even explain. Such wounds are invisible, affecting the spirit, but every bit as painful as those to the body. Sometimes they never heal.

So it was with Andrew Jackson. Although he was only fourteen when the Revolutionary War ended, it stayed with him to the end of his days. The war had claimed those dearest to him, his mother and brothers. A brutal officer had nearly killed him; so had a cruel disease, smallpox. Men had died horribly before his eyes. As with so many war veterans throughout history, such ordeals did not make them less violent, but more. War toughened them, burning all fear out of them.

Having overcome the revolution's horrors, Andrew acted as if he could overcome anything life threw his way. More than that, danger and excitement became stimulants, which he seemed to crave as if they were drugs. Fighting Indians. Street brawls. Pistol duels. Another war. Political feuds. All show a willingness, even an eagerness, to court danger. As Andrew grew older, he came to understand more about himself. "I was born for storm," he would say, "and calm does not suit me."[1]

After regaining his health, he faced the questions we all must answer in growing up. Who am I? How shall I earn a living? What path should I take in life? Andrew did not record his thoughts on these matters. Perhaps he did not think about them in so ultimate a way—at least at the age of fourteen. Perhaps he preferred to drift, allowing events to take him where they would. Nobody knows exactly. We do know that he remembered his mother's last words to him, spoken before she left to nurse the American prisoners at Charleston. He often repeated and always tried to live by those words. We also know that he took a job as an assistant to a saddler, a craftsman who made saddles and other horse gear. The job lasted six months, until he found more exciting ways to spend his time.

Several well-to-do Charleston families had fled to the Waxhaws during the British occupation of their city. The young men of these families called themselves "gentlemen." An eighteenth-century gentleman did not merely speak nicely and have proper manners. The term applied to a man of "good family," one of high social standing, who did not have to do physical labor. Andrew soon became friendly with these newcomers. He found that he liked the same things as they—riding horses, running footraces, betting on cockfights—only he usually came out ahead. When British forces evacuated Charleston in December 1782, the refugee gentlemen returned. Andrew came with them. Back in Ireland, his grandfather had recently died, leaving him some money. He meant to spend it.

For the backcountry youth, visiting Charleston was like stepping into another world. Although he left no written account of this bustling port city, others did. A sailor-poet described it this way:

> Whites & blacks, all mixed together,
> Unconstant strange unwholesome weather,
> Burning heat . . .
> Dangerous to both young and old. . . .
> Mousquetous on the skin make blotches,
> Centipedes & large cockroaches.
> The water in the wells is bad,
> Which makes the inhabitants full sad. . . .
> Frightful creatures in the waters,

> Porpoises, sharks & alligators.
> No lamps of light, but streets of sand,
> And houses built on barren land. . . .
> Many a bargain, if you'll strike it,
> This is Charleston, how do you like it?[2]

Andrew liked it very much. Until then, the largest settlement he had ever seen was Camden, a village of about four hundred. Charleston was something else! He could hardly imagine so many people (16,359 in 1790) gathered in the same place at once. The city pulsed with energy and excitement. Ships lined the waterfront, their holds crammed with cargo, their masts slim wooden fingers pointing skyward. Scents of sweat and whiskey, tobacco and spices, blended in the humid air. Music and laughter came from taverns and gambling dens. Streets echoed with a babble of tongues—French, Spanish, Portuguese, and Dutch, mixed with the accents of West Africa.

Charleston was a center of the slave trade; over half its population was of African descent. Posters advertised the sale of men, women, and children, often mentioning they had survived smallpox in their native land. Since smallpox was so contagious, buyers tried to protect their investments by making sure new slaves had already had the disease. After being auctioned to the highest bidders, most did heavy labor on farms and plantations. A tiny elite became body, or personal, servants. Everyone of good family had at least one slave servant, who waited on them hand and foot. Servants helped them bathe and dress. Servants fetched whatever they wanted, carried packages, and stood behind their chairs at meals.

Andrew had grown up with slavery in the Waxhaws. Both his uncles had slaves, though probably just a few. Slave traders from Charleston marched their "chattel" up the post road, past the tiny settlement, to auctions in Charlotte, North Carolina. The youngster could not have avoided seeing these pitiful processions. Yet we can read Jackson's letters—thousands of them—without finding a hint that what Southerners called their "Peculiar Institution" ever troubled his conscience, or that he gave any thought to its morality. Slavery, for Jackson, simply *was,* a reality he accepted unquestioningly as a white man's God-given right to impose upon others.

The growing boy probably noticed that wealthier slaveholders, with more land and more slaves, were often community leaders. "A man's merit in this country," a Southerner wrote, "is estimated according to the number of Negroes he works in the field." Slaves were more than property, "hands" that worked. They were status symbols, like private jets and sleek sports cars are today. Slaves were hallmarks of the gentleman, living proof of his intelligence, ambition, drive, discipline, and success. A big-time slave owner could be said to have "arrived" in society, however humble his background. People looked up to him. He was "somebody" in the South, a person worthy of trust and respect.[3]

An ambitious man could follow a well-marked path into the Southern ruling class. Start by getting a profession: law, medicine, the ministry. Save your earnings, or borrow money from a bank or a prosperous neighbor, to buy some land and a few slaves. Grow cotton and sell it, investing the profits in more land and more slaves, increasing your human "stock" as they had children. Finally, leave your profession. Take up planting full-time, become a gentleman, and enter politics. The Scotch Irish did it this way. As poor immigrants, most opposed slavery at first. As they prospered, however, they accepted slaveholding as a means to an end and a measure of their success. Scotch-Irish settlers were, a backcountry traveler wrote, "certain in a few years to acquire money enough to buy a Negro, which they are . . . invariably ambitious to possess."[4]

Andrew admired his Charleston friends' manners, their clothes, and the respect others showed them. Somehow, he learned the latest dances; light on his feet, he enjoyed dancing. He also learned the social graces, how to dress, eat, and carry himself properly. In short, he came to see himself as a gentleman.

Meanwhile, the friends gambled and generally had a wild time. Yet, try as he might, Andrew could not keep up. Living as a gentleman cost money, something he had less and less of each day, as he lost most of his grandfather's legacy at rattle and snap, a popular dice game. Before long, he owed his landlord back rent, which he could not pay. Desperate, he bet a gambler two hundred dollars which he did not have, against his horse. If he lost, he would give the landlord his saddle and beg him to let him repay anything beyond their value later. Andrew won. Years later, he recalled leaving the table, grinning from ear to ear. Yet he had learned a lesson. "From that moment to the present time," he said, "I have never thrown dice for a wager."[5]

Back in the Waxhaws, Andrew turned to schoolteaching. Frontier school-masters seldom had good educations; they did not need them, for they only taught the basics of reading, writing, and "casting sums"—arithmetic. Preparing for class was a simple matter of staying a lesson ahead of their pupils. Discipline counted more than knowledge. Older boys might decide to test their strength against a teacher's, especially one close to them in age. For the students to learn, the teacher first had to show who was boss. This he might do with a stick, even a fistfight. Occasionally, he kept a pistol on his desk, quietly making his point. Since Andrew was a war veteran, and with such a violent temper to boot, he probably had no trouble keeping order. After a year, he tired of teaching, too; it would never give him the income to live as a gentleman. So, late in 1784, he decided to study law.[6]

The law profession held several attractions for a youngster wanting to make his way in a slaveholding society. Society considered lawyers gentlemen. There were no age or education requirements. Since the nation had few law schools, the vast majority of lawyers had never attended regular classes. You simply found an established attorney and "read law" in his office; that is, read his books under his guidance, for the books often used technical language that required explaining by a professional. To earn your keep, you copied piles of legal documents "in a fine hand." When you were ready, you took on oral examination given by a panel of district judges.

Andrew set out for Salisbury, North Carolina, seventy miles from the Waxhaws. There he entered the office of Spruce McCay, a wealthy attorney who owned twenty slaves. He lived in a tavern with other young men, also McCay's students, which suited him just fine.

Years later, townspeople described two Andrew Jacksons. One read law and attended court with his teacher. After work, however, the other Andrew would appear and go on a "tear." Soon he gained a reputation as "the most roaring, rollicking, game-cocking, horse-racing, card-playing, mischievous fellow, that ever lived in Salisbury . . . the head of all the rowdies hereabouts." He threw the "long bullet," a cannonball flung with a leather sling. He courted the girls, drank corn whiskey, smoked a pipe, and "chawed"—chewed tobacco. Andrew and his friends played practical jokes, like stealing outhouses, small sheds having one or two holes in a seat built over a pit used as an outdoor toilet. Once they smashed all the glassware in a tavern. Since Andrew received no salary, he probably paid his expenses with winnings from gambling.[7]

None of this troubled the examiners. In 1787, two judges found "Andrew Jackson a person of unblemished moral character," with "a competent degree of knowledge in the Law." Now, at age twenty, he was a full-fledged attorney.[8]

Although nobody ever described him as handsome, Jackson was an impressive figure. He had fair skin, a long narrow face with freckles, thin lips, and fine reddish-brown hair. Large blue eyes seemed to look clear through you. Oh, those eyes! If he fixed you with them, they held you in a viselike grip. His eyes mirrored his moods. When he got angry, they blazed, signaling the explosion to come. Wise men got out of the way then—fast! Thin as a toothpick, he stood six feet one inch in his stocking feet. At a time when poor diet stunted most people's growth, he towered over others, forcing them to look up when speaking to him.

Native Americans called Jackson "Sharp Knife" because he always seemed so fierce. In this engraving, we see him, sword in hand, ready for action.

Years later, Nancy Jarret, of Salisbury, drew a marvelous word portrait of the young attorney. She spoke for herself and her girlfriends; they were all about his age, and most had a crush on him.

. . . he was always neat and tidy and carried himself as if he was a rich man's son. . . . I have talked with him a great many times and never saw him avert his eyes from me for an instant. It was the same way with men. He always looked them straight in the eye, as much as to say, "I have nothing to be ashamed of and I hope you haven't." This and the gentle manner he had made you forget the plainness of his features. When he was calm he talked slowly and with very good selected language. But if much animated [excited] by anything, then he would talk fast with a very marked North-Irish brogue. . . . But either calm or animated there was always something about him I cannot describe except to say that he had *a presence,* or a kind of majesty I never saw in any other young man. . . . This I and all the other girls in Salisbury talked about among ourselves.[9]

A presence. A kind of majesty. Today, we would say Jackson had charisma; that is, personal magnetism, an ability to connect emotionally with others and bond with them. There was always a hint of danger about him, too. Although always polite to women, with men he might, if provoked, shift instantly from calm good humor to stunning violence.

John McNairy, son of a wealthy North Carolina family with political connections, was his best friend at this time. It so happened that the state's Western District stretched from the Appalachian Mountains to the Mississippi River. To pay its share of the cost of the Revolutionary War, North Carolina planned to sign over this vast area, the future state of Tennessee, to the federal government. Meanwhile, its legislature created a superior court to help keep the peace there. McNairy's family saw to it that John became the court's first judge. As a favor to his friend, he named Jackson public prosecutor.

In the 1780s, the Western District of North Carolina was the Wild West. It lay hundreds of miles beyond the settled frontier. Just getting there was dangerous; "gone west" became a slang expression for anyone who died violently, particularly at the hands of Indians. Seeking safety in numbers, settlers traveled in groups of a dozen families or more.

While waiting for a large enough group to assemble, Judge John McNairy and his friend Andrew went to Jonesborough in the eastern part of the district. Jackson rode into the village in style, as he thought a gentleman should, wearing a long coat, ruffled shirt, skintight breeches, and high riding boots shined mirror bright. He had two fine horses and a pack of purebred hunting dogs. With him also came a black woman of about eighteen, Nancy, a slave he bought for two hundred dollars, probably with money from his budding law practice or gambling. Most likely, buying Nancy had less to do with his need for a full-time servant than with the image he wished to project. Owning a slave, as we have seen, said something about one's drive, character, and abilities. Nancy surely did Jackson's housekeeping. She may also have been his sex partner, although we cannot know this for certain. Yet, as chattel—property—

we do know that, by law, slaves did not own their own bodies; their bodies were for their masters to use as they pleased. Most likely, Jackson's main reason for buying the young woman was to show off his moneymaking ability, proving that clients could trust him with their affairs.

One of the most important developments in American history occurred during Jackson's stay in Jonesborough. In July 1788, the states approved the U.S. Constitution, which set out the organization, powers, and duties of the national government. Working in Philadelphia, the framers of the Constitution created a republic, a country with a representative lawmaking body and chief of state who is not a monarch; we still pledge allegiance to the flag "and to the republic for which it stands."

Distrusting the full mass of the people—the unlanded, unlettered, unskilled, illiterate—the framers did not create a simple democracy, or government only by majority rule. A series of checks and balances prevented this by providing for a "federal system," one in which the national government shared power with the states. In turn, each branch of the national government—legislative, executive, judicial—had the power to curb, or check, the others' actions.

The legislative branch, or Congress, would make the laws. It would be "bicameral," or two-chambered. Male voters—only white men over eighteen years of age could vote—elected the first chamber, or House of Representatives, the number of representatives to be elected from each state depending on its population. To assure that representation kept pace with population, the Constitution mandated a census every ten years. Since most black Americans were enslaved, they could not vote; yet, for purposes of deciding how many representatives a state could have, each slave was counted as three-fifths of a person. Native Americans were not allowed to vote nor were they counted in the census. *State legislatures* elected the second chamber, or Senate. State residents would not vote for their senators directly, as we do today, until the year 1913. Acting together, both chambers would pass laws for the entire nation, raise taxes, and declare war.

The executive branch, led by a president, was designed to be the servant of Congress. Known as the chief executive, the president would sign laws passed by Congress to make them official, carry out the laws, be commander in chief of the armed forces, and conduct foreign affairs. Although the Constitution did not give them any role beyond that of managers, under George Washington the heads of the main executive departments became the president's cabinet, or advisers. (In the early days of the republic, the cabinet included the secretaries of state, treasury, war, navy, the postmaster general, and the attorney general, the government's chief lawyer.) Finally, a system of courts headed by the Supreme Court ruled on whether the government and states acted legally. Although the Constitution looked good—on paper—nobody knew whether the system it created would actually work. In 1788, the fate of the United States was still very much in doubt.

In September, Jackson and McNairy joined the first wagon train to use the Cumberland Road, the nation's new "highway to the West." Their destination, a tiny settlement called Nashville, lay on the east bank of the Cumberland River, a tributary of the Mississippi River.

It was an exciting journey. One night, as the party slept in a clearing, Jackson lay on his blanket smoking his pipe and gazing up at the stars. His eyelids grew heavy, and he heard "owls" hooting in the surrounding forest. Then he heard a louder hoot nearer the camp. Something about it troubled him. He grabbed his rifle and nudged the man snoring beside him.

"Searcy," whispered Jackson, "raise your head and make no noise."

"What's the matter?" Searcy grumbled, rubbing the sleep from his eyes.

"The owls—listen—there—there again. Isn't that a little *too* natural?"

"Do you think so?"

"I know it. There are Indians all around us. I have heard them in every direction. They mean to attack before daybreak."

Quietly, they awoke the camp. Leaving the fires burning, the settlers hitched their horses to the wagons and left without seeing Indians or, apparently, being seen by them. An hour later, a party of hunters found the abandoned campsite and fell asleep beside the fires. Before dawn, Indians killed all but one, who lived to tell the story. Had it not been for Jackson, the entire wagon train might have been wiped out.[10]

After six weeks on the Cumberland Road, the party reached Nashville in late October. Jackson did not know it then, but it would be his home for the rest of his life. In 1788 the village had a few hundred citizens, a few dozen log cabins, a shabby log courthouse, and two taverns. It had existed for nine years, yet nobody felt safe there. For Nashville lay deep in Cherokee country, a land ravaged by war.

That war was part of a conflict that began with what historian Francis Jennings has called "the Invasion of America." Everywhere in the New World, the coming of Europeans brought enormous change to the lives of native peoples, not least in the way they made war. Traditionally, in North America, Indian warfare in the woodlands east of the Mississippi River was not a nightmare of butchery. Although some tribes fought often, even then they tried to limit war's effects. That made sense, for tribes were small, and heavy losses threatened the survival of everyone—including the "winners." Thus, warriors did not destroy an enemy's food, because that would starve innocent women and children, especially during the winter. Nor did they rape women, let alone deliberately kill them or their children. "We have never heard that they have ever permitted women or children to be killed," said a Dutch soldier of the tribes of colonial New Netherland, the future New York.[11]

Battles among Native American warriors were more like deadly games to gain honor for courage than struggles against enemies who wished to exterminate one another. The early colonists noticed that Native Americans always seemed to fight with moderation. For example, an English soldier, writing in the 1630s, said Indian warfare "is more for pastime, than to conquer and subdue enemies." At about the same time, Roger Williams, a clergyman, noted that war among the New England tribes was "farr lesse bloudy and devouring than the cruell Warres of Europe." Warriors broke off attacks that might be too costly to themselves, sparing the enemy, too.[12]

Mercy made sense, as it always does. If a relative died, whether in a fight or from natural causes, the family might adopt a captive in their place. Widows often married male captives. "Washing away" their past in a stream made captives cherished members of the tribe and their new families. In this way, tribes kept strong by replacing lost members with outsiders. It made no difference whether the outsiders were Indians, whites, or escaped black slaves. Most adoptees came to love the Native American way of life. When recaptured and offered the chance to rejoin white society, whites often refused.[13]

Europeans made war differently. For centuries, long before Columbus set sail, European armies fought *ad terrorem,* Latin for terrorism. Roving armies destroyed enemy food supplies, burned cities, and slaughtered their inhabitants. Whites brought this style of warfare to the New World.

Starting with the first colonies in Virginia and Massachusetts, settlers went in for wholesale terrorism. During the Pequot War of 1637, for example, the Puritans of Connecticut set fire to a sleeping village beside the Mystic River and shot those who managed to escape the flames. About the same time, Dutch soldiers in New Netherland used terror to drive Indians from their lands. A Dutch writer accused his countrymen of "murdering so many in their sleep," sparing no one. "Infants were torn from their mothers' breasts, and hacked to pieces in the presence of their parents." During the Revolutionary War, many tribes joined the British in hopes of protecting their lands. Patriots struck back—hard. George Washington set the example for ruthlessness. The Iroquois of New York had a name for him: the Town Destroyer. This was no exaggeration. At the mention of his name, a chief said, "Our women . . . turn pale and our children cling to the necks of their mothers." By then, however, some warriors in some tribes began to violate the traditional rules, copying white methods. Even so, Indian warfare was never the nightmare of savagery portrayed in the "captivity narratives," bloodcurdling yarns similar to today's horror movies, and equally false.[14]

Centuries before the first Europeans crossed the "great salt water," or Atlantic Ocean, the Cherokee had lived in Tennessee, or Tinnase, named for a famous chief. The largest and most powerful Native American tribe in the region, the Cherokee combined hunting with growing crops like corn, squash, and melons. They lived in towns built in forest clearings. These towns were larger, often with more than a thousand inhabitants, cleaner, and better organized than most white frontier settlements at their outset. Each had a council house, regular streets, storage buildings, and a central plaza used for ceremonies. For safety, tribesmen surrounded their towns with palisades, or logs driven upright into the ground side by side to form a high wall.

The Cherokee were noted for their courage in battle. Their warriors, trained to fight as youths, fought in self-defense and for revenge. A distant tribe might attack a party of trespassing Cherokee hunters. Perhaps a man died in a fight while visiting another Cherokee town. In either case, the victim's family, and often his entire town, felt obliged to take revenge. The coming of the whites, with their guns and land hunger, threw the Cherokee world into turmoil. Settlers seized tribal lands, cutting down vast stretches of forest to clear the way for planting. Where Cherokee hunters took only enough game to feed their families, and then with prayers to the animals' spirits for forgiveness, settlers killed vast numbers of animals for food and "sport." Worse, traders corrupted many Native Americans with "rotgut," cheap whiskey. In the early 1800s, William James, an English traveler, reported:

> Fatal day! When the 'Christian people' first penetrated the forests, to teach the arts of 'civilization' to the poor Indian. Till then, water had been his only beverage. . . . Now, no Indian opens his lips to the stream that ripples by his wigwam . . . [But] he and his [family] wallow through the day in beastly drunkenness.[15]

To save themselves, then, the Cherokee fought, as any people would, when they saw strangers threatening to take everything that belonged to them.

Arriving in Nashville, Jackson found the frontier aflame, as his ancestors had found the Scottish Lowlands. Old records read like catalogs of horrors. "Indians attacked the house of Mr. Thompson," says one, "killed and scalped the old man, his wife, his son and a daughter, and made prisoners of Mrs. Caffrey, her son, a small boy and Mrs. Thompson." Another tells how Indians "killed Benjamin Williams and party, consisting of eight men." Striking within seven miles of Nashville, Cherokee war parties killed about one person every ten days.[16]

Extended families often lived in "stations," clusters of log cabins surrounded by a palisade. They always "forted" one cabin, called a blockhouse, in case Indians broke through the palisade. A blockhouse had heavy wooden shutters over the windows, loopholes drilled at different levels in the walls, and the inner walls lined with sandbags. A cellar provided shelter for the youngest children and a fireproof storeroom. During an attack, women and older children loaded and passed rifles to the men at the loopholes. Water buckets stood ready, should the attackers use flaming arrows.

Jackson reached Nashville spoiling for a fight. This, partly, was due to his

Frontier Tennessee was a scene of constant strife between Native Americans and white settlers. Here Cherokee warriors attack a "station," a tiny outpost surrounded by a wooden palisade. From Amos Kendall, Life of General A. Jackson, 1843.

own feistiness and his struggles during the American Revolution. Equally important, surely, was his upbringing. From an early age, Jackson had disliked Indians. While the Waxhaw tribes could no longer threaten war, occasionally raiding parties from the west and north came too close for whites' comfort. Meanwhile, settlers and local Indians quarreled over all sorts of petty things, like broken fences and stray farm animals. More than that, Betty instilled in her sons racist beliefs, typical on the frontier, toward Native Americans. She taught that Indians were bad—all Indians. We do not know if she bore them a special grudge; neither she nor her family appear to have suffered at their hands. Still, a neighbor recalled, she was "at dreadful enmity with the Indians." Just as she encouraged her sons to despise the British, she made them into "inveterate haters of the Indians." In effect, she poisoned their minds with racial hatred.[17]

The poison had its effect. Friends remembered Andrew as "always ready to pursue a party of Indians" that ventured close to Nashville. One described him as "mad upon his enemies"; another said he had "a great ambition for encounters with the [Cherokee]." Several times he joined attacks on Cherokee villages. Later, tragically, he would bring more suffering to Native Americans than any single white person in American history, an evil which must forever stain his memory. Yet that lay in the distant future. Little did he know, in 1788, that he was approaching another turning point in his life.[18]

Lawyer Jackson did not work out of a regular office, but from living quarters he rented at the Donelson family station. John Donelson, a founder of Nashville, had come from Virginia with his wife, Rachel, and their eleven children. When Indians or white bandits killed him in the forest, his widow decided to take in boarders. She wanted them not for the money, but because more men meant more rifles for defense. Jackson shared a cabin with another lawyer, John Overton. The two men formed a lifelong friendship, and Overton would later become one of Jackson's earliest backers for the presidency.

Widow Donelson had a daughter, also named Rachel. She was born in June 1767, just three months younger than Andrew Jackson. Friends described Rachel as short, with "lustrous dark eyes," a lovely figure, "full red lips," and an oval face "rippling with smiles and dimples." Poorly educated, she could barely write a complete sentence. Yet she was "a rattle," a fun-loving person fond of telling stories, dancing, and riding horses at breakneck speed. Young men adored her.[19]

When Rachel turned seventeen, she married Lewis Robards and went to live on his Kentucky plantation. It was not a happy marriage. Insanely jealous, Robards falsely accused Rachel of unfaithfulness. Finally, he sent her back to her mother with orders "never to show her face in his house again," an insult to the entire Donelson family. Jackson arrived at the Donelson station a few weeks after Rachel's return. Although he may have been attracted to her then, we do not know that for sure. In any case, if so, it would not have been proper to show affection for another man's wife.[20]

The following year, 1789, Robards offered Rachel another chance to prove *her* devotion to him. She accepted, and he joined her at the Donelson station. Things went well—for about a week. One day, Robards saw his wife speaking to Jackson. Aha! He had "caught" her again! In the privacy of their cabin, she later said, he ranted and raved. She cried. Nothing she said could tame his jealousy. Yet the man was a hypocrite. While demanding his wife's loyalty, he used slave women as objects to do with as he pleased, whenever he pleased. A neighbor recalled that he often enjoyed "spending the night with the negro women" in the slave cabins. After all, as "property," they had no right to refuse his attentions, however much they despised them.[21]

To keep the peace, in 1790 Jackson found another place to live. Yet Robards continued to storm and swear, accusing him of coming between him and his wife. Jackson did not take these charges lightly. He and Rachel were innocent, he said; they had done nothing wrong. If Robards connected his name to Rachel's again, Jackson swore to "cut his ears out of his head." The irate husband replied by getting an arrest warrant, which he enforced with the help of several court-appointed deputies. On the way back to the courthouse, Jackson asked a deputy to see his hunting knife, saying he meant no harm. The man handed it over. Calmly Jackson ran his finger along the slender blade, all the while fixing Robards with his eyes. Robards ran away. Shortly afterward, he left for Kentucky.[22]

Before leaving, he told Rachel she would never be free of him; he would "haunt" her until the day she died. Fearing violence, she decided to flee to Natchez, a town on the Mississippi River. The Donelsons had friends there who would look after her. Jackson volunteered to go along to protect her from Indians and river pirates. It was a move sure to raise questions about their relationship. Perhaps, gossips said, Robards had rightly accused his wife of unfaithfulness.[23]

From Nashville, they headed down the Cumberland to the Ohio River, then into the Mississippi River. They went by flatboat, a log raft seventy feet long by sixteen feet wide with a bulletproof cabin on deck. Besides passengers, flatboats carried the wealth of a continent: wheat, timber, furs, cattle, hogs, even buffalo robes from the Great Plains to the west. All went downstream, to the docks of New Orleans, and from there by ship across the Atlantic. Natchez and New Orleans lay in Louisiana, then a Spanish possession. Americans resented Spain's presence, for whoever controlled the "Father of Waters" and its tributaries had a stranglehold on more than half the nation's territory.

As the flatboat drifted southward, it became clear why boatmen called the Mississippi a "wicked river" and "this foul stream." An English traveler de-

A flatboat making its way down the Mississippi River to New Orleans, as depicted in a drawing by Charles A. Lesueur. Americans feared they might lose access to the great seaport at any moment while it was in Spanish hands.

scribed it as "an enormous ditch, sometimes two or three miles wide, running liquid mud, six miles an hour; its strong and frothy current choked and obstructed everywhere by huge logs and whole forest trees, now twining themselves together in great rafts . . . now glancing singly by like giant leeches." Ducks, geese, and pelicans swarmed along the shores. Enormous alligators sunned themselves there as well. High overhead, eagles made lazy circles, searching for prey.[24]

Nobody can say if Andrew and Rachel loved each other when they left Nashville. If not, they surely did by the time they reached Natchez. Yet they could not show their love openly. Rachel was still a married woman, and society expected her to act like one, no matter how she felt. Jackson left her with her friends and headed back to Nashville. Most likely, they agreed to marry if the chance came—a big if.

Yet luck seemed to favor them. Somehow Jackson's Nashville friends heard that Robards had asked for a divorce and that the Virginia legislature had granted it to him. Since Kentucky was still part of Virginia, only the Virginia legislature could end a marriage by passing a special act in each case. Jackson took the news as a gift from heaven. Immediately, he asked Widow Donelson's permission "to offer his hand and heart" to her daughter. She gave it, gladly. He rushed back to Natchez and married Rachel, although no record of their marriage—if there ever was one—exists today. Then the newlyweds returned to Nashville.[25]

For two years they lived happily. In 1793, disaster came in the form of an official divorce decree. Jackson, a practicing attorney, had made a terrible mistake. Instead of getting written proof that the "divorce" was real, he had asked for Rachel's hand. Yet it turned out there had been no divorce—in 1791. The Virginia legislature had merely invited Robards to present a court with proof of his wife's unfaithfulness. Her "marriage" to Andrew gave Robards the necessary proof. Finally, after the court found in his favor, the legislature granted the divorce because Rachel "hath and doth live in adultery with another man." She took the news hard. "I expected him to kill me," she cried, "but this is worse," for he had shamed her. John Overton urged the couple to marry again at once, but they hesitated for over a year, not wanting to admit they had done wrong. Yet to continue as they were branded them as sinners. Finally, on January 24, 1794, they repeated their marriage vows.[26]

Their marriage released a storm of gossip. Until the day she died, the charge of adultery haunted Rachel, making her miserable. And whatever hurt her, hurt her husband. Never one to overlook an insult, Jackson defended her with words and bullets. Still, the couple had no regrets. Nor did those who counted most with them—family, friends, neighbors. Major William B. Lewis, a neighbor and a friend, said it best. Although they might have acted rashly, "no one believed they acted criminally; the whole course of their lives contradicts such an idea."[27]

If anything, their love grew stronger with time. Jackson could not imagine life without Rachel, nor she without him. Throughout their marriage, there was never a hint of infidelity. Even Jackson's political rivals, who would have jumped at a chance to discredit him, never suggested such a thing. We have no record of an angry, rude, or harsh word passing between them. In public, they spoke to each other formally, a mark of respect among married people in those days. No one ever heard him call her Rachel; it was always "Mrs. Jackson" or "wife." However, he often began private letters with "My Love" or "My Dearest Heart"; some of her letters to him start with "My Dearest Life." She called him "Mr. Jackson," not "Andrew." Nobody dared call him "Andy" to his face; he thought it too informal, a discourtesy.[28]

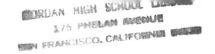

Rachel was a good influence. Her soft, lilting voice acted as a tranquilizer to her husband's violent temper. There was nothing he would not do for her, including watch his language, at least in her presence. Swearing caused her actual physical pain, like a slap in the face. A deeply religious person, she thought phrases like "by God!" used the Lord's name improperly. When Jackson said it, she would look away, blushing. Realizing his error, he would correct himself, saying, "By Jupiter!" When she was not around, to make a point he would often slam his fist into his palm and cry, "By the Eternal!"[29]

Rachel brought her man more than love. She brought an extended family of brothers, sisters, aunts, uncles, cousins, nieces, and nephews. All accepted him warmly, for marrying Rachel made him "kin." More than that, the Donelsons had a network of business and political connections throughout western Tennessee. These combined with Jackson's drive and ambition to set him on the road to success.

Jackson was exactly the kind of man Nashville's merchants needed. On the frontier, where the legal system had not yet put down deep roots, some settlers took to borrowing goods or money and then defying their creditors—refusing to pay back the debt. In Nashville, a group of debtors formed a kind of alliance, threatening violence should any creditors try to collect what they were owed. A lawyer who sued for payment on behalf of a creditor risked a beating or, worse, a bullet in the back. Now, Jackson was both a public official and a private attorney. In his attorney's role, merchants who could not collect their debts turned to him for help. To succeed, however, he first had to win the community's respect.[30]

Debtors tested Jackson, trying to scare him off. They quickly learned that nothing scared this war veteran. Years later, he recalled how, during a court recess, a man stepped on his toes. It hurt. Yet he thought it an accident, until someone whispered that the fellow wanted to pick a fight. In Jackson's words,

He was a man of immense size, one of the biggest men I ever saw. As quick as a flash, I snatched a small rail from the top of the fence, and gave him the point of it full in the stomach. Sir, it doubled him up. He fell at my feet, and I stamped on him. Soon he got up *savage,* and was about to fly at me like a tiger. The bystanders made as though they would interfere. Says I, "Gentlemen, stand back—give me room, and *I'll* manage him." With that I stood ready with the rail pointed. He gave me *one* look, and turned away, a whipped man, sir, and feeling like one. So, sir, I say to you, if any villain assaults you, give him the *pint* in his belly.[31]

In that rough frontier society, refusing a challenge would have branded Jackson a coward, destroying confidence in his ability and ending his career. After this violent display, would-be clients felt they could trust him with their business. Indeed, he became an ally of society's "haves," who provided the bulk of his livelihood. Jackson wanted money, since he felt it would give him the material possessions and respect he craved—make him a real gentleman. Yet that did not mean he would do anything, sell his good reputation, to make a dollar. Nothing in his writings suggests that he accepted a client whose claim he thought unfair or unjust. In also representing society's "underdogs"— small-scale farmers, the landless, assault victims—admittedly a tiny portion of his legal practice, he pursued justice even if it meant a low, or no, fee. As an attorney, Jackson stressed justice above legal technicalities. Later, when he was a judge, one comment expressed his entire legal outlook. "Do what is *right* between these parties," he instructed juries at the end of trials. "That is what the law *always* means." It is still a good rule to follow, though it is not always a simple matter to see what is right.[32]

Most settlers lived not in Nashville, but in stations far from town. Here, as throughout frontier America, if you could not come to the law, the law must come to you. For several weeks in the spring, summer, and fall, the judge "rode circuit," that is, traveled from one district to another, holding court in each. Lawyers, to make a living, had to join the judge on his rounds.

Before setting out, Jackson packed a few clothes, his pistols, pens, ink, and a supply of heavy writing paper. Attorneys used this paper for briefs, documents containing the facts and points of law involved in a case, which they filed before arguing it in court. Several lawyers usually rode with the judge for company and safety. After reaching a village, they piled into the local tavern, a crowded, dirty log cabin with crude furniture. There they ate, drank, joked, smoked, spat, gambled, argued, and shared flea-infested beds. Circuit lawyers formed a kind of social club. Although they might argue opposite sides of a case, they generally remained friends.

Attorney Jackson specialized in getting court orders to repay debts and to settle disputed land claims. Since he seldom lost a case, his practice grew steadily. Within six years of his arrival in Nashville, he was handling more cases than all his fellow lawyers combined. In 1794, the court heard 397 cases; Jackson appeared in 288 of them.[33]

Jackson usually took his fees in land, not cash. This was a clever business move, for as the desire for a better life drew more settlers westward, demand for farmland skyrocketed. Before long, Jackson owned large tracts of Tennessee land, usually former tribal lands seized by settlers, or settlers' lands taken over by creditors in payment of debts. Jackson then sold these to Eastern speculators, men who took big risks in hopes of making big profits by cashing in on the rising demand for land; a profit of five cents an acre on a vast tract added up to a fortune. People knew Jackson as a sharp businessman, always out for profit, but an honest one. If you needed credit, you would draw up an IOU and try to persuade others to sign it; thus they promised to pay if you could not. Creditors considered Jackson's name on an IOU a sure thing. Always as good as his word, he never went back on a commitment.[34]

Jackson's reputation spread across Tennessee. When it prepared for statehood in 1796, he was chosen to help write its constitution. Soon afterward, William Blount, a political strongman on the frontier and a Donelson family friend, asked Jackson to run for the state's only seat in the U.S. House of Representatives. Voters elected him without opposition.

In December, Tennessee's first congressman rode into Philadelphia, Pennsylvania. Congress met there until the year 1800, when it moved to the District of Columbia, on the east bank of the Potomac River between Virginia and Maryland. Meanwhile, work on the permanent capital, Washington, D.C., proceeded under the direction of President Washington himself.

Congressman Albert Gallatin, of Pennsylvania, claimed that Jackson's appearance shocked him. Gallatin described "a tall, lank, uncouth-looking personage, with long locks of hair hanging over his face, and a queue down his

Lawyer Andrew Jackson, Tennessee's first congressman, arrives in Philadelphia to take his seat in the House of Representatives in 1796.

back tied in an eel skin; his dress singular, his manners . . . those of a rough backwoodsman." As with any historical source, we should not take this one at face value. People do not always see the same thing in the same way. More than that, they may have special, hidden reasons for what they say. Gallatin's statement is misleading, if not deliberately false. We know he disliked Jackson. We also know Jackson had a top Philadelphia tailor make him a fine set of clothes before the congressional session began. As for Jackson's manners, friends, even casual acquaintances, never described them as anything other than those of a gentleman.[35]

In September 1796, three months before Jackson arrived in Philadelphia, President Washington's farewell address appeared in a local newspaper. Out of respect, the House drafted a resolution thanking him for his services to the nation. Nowadays, we look upon Washington as brave, honest, and truthful. Yet back then, not everyone loved "the Father of His Country."

After the Revolutionary War, Washington tried to make peace with the Native American tribes in the area of the frontier settlements. One treaty, with the Cherokee, bound the government to respect tribal land rights; it even allowed the Cherokee to punish white intruders. This infuriated whites, none more so than the always land-hungry Andrew Jackson. He simply could not see, let alone admit, that Native Americans had *any* right to their lands. The Cherokee, this "Savage Tribe" as he called it, simply stood in the way of progress. When violence erupted, Washington blamed the whites and refused to send troops.

Frontier people never forgave Washington for that, saying he had innocent blood on his hands. So did the Tennessee militia. Militia units attacked the Cherokee indiscriminately, burning peaceful towns as well as hostile ones. Where Indians were concerned, Jackson, like many other frontier people, believed in collective guilt—punishing all for the acts of a few. "The whole Cherokee Nation ought to be scourged," he insisted, for resisting white claims. He once joined a raiding party led by a Lieutenant Telford. Ambushed, the officer died; Jackson barely escaped with his life. So, when the resolution thanking the first president came up for approval, Jackson was in no mood to praise him. Instead, he joined eleven other Westerners in voting "nay." They lost badly. Jackson, however, did succeed in getting Congress to repay Tennessee for its campaign against the Cherokee.[36]

Despite this small victory, Jackson hated his time in Congress. He was lonely, missing Rachel desperately, and he knew his absences made her miserable. She tried to accept them for his sake and the good of the country. Yet whenever he left, she grew depressed. While away, he wrote her as often as possible. One of his letters from Philadelphia was as loving as he ever got in writing. Here is part of the letter, with his own punctuation, or lack of it:

> My Dearest Heart:
> With what pleasing hopes I view the future when I shall be restored to your arms there to spend My days . . . with you the Dear Companion of my life, never to be separated from you again. . . . Could I only know you enjoyed Peace of Mind it would relieve my anxious breast . . . until . . . I am restored to your sweet embrace which is the Nightly prayer of your affectionate husband.[37]

At the end of the congressional session, Jackson rushed back to Rachel, vowing not to seek reelection. He was finished with politics, he said. Yet politics had not finished with him.

In September 1797, the U.S. Senate expelled William Blount for crooked land dealings. Since he remained powerful in Tennessee politics, his allies in the legislature appointed Jackson to serve the remainder of his term. Jackson agreed out of duty to his state, and for the honor of sitting in the upper house. Still, he hated every moment of it. Having left Rachel *"Bathed in Tears,"* as he wrote a friend, he felt guilty. Some investments had failed as well, leaving him in debt.[38]

Jackson reached Philadelphia full of regret, worry, and anger. Sometimes anger got the best of him. "His passions were terrible," Thomas Jefferson recalled years later. "When I was President of the Senate, he was Senator, and he could never speak on account of the rashness of his feelings. I have seen him attempt it repeatedly, and as often choke with rage." Jackson stuck it out for seven months. Then he returned home and resigned. His Senate record is a blank, as he did nothing there but embarrass himself.[39]

A high legal post was more to Jackson's liking. Thanks to William Blount, who still had many powerful friends, in September 1798 the Tennessee legislature named Jackson a judge in the Superior Court, Tennessee's highest court. The generous salary, $600 a year in gold, only $150 less than the governor's, helped settle his debts. For the next six years, he rode to district courts across the state. Since Tennessee courts kept no records during the first days of statehood, he wrote no legal decisions. Yet we can imagine him giving juries that favorite bit of advice about the law always commanding them to do *right* between the parties.[40]

A bully never stood a chance with Judge Jackson. In one backcountry village, Russell Bean, a "great, hulking fellow," had quarreled with his wife. She had, Bean claimed, given birth to a child by another man. To teach her a lesson in loyalty, he cut off the infant's ear during a "drunken frolic."

The sheriff hauled Bean into Jackson's court, a shack with sawdust and spit on the floor. Court! Bean would have none of it. He stomped around the room, cursing everyone, then stormed out. Jackson ordered the sheriff to bring him back, but he failed. Bean, he explained, had threatened to shoot the "first skunk that came within ten feet of him." Nobody would tangle with him.

His Honor called a ten-minute recess and left the courthouse. He found Bean in the street, at the center of a crowd, cursing and waving a pistol in each hand.

Jackson had his own pistols. Elbowing his way through the crowd, he stared into Bean eyes. "Now, surrender, you infernal villain, this very instant," he roared, "or I'll blow you through!"

Bean lowered his pistols. "There, judge," he said, meekly, "it's no use, I give in."

The sheriff, regaining his courage, led him away.

No one had expected Bean to give up so easily. "Why," Bean explained a few days later, "when he came up, I looked him in the eye, and I saw 'shoot' . . . and so I says to myself, says I, hoss, it's time to sing small, and so I did."[41]

When the bully Russell Bean ran out of court and threatened to kill anyone who tried to bring him back, Judge Jackson promised to shoot him if he continued to defy the law.

By all accounts, Jackson was an able judge, firm, fair, and honest. Despite his success on the bench, however, he was restless. Ever ambitious, he decided to go after another post: major general of the Tennessee militia. One gained that military rank, the highest in the state, through election by the militia field commanders. Jackson knew most of these men from riding circuit as a lawyer and a judge. So, when the current major general died in 1802, he made his move.

Jackson faced stiff opposition from John "Howling Jack" Sevier. A Revolutionary War hero and leader of thirty-five raids on the Cherokee, Sevier had earned his nickname by charging into battle with a bloodcurdling war cry. Since he was a three-term governor, Tennessee law prevented him from serving a fourth consecutive term. Instead, he decided to become major general.

Sevier seemed like a sure winner. After all, he had battle experience, while the judge had been a mere boy during the war. The voting, however, reflected Jackson's growing influence. It produced a seventeen-to-seventeen tie, a blow to Sevier's pride. Under state law, Archie Roane, the new governor, had to break the tie. Roane was another of William Blount's political allies, and he cast his vote for Jackson. Thus, at the age of thirty-five, Judge Jackson also became Major General Jackson. He took the new post seriously, supervising drills, tightening discipline, and studying French army regulations (in translation) to learn how to manage military units. When it came to war, he admitted to being an amateur. Yet he had the makings of a fine commander. In years to come, no American general prepared for battle more carefully, or acted more quickly to surprise the enemy, than Jackson.

Sevier was outraged at losing to "a very wicked, base man, and a very improper person for a Judge." The next gubernatorial election made him angrier. Now eligible to seek another term, in 1803 he challenged Archie Roane. Meanwhile, Jackson had found damaging information about the would-be governor. Eager to help an ally, he published evidence of Sevier's role in a phony land deal. Sevier did what politicians often do when faced with embarrassing truths: he changed the subject. While praising his war record in lavish terms, he blasted the opposition for playing dirty politics.[42]

On October 1, 1803, Sevier and Jackson met in Knoxville, the state capital. As Jackson left the courthouse, he found the candidate giving a speech in the town square. Sevier was verbally patting himself on the back, boasting of his services to Tennessee. Seeing Jackson, he scolded him for questioning his honor. Flustered by the sudden attack, Jackson stammered that he, too, had done valuable service for the state.

"Services?" Sevier sneered. "I know of no great service you have rendered the country, except taking a trip to Natchez with another man's wife."

If Sevier expected to get a rise out of Jackson, he succeeded. "Great God!" His Honor roared, his eyes blazing, the veins in his throat bulging. "Do you mention *her* sacred name?" As always, Jackson was sensitive to "insults," and could not bear to hear *anything* that reflected badly on his wife's reputation.[43]

Candidate and judge squared off like thugs in a street brawl. Curses split the air. Pistols appeared. Shots rang out. A bullet grazed a bystander. The crowd fled in panic. Friends separated the two men before they could do serious harm.

Yet Jackson would not let the matter end there. Sevier had insulted Rachel! Only his blood could make things right, could cleanse the "Sacred Name!" The encounter that followed reveals something of the dark side of the early American republic. It shows how even responsible men, community leaders, often placed their idea of "honor" above the law.

To provoke a duel, Jackson printed insulting letters in the local newspaper, calling Sevier "a base coward." Dueling was a carryover from old Europe, where knights would defend their "good names" on the "field of honor," with sword and lance. Any sign of disrespect, even a casual remark or a harsh glance, might provoke a duel. On the American frontier and throughout the South, calling someone a "puppy," or staring at him while biting your thumb, were serious challenges, too. Because a gentleman could only fight his social equal, he would not lay hands on "crackers," "rednecks," and "peckerwoods," terms for poor whites. If they gave offense, he struck out with his cane or horsewhip—or a fence rail. Dueling, however, was illegal throughout the nation, for it promoted violence and disorder, thus weakening the nation. Killing an opponent was defined as murder. Yet that did not matter; scores of men died in duels every year. Lawmen, however, were usually tolerant and ignored these killings. Very few duelists were tried, and still fewer punished.[44]

Jackson, a judge sworn to uphold the law, believed in dueling. His mother, let alone his Scotch-Irish tradition, had taught him never to tolerate an insult. Insult was worse than murder for him. "The murderer only takes the life of the parent and leaves his character as a goodly heritage to his children," he said, "whilst the slanderer takes away his good reputation and leaves him a living monument to his children's disgrace." After Jackson became president, he advised a West Point cadet to wish for "death before dishonor." Like a good soldier, the cadet must obey a superior's orders. "But if the Superior attempts either to strike or kick you, put him to instant death. . . . Never . . . outlive your honor. Never do an act that will tarnish it."[45]

Yet dueling did not necessarily mean killing. Jackson's first duel, in 1788, was with a lawyer who had mocked his argument in court. Jackson had no intention of harming a person who could not properly defend himself. Yet he believed his honor demanded a duel. As if by silent agreement, both men fired into the air. Having satisfied their honor, they bowed and shook hands. Jackson would fight a dozen duels, killing only one opponent. But that opponent was not Sevier.[46]

The former governor met Jackson's insults with insults of his own. The judge replied in kind, turning up the heat. After ten days of insult and counter-insult, they agreed to fight in a forest clearing. Each man set out with armed companions, called seconds, who would see that the duel went according to the rules.[47]

What followed did neither man credit. The moment Jackson saw his opponent, he leaped off his horse and ran toward him with a drawn sword, swearing loudly. Sevier leaped off his horse, too, but it took fright and ran off with his pistols. Sevier ducked behind a large tree for cover. His son drew a pistol on Jackson, shouting he would protect his father with his last breath. To protect the judge, a friend, Dr. Thomas Van Dyke, drew on young Sevier. Round and round the tree they ran, each swearing and waving weapons. It was ridiculous. Finally, exhaustion and the urging of their more sensible companions won the day. Both parties rode toward Knoxville together, agreeing to let bygones be bygones.[48]

Sevier won the election. Jackson returned to the routines of court, militia, and home.

After the Jacksons married, they lived in Widow Donelson's blockhouse. Andrew soon bought Poplar Grove, a small plantation nearby, along with the slaves to work it. As his land deals began paying off, he bought a larger place, Hunter's Hill, a plantation along a bend of the Cumberland River. On each plantation, cotton was his chief moneymaker, but he also grew wheat and raised farm animals.

An economic downturn and bad investments threw Jackson into debt again. Yet just when he needed it most, he seemed to find a way out of his troubles. In 1800, the French dictator Napoleon Bonaparte forced Spain to give Louisiana back to France. Yet France did not keep it for long. Fearing a British attack in America, and desperate for money to fight his European wars, Napoleon offered to sell Louisiana to the United States. Thomas Jefferson, our third president, saw a chance to double the nation's size with the stroke of a pen. So, in 1803, he completed the Louisiana Purchase. For $15 million, or three cents an acre, he bought over 800,000 square miles of land between the Mississippi River and the Rocky Mountains, except for Spain's territories of Texas, Arizona, and New Mexico. Jackson wanted to become governor of the Louisiana Territory, a bid supported by Tennessee's congressional delegation. Jefferson, however, gave the post to someone he thought better qualified.

In the face of mounting debts, Jackson had to use all his energy to avoid bankruptcy. To raise cash, he sold his two plantations and other land holdings.

In July 1804, he resigned as judge, but did not return to his law practice. A week later, he bought 420 acres of fields and woods ten miles from Nashville. Why Jackson chose to call the place "The Hermitage" remains a mystery. Whatever the reason, it had a two-story log house and three cabins nearby for guests. He and Rachel moved into the twenty-four-by-twenty-six-foot house. The first floor was a single room that served as living room, dining room, and kitchen, with the meals cooked in a stone fireplace. A narrow passage at the back led to a lean-to with a pantry and bedroom. There were two tiny bedrooms upstairs.[49]

Jackson steadily chipped away at his debts. He built a whiskey distillery, always a moneymaker, and a small racetrack with a tavern and betting booths. With two partners, he opened three stores in neighboring towns. These carried everything from grindstones to gunpowder, cowbells to silk handkerchiefs. In payment, the partners took farm products, which they sold in New Orleans. Although the stores eventually failed, they and Jackson's other ventures earned enough to pay off his debts and buy more slaves.

The Hermitage was Jackson's safe place in the world. Rachel was there, always calming, always comforting. In the evening, they would sit by the fireside, talking softly or wrapped in their own thoughts, silently puffing their pipes. Unlike most American women then, the Donelson women smoked tobacco. When Andrew was away, Rachel's favorite sister, Jane Hays, kept "dear sister Jackson" company. They would, said Jane, "smoke our pipes, laugh and talk over occurrences of former days, each one taking the words out of the other's mouth." Rachel also smoked "Spanish segars," lumpy black things that gave off smoke no mosquito could stand.[50]

Jackson always made time for his favorite sports. While he gave up footraces and throwing the long bullet, he played billiards and cards. Visitors to The Hermitage recalled that cockfights put him into a roaring, rollicking mood. "Hurrah! My Bernadotte!" he would shout, flinging down coins as a favorite bird tore into a challenger's with beak and claws. "Twenty dollars on my Bernadotte! Who'll take me up? Well done, my Bernadotte! My Bernadotte forever!"[51]

Yet, for pure joy, nothing compared to his horses. The master of The Hermitage bred them, trained them, and bet on them. Although he did not ride them in races himself, he had several black jockeys, all slaves, small wiry men who loved the mighty animals as he did. Jackson knew all the jockeys' tricks. "Now, Simon," he told an opposing jockey before a race, "when my horse comes up and is about to pass you, don't spit your [chewing] tobacco juice in his eyes, and in the eyes of his rider, as you sometimes do." Simon smiled, saying, "I've rode a good deal agin your horses, but none was ever near enough to catch my spit." Jackson took this as a compliment and smiled, too.[52]

Jackson was no bookworm. While he read the Bible constantly and enjoyed only one English novel, *The Vicar of Wakefield* by Oliver Goldsmith, he did not care much for books. Newspapers were another matter. A fanatical newspaper reader, he subscribed to no fewer than twenty, which kept him informed about events in America and overseas.[53]

Since the South had few hotels, and these were far apart, Southerners became famous for their hospitality. Opening one's home, even to strangers passing through the neighborhood, was a social obligation. Known as "the prince of hospitality," Jackson prided himself on being a good host at The Hermitage. He welcomed everyone who came to his door, provided they behaved, making them feel at home. One evening, an invited guest, James Alexander Hamilton, recalled "there drove up a farmer with wife [and] children . . . to stay the night; such was the usual course of things." Basically, Hamilton explained, "He kept a tavern without the privilege of making a bill."[54]

A young Virginian, Henry A. Wise, reported that Jackson felt totally at ease with company. "He affected no style, and put on no airs of greatness, but was plainly and simply . . . polite to all." Women especially adored him. He always seemed to know just what would make each one feel comfortable. For example, "a homely young girl" once stayed at The Hermitage. She kept to herself, a shy wallflower, barely speaking to anyone. To set her at ease, Jackson "caught her by the arm and introduced her with so much earnestness" that the others had to pay attention to her. She remembered her visit as a high point in her life.[55]

Rachel was "Aunt Rachel," everyone's favorite—generous, outgoing, and caring. Should a poor family need clothes or a woman need help giving birth, nobody hesitated to knock at her door, day or night. Aunt Rachel made it her business to learn about her guests, their names, their likes and dislikes. A few words from her could melt the reserve of the iciest fellow. She would light her pipe, take a few puffs, and offer it, saying, "Honey, won't you take a smoke?" In the evening, she might lead guests in a sing-along; Jackson's favorite song was "Auld Lang Syne." At dance parties, they broke the ice with a Virginia reel, a favorite dance.[56]

Yet Rachel was more than a wife and hostess. She was her husband's business partner. An able manager, she ran The Hermitage during his absences. Always frugal, she never spent more money than necessary. Jackson trusted her completely and paid her the highest tribute. More than once, he wrote, "nothing but her care and industry, with good economy, could have saved me from ruin."[57]

However, Jackson's sensitivity to Rachel's reputation brought a Nashville man to his ruin. Charles Dickinson, a wealthy landowner proud of his skill with a pistol, had a racetrack argument with Jackson. To make matters worse, in a tavern he made a nasty remark about Rachel. For that, Jackson wanted him dead. As with Sevier, he was not acting as a man of law but lawlessly, yet according to the prevailing idea of honor in his community.

Portrait of Rachel Jackson, by Ralph E.W. Earl, resident artist at The Hermitage, about 1827, the year before her death.

Jackson placed a notice in a local newspaper demanding "satisfaction" and calling Dickinson a "blackguard," a person without honor. Dickinson placed his own notice, calling Jackson "a worthless scoundrel." Each man then chose his seconds.

On the chosen day, May 29, 1806, the duelists left home at the crack of dawn. Jackson did not tell Rachel what he was up to, although she probably knew. If so, she may well have had doubts about the coming encounter. Dickinson, everyone said, was a master with the pistol. Nashville knew him as a "snap shot," quick to aim and put a bullet into a bull's-eye eight yards away, the usual dueling distance. Dickinson's wife was also pregnant, and Rachel had always shown tenderness to widows with small children. Dickinson also kept the encounter secret. "Goodbye, darling," he told his wife. "I shall be *sure* to be at home tomorrow night."

Since Jackson was no snap shot, he knew it was useless trying to fire first.

He was sure to take a bullet, he told his seconds, but hoped it would not hit a vital spot. If he survived, he would steady himself, aim carefully, and kill Dickinson. Jackson had a special advantage, but did not realize it yet. The baggy coat he wore veiled his scrawny figure somewhat.

Facing each other, the duelists raised their pistols. As expected, Dickinson fired first. A puff of dust rose from Jackson's coat as the bullet struck. Yet Jackson did not go down. Slowly he raised his left arm and placed it across his chest, tightly. Dickinson had misjudged his aim, thanks to the baggy coat.

"Great God! Have I missed him?" he cried.

Now it was Jackson's turn. He could have spared the defenseless man, as he had other opponents. But Dickinson had insulted Rachel and given him an awful pain in the chest.

Jackson raised his pistol, aimed, and pulled the trigger. Nothing! The hammer that struck the flint that set off the gunpowder in the barrel had stopped halfway down. Jackson calmly drew it back, aimed, and fired. The bullet entered below Dickinson's ribs, passing clear through his body and causing him to bleed to death.

Several townsmen, duelists themselves, accused Jackson of cold-blooded murder. Yes, Dickinson had shot him. And, yes, Jackson had the right to take the next shot, although Dickinson could not defend himself. That was the rule. However, when Jackson's gun failed to fire, they argued, he should have taken it as God's judgment and, like a gentleman, spared his opponent's life.

Jackson had no regrets. "I should have hit him, if he had shot me through the brain," he said. Dickinson's bullet changed Jackson's life. Breaking two ribs, it lodged in Jackson's chest, too close to the heart for surgeons to remove. He recovered, due chiefly to his wife's care, but the wound would be a constant source of infection.[58]

Although the Jacksons had each other, something was missing from their lives. By 1806, they had been legally married eight years. They loved children, but they had none, nor ever would. When Rachel's sisters and sisters-in-law gave birth, she was happy for them. But deep down she felt a mixture of sadness and envy. Upon learning of Dickinson's death, Rachel cried out: "Oh, God, have pity on the poor wife [and] the babe in her womb!" That outburst was as much for herself as for the widow. At least *she* would become a mother.[59]

To fill the void in their lives, the couple filled The Hermitage with other people's children. Flocks of nieces and nephews visited for months on end. Strangers knew Jackson's fearsome reputation. When they first arrived, they expected to find a gun-toting ogre with blazing eyes. Instead, they met a loving man who thrilled at holding infants, even as they poked sticky fingers into his eyes, nose, and mouth.

Thomas Hart Benton was a lawyer who would have his ups and downs with Jackson over the years. One unforgettable night, about 1808, he saw a man outsiders could not imagine. "I arrived at his house one wet chilly evening, in February, and came upon him in the twilight, sitting alone before the fire, a lamb and a child between his knees. He started a little, called a servant to remove the two innocents to another room, and explained to me how it was. The child had cried because the lamb was out in the cold, and begged him to bring it in—which he had done to please the child . . . then not two years old. The ferocious man does not do that!"[60]

Jackson became guardian to orphans and children whose parents were unable to raise them. His favorite was his nephew, Andrew Jackson Donelson, known to everyone as "Jack," the son of Rachel's brother Samuel. Yet this did not satisfy Rachel. "Oh, husband!" she blurted out once, bursting into tears. "How I wish we had a child!" Jackson held her tightly. "Darling, God knows what to give and what to withhold."[61]

On December 22, 1809, the wife of Rachel's brother Severn had twin boys. Since their mother was sickly and unable to nurse them both, she gave one to the Jacksons three days after its birth. They legally adopted the infant, naming him Andrew Jackson Jr. From then on, Jackson always spoke of "my son."[62]

Jackson had every reason to be happy. Life was good. Prosperous and respected, he was now a family man, too. Yet he was also a patriot. His newspapers told of gathering clouds. War was in the air. One day soon, the United States would have to defend its independence on the battlefield.

Since Andrew and Rachel could not have children of their own, they adopted one of her nephews, naming him Andrew Jackson, Jr. From a painting by Ralph E.W. Earl.

III

"IMMORTAL JACKSON"

Come all ye sons of freedom
Come all ye brave who lead 'em
Come all who say God speed 'em
And sing a song of joy!
To Jackson ever brave
Who nobly did behave—
Unto Immortal Jackson,
The British turn'd their backs on,
He's ready still for action,
O Jackson is the boy!
—SONG, 1815

In May 1806, while riding to his duel with Charles Dickinson, Jackson discussed foreign affairs with his seconds to pass the time. He saw these matters as a militia commander, a patriot, and one who bore a lifelong grudge against England. "We must fight England again before long," he said, as if stating a fact everyone knew. "I wasn't old enough to be of any account the last time. I only hope we'll go to war before I'm too old to fight."

"What age do you think that will be?" John Overton asked, smiling to break the tension.

"About a hundred years, if England's the enemy!" said Jackson, grimly.[1]

A gigantic conflict had already been gathering. Although its roots lay deep in European history, it eventually drew in the United States. In July 1789, a mob in France stormed the Bastille, the hated prison-fortress in Paris, starting the French Revolution. During the chaos that followed, Napoleon Bonaparte seized power. The nations of Western Europe quickly fell under this military commander's control—all, that is, except Great Britain. While Napoleon commanded vast armies, he could not command them to walk on water. While her Royal Navy ruled the seas, the island kingdom of Great Britain remained safe.

British sailors impress an American for service aboard a warship. Impressment was a chief cause of the War of 1812.

To destroy each other's overseas trade, Great Britain and France seized each other's ships. They also seized the ships of neutral nations bound for the other's ports, most often ships sailing under the Stars and Stripes. Americans became angrier with Britain than with France over this, for Britain seized more than ships' cargoes. Most American families traced their roots back to the British Isles. Both peoples looked pretty much alike and spoke English in similar accents. It was only natural, then, for search parties to mistake American sailors for Royal Navy deserters. Ignoring threats of war, Britain "impressed" about six thousand American seamen between 1803 and 1812, that is, forced them to serve aboard its warships.

Merchants in the northeast United States wanted peace at almost any price, arguing that war would destroy their trade. However, a group of Southern and Western congressmen, dubbed the War Hawks by Thomas Jefferson, disagreed. Today, we say that anyone eager to use military force in foreign affairs is "hawkish," a term derived from the original War Hawks.

The War Hawks wanted to accomplish two things at once: drive all European powers off the North American continent and profit economically. To the north lay Canada, an English possession. Americans had tried and failed to conquer Canada during the Revolutionary War. Conquering it would remove a dangerous enemy, one who might join with hard-pressed Native American tribes to destroy the young nation. American settlers and land speculators also wanted to exploit Canada's vast, fertile lands. War Hawk leaders, Henry Clay of Kentucky and John C. Calhoun of South Carolina, boasted that a few hundred militiamen could easily overrun Canada. So did Thomas Jefferson. In 1812, the former president declared: "The acquisition of Canada this year as far as the neighborhood of Quebec, will be a mere matter of marching, and will give us experience for the attack on [the vital seaport of] Halifax the next, and the final expulsion of England from the American continent." Looking southward, War Hawks wanted to take Florida from Spain, driving more Native Americans from their lands. This, in turn, would allow the area available for growing cotton, and thus slavery, to expand.[2]

Jackson wanted everything the congressional War Hawks did. Yet he wanted more. Like many others, including President James Madison, he saw war as the only way for the young nation to gain the world's acceptance. Many Europeans regarded American independence as an accident. Had it not been for French intervention, they argued, the rebellious colonies could never have defeated Great Britain. America, then, had yet to prove that it deserved to exist, that it had a rightful place in the family of nations. Jackson understood the importance of respect; however wrongheadedly, he had fought, even killed, to preserve his "honor" since childhood. Now he saw his country as about to fight for the same ideal. In a printed address to the Tennessee militia, he asked: "*Who are we?* and for what are we going to fight? Are we the . . . slaves of George the third? the military conscripts of Napoleon the great? or the frozen peasants of the Russian czar? No—we are the free born sons of America; the citizens of the only republick now existing in the world; and the only people on earth who possess rights, liberties, and property which they dare call their own."[3]

On June 18, 1812, Congress passed, and President Madison signed, the declaration of war on Great Britain. The declaration recited the familiar grievances—stopping American ships on the high seas, seizing cargoes, impressments. About the other, hidden agenda—territorial expansion—it said nothing. Anyhow, that night a messenger named Billy Phillips, whom Andrew Jackson had taught to ride horses, rode south from Washington, D.C. At every settlement he passed, he shouted: "Here's the Stuff! WAR WITH ENGLAND!! WAR!!"[4]

Americans soon began to relearn a painful lesson, one as old as warfare itself. Wars are easier to declare than to win. War Department planners hoped to seize Canada in a lightning move, forcing the enemy to sue for peace. Before the invasion began, however, the British struck the first blow. In August, Fort Detroit surrendered to a tiny force of redcoats from Canada, threatening the entire area south of the Great Lakes. Fuming at the regular army commanders—"imbeciles" he called them—who had lost this key position, Jackson offered to lead his militia wherever the War Department ordered. "I owe to Britain a debt of retaliatory vengeance," he told Rachel. "Should our forces meet, I trust I shall pay the debt."[5]

Although less qualified men, said Jackson, got military commands, the War Department ignored him. Given his performance in Congress, he seemed undependable. However, in October 1812, the War Department asked Tennessee governor Willie Blount, William's younger brother, for volunteers to reinforce army units at New Orleans. Their leader would have the rank of major general of United States volunteers. Blount promptly wrote Jackson's name on the commission.

John Coffee was one of Jackson's closest personal friends and military aides. Portrait by Ralph E.W. Earl, about 1825.

Naming him had a magical effect. Instead of the 1,500 men called for, 2,500 volunteers showed up at Nashville. They came from the backcountry, singly or in groups, on foot or on horseback. Most were of Scotch-Irish descent, the sons and grandsons of Revolutionary War veterans. Their officers included men like the young lawyer Thomas Hart Benton, a Jackson protégé, and Jackson's neighbor William B. Lewis. John Coffee, a bear of a man, over six feet tall, had recently married a niece of Rachel's.

While Coffee led the cavalry overland, the main force of Tennessee volunteers boarded flatboats at Nashville. After they reached Natchez in January 1813, orders came for Jackson to make camp and await further orders. The army waited—and waited. Supplies began to run low. Homesickness spread like a disease of the spirit, with none more "sickly" than the general.

Jackson's absence tormented his wife. "Do not my beloved husband let love of country, fame and honor, make you forget [me]," she wrote. "You will say this is not the language of a patriot, but it is the language of a faithful wife. . . . Our little Andrew often does he ask me in bed not to cry, papa will come again and I feel my cheeks to know if I am shedding tears." Deeply moved, he promised his "dearest friend on earth" to wear her letter "near my bosom." As for their son, "Kiss him for his papa and give him nuts and ginger cake."[6]

Fresh orders came early the next month. Jackson's soldiers were "dismissed from public service" because they were no longer needed. The general had to let them make their own way home.

By the Eternal! Orders or no orders, Jackson would not leave "his" men stuck in the middle of nowhere. Jackson admired the old-time Scottish chiefs, and he knew what William Wallace would have done in the same situation. Like Wallace, he understood that a warrior chief must be for his men—and they must know it. That is the first rule of leadership.

Jackson did not hesitate to disregard orders when they disagreed with his own ideas of what was right. If he succeeded, he believed his disobedience would be overlooked, for nobody could quarrel with success. If he failed, he would accept the consequences. But he did not intend to fail. Jackson called an officers' meeting. Those soldiers trusted him; he knew many by their first names, or had business dealings with their folks, he said. To leave them flat, without pay or food or medicine, was unthinkable. He would use his own money to buy wagons and supplies, even write to Nashville to borrow money on his personal credit. "It is . . . my duty," he wrote Rachel, "to act as a father to the sick and the well and stay with them until I march them to Nashville."[7]

Even so, a march of over five hundred miles in midwinter was no picnic. Shivering, their fingers frozen, men hacked trails through the woods and pulled wagons out of the mud. Their general was everywhere, seeing to everything. "Where am I?" asked a youngster delirious with fever. "On your way home!" Jackson sang out. Men struggling nearby cheered; the youngster reached home to make a full recovery.[8]

Exhausted, Jackson pushed on, forcing his body to obey his mind. "Tough!" a man remarked after he passed by. "Tough as hickory," said another. "Tough as *old* hickory," another chimed in, correcting his friends. Old, seasoned hickory wood was the hardest wood these frontiersmen knew. Their general was just like it: tough, dependable, supportive. The nickname followed Jackson the rest of days.[9]

Nashville welcomed Old Hickory as a hero, who had saved its men despite the War Department. Back at The Hermitage, his family fussed over him. He fussed over the newspapers, which told of further defeats. Old Hickory begged the government for another assignment. While waiting for a reply, he had a row that became part of Nashville folklore.

Tom Benton's younger brother, Jesse, had challenged Billy Carroll, a fellow officer, to a duel. Billy asked the general to be his second. Sensibly, Jackson tried to back off, saying, "I am too old" for that sort of thing anymore. Yet Billy refused to take no for an answer, and Jackson agreed to serve. At the signal to fire, Jesse Benton suddenly squatted down to make the smallest target possible. As he did, he fired, his bullet grazing Billy's thumb. In reply, Billy's bullet made "a long, raking wound" on Jesse's buttocks. Shot in the backside! Overnight, Jesse became a laughingstock, the butt of coarse jokes.[10]

Tom Benton and Old Hickory had always liked each other. The duel made them enemies. Angrily, Benton accused his former friend of conducting the duel in a "savage, unequal, unfair and base manner." Answering in kind, Jackson promised to horsewhip Benton "on sight." Three months later, on September 4, 1813, they met at the front door of a Nashville hotel. In the brawl that followed, the Benton brothers shot Jackson twice: one bullet struck his left shoulder, the other shattered his left arm. Had John Coffee not charged to the rescue, they would have killed Jackson.

Friends carried Old Hickory to his room at the Nashville Inn nearby. Every doctor in town came to try his skill. Although they finally stopped the bleeding with a paste made of leaves from the slippery elm tree, a Cherokee recipe, the patient grew weaker. Fearing for Jackson's life, the doctors wanted to amputate his arm. "I'll keep my arm," he growled. They did not try to remove the bullet; it stayed in his arm for twenty years, when a surgeon finally removed it. Meanwhile, the Bentons left Tennessee in a hurry. Jackson had lots of friends, and they were all gunning for the brothers.

While Jackson's friends worried over his life—he did not leave his bed for a month—others went in fear of their lives that summer. Panic gripped America's entire southeastern frontier. To understand why, and how it touched Old Hickory, we must turn to a giant in Native American history.

Tecumseh, the Shawnee chief, dreamed of uniting the Native American tribes to block the westward advance of the United States and preserve their ancestral lands. From a drawing by Benson J. Lossing, in Pictorial Field-Book of the War of 1812, *published in 1868.*

His name was Tecumseh, or Blazing Comet. Tecumseh was chief of the Shawnee, a tribe whose domain stretched from the Great Lakes to the Ohio Valley. He was born in 1768, the year after Jackson, and his earliest memories were of wars with settlers, who killed his father. Although still a child, like Jackson he fought in the Revolutionary War, but on the British side.

A tall, erect man, throughout 1810 and 1811 Tecumseh traveled constantly, visiting the tribes along the Great Lakes and to the south. Although

Native Americans had no written language, news of faraway happenings passed quickly through the forests, carried from tribe to tribe by native warriors, travelers, and traders. Oral tradition then kept the events alive through the generations. As a youth, through conversations with older chiefs and wise men, Tecumseh had learned his people's history. He learned about the first white settlements at Jamestown, Virginia, and Plymouth, Massachusetts. He learned about the whites' hunger for land, their broken treaties, their corruption of Indian society. That history convinced Tecumseh that, unless native people, who "all belong to one family," forgot their petty squabbles and formed a single nation, the invaders would not only take their lands but destroy their entire way of life. In other words, for Native Americans, it had become a matter of fight or die.

Tecumseh had a booming voice that echoed in his listeners' ears and a message that stirred their hearts.

. . . What need is there to speak of the past? It speaks for itself and asks, Where today are the Pequoit? Where the Narraganset, the Mohican, the Pocankoet and many other once powerful tribes of our people? They have vanished before the avarice and oppression of the white man, as snow before the summer sun. . . . Look abroad over their once beautiful country, and see what you have now? Nought but the ravages of the paleface destroyers . . . Soon your mighty forest trees . . . will be cut down to fence in the land which the white intruders dare to call their own! Soon their broad roads will pass over the graves of your fathers, and the place of their rest will be blotted out forever. . . .

The annihilation of our race is at hand, unless we unite in one common cause against the common foe. . . . Our broad domains are fast escaping from our grasp. Every year the white intruders become more greedy, more exacting, more oppressive and more overbearing. . . . Before the palefaces came among us, we enjoyed the happiness of unbounded freedom and were acquainted with neither wants nor oppression. How is it now? Need and oppression are our lot. . . .

To fight or to be exterminated is now our only choice. . . . Let the white race perish! They seize your land, they corrupt your women, they trample on the grass of your dead. Back whence they came, upon a trail of blood, they must be driven. Back, back, aye, into the great waters whose accursed waves brought them to our shores. Burn their houses, destroy their stock! . . . War now, war forever! War upon the living, war upon the dead. Dig their bones from the grave. Our country must give no rest to the white man's bones. This is the will of the Great Spirit. . . . Two mighty tribes across the great waters [England and France] will send us guns, powder and lead. . . .[11]

In October 1811, Tecumseh visited the Muskogee, known to whites as the Creeks, because their towns lay along waterways in present-day Georgia, Alabama, and Mississippi. For over a century, white traders and fur trappers had lived among the Creeks, as among other Southern tribes. Often they married Creek women; fellow whites called their children "mixed bloods," as opposed to "full-blooded" Indians. Mixed bloods often kept their fathers' names, spoke English, and adopted white ways, like cloth dress and keeping enslaved black people. Yet they considered themselves Indians, even became chiefs. This explains why some chiefs had names like Hicks, Howard, Walsh, McGillvery, McIntosh, and McQueen.

Tecumseh's visit began a bitter debate among the Creeks. Two factions formed, each containing mixed bloods and full bloods. One faction, called the Red Sticks, from the color of their war clubs, wanted to fight the Americans. With white people heading for war, the Red Sticks expected British help in their war. Their opponents, however, argued that siding with the British during the Revolutionary War had cost Native Americans dearly. Remember what George Washington had done to the Iroquois! Instead, they believed that adopting white ways would best protect their people. These disagreements led to violence, as the Red Sticks began to attack opponents' villages.[12]

In 1812, this Creek civil war became part of the larger conflict between the whites. Red Stick warriors looked to the Spanish possession of Florida for support. Spain was Britain's ally against Napoleon. At that very moment, a British army under the Duke of Wellington was helping Spain drive Napoleon's forces from its soil. Although it claimed to be neutral in the American war, Spain's neutrality was a farce. British warships used the harbor of Pensacola, then Florida's capital, and British officers sent weapons to the Red Sticks to use against their Creek enemies and the Americans.

The Red Sticks used these with deadly effect. Their leader, a mixed blood, had two names: Red Eagle, his Creek name, and William Weatherford, his Scotch grandfather's name. Although the chief believed Indians must fight for their rights, he thought it wrong to kill civilians. However, Red Eagle agreed to lead a thousand warriors against Fort Mims in Alabama, then part of the Mississippi Territory, near the Florida border. Local people, frightened by earlier raids, had crowded into the fort for safety. Since it had a strong log palisade, Red Eagle did not expect to capture it; Indians had never stormed a fort. He expected the warriors to make a token attack, then retreat to avoid heavy losses. Failure would avoid a massacre while preserving his reputation as a leader and the warriors' honor as fighting men.

August 30, 1813, dawned hot and humid. As the sun rose, Red Eagle could scarcely believe his eyes. Those crowded into Fort Mims lazed about in the shade. Guards took it easy, too, and the gate stood wide open! Red Eagle could not hold his men back. All he could do was watch, horrified, as they burst from the tall grass and rushed the entrance. Of the 553 people inside, forty escaped, thanks to the mercy of individual warriors. Their companions killed everyone else, including women and children.[13]

The Fort Mims massacre sent waves of panic across the frontier. Wherever whites gathered, they spoke of "bloodthirsty savages" aided by British "demons." When the news reached Nashville, citizens demanded a war to "exterminate the Creek Nation." Governor Willie Blount called for volunteers to punish the "barbarous sons of the woods." Andrew Jackson must lead them, said Blount.[14]

At that time, Old Hickory lay in bed, swathed in bandages, recovering from wounds the Benton brothers had inflicted. Yet the promise of action acted as a tonic. "By the Eternal!" he wrote, using a pillow for a desk. He would

Creek warriors, led by Chief Red Eagle, also known as William Weatherford, stormed Fort Mims, Alabama, killing nearly all the settlers and soldiers.

avenge Fort Mims and protect the frontier people. "The health of your general is restored. He will command in person."[15]

Some 2,500 white men volunteered to serve under his command. These included veterans of the Natchez expedition and a motley crew of adventurers like Sam Houston and Davy Crockett, soon to be famous in their own right. Over five hundred Indians enlisted, too. Among them were Creeks opposed to the Red Sticks; Choctaws, longtime enemies of the Creeks, also came, led by Chief Pushmataha. Cherokees and Chickasaws joined in the hope that grateful whites would spare their tribal lands.

On October 7, Jackson, his shoulder and arm bandaged so tightly that only a little blood seeped through, led his army out of Nashville. Although he did not know it then, two days earlier Tecumseh had died while fighting alongside British troops in Canada. As Jackson had explained to Governor Blount, his Indian-fighting tactics would be simple—and brutal—as had been usual for generations in frontier warfare. He would march into Creek country, "laying waste their villages, burning their houses, killing their warriors and leading into captivity their wives and children."[16]

As Jackson advanced, he built forts as supply bases and to control the surrounding countryside. On November 3, 1813, he drew blood at the Creek town of Tallushatchee. In a dawn attack, his troops burned houses, ignoring the screams of those trapped inside. The few who escaped tried to resist, but it was no use. "We shot them like dogs," without mercy, said Davy Crockett. At least 186 warriors died; scores of women and children also died. Fifteen whites lost their lives.[17]

Old Hickory kept up the pressure. On November 9, John Coffee's cavalry stormed another town, Talladega, killing over three hundred Creeks while losing a dozen of his own troopers. From then on, the Creek called Coffee's boss Sharp Knife. Although Jackson was their ally, Choctaw warriors called him the Devil because he seemed to fight with demonic ferocity.[18]

Yet Jackson was not entirely devilish. Amid the mayhem he created, he could also feel sudden bursts of humanity. For example, his men had found a dead mother still clutching her crying infant, a boy, in her arms. When asked to care for him, the Creek women refused, saying all his relatives were dead, so the general should kill him, too. Old Hickory always had what he called "unusual sympathy" for orphans, seeing his early losses reflected in them. He took the infant in his arms, dissolved some brown sugar in water, and coaxed him to drink. After naming him Lyncoya, he sent him to The Hermitage as a gift for Andrew Jackson Jr. "Tell my dear little Andrew to treat him well," the general wrote his wife. "Charity and christianity says he ought to be taken care of." But Jackson's racism showed through even his act of humanity. He warned Rachel to keep the infant in the house, because "he is a Savage." However, the Jacksons raised the orphan as a member of their family. Later, in personal letters, the general referred to "my little sons, including Lyncoya."[19]

With supplies nearly gone, Jackson headed back toward Fort Strother near the Tennessee–Alabama border. Hunger gripped the army. Tempers flared. A private stood before the general, screaming for food as if he had taken leave of his senses. The general took it in stride; he knew how the private felt. "I will most cheerfully divide with you what I have," he replied, politely, offering a handful of acorns. The man stepped back into the ranks without saying another word.[20]

Supplies reached Fort Strother, but not nearly enough to meet the army's needs. Discipline began to crack. One day, several companies decided they'd had enough of soldiering. They had enlisted to fight Indians, they said, not to become walking bags of bones. Whatever the general might think, they were going home.

When they started to leave, Old Hickory's temper flared. Grabbing a musket from a soldier, he rode into their path. Resting it across his horse's neck, he swore to shoot the first man who took another step. He still wore a sling, and his left arm ached terribly. The men looked at him, and at one another, then returned to the fort. The general's eyes said "shoot," and everyone knew he would. He returned the musket, only to be told, "Why, Ginral, that gun ain't loaded." "Never mind," he said, "it has answered my purpose as if it had been loaded . . . to the muzzle."[21]

Later, Private John Woods, age eighteen, refused to clean up around his tent. When an officer ordered his arrest, Woods threatened to shoot anyone who came near him. Told of the incident, Jackson stormed out of his tent, shouting, "Which is the——rascal? Shoot him! Shoot him! Blow ten balls through the——villain's body!" Meanwhile, an officer persuaded Woods to hand over his weapon.[22]

A court-martial—military court—found Woods guilty of mutiny. Its

sentence: death by firing squad. Jackson, as commander, could have reduced it to a whipping or a few days of hard labor. When his temper cooled, he began to wrestle with his conscience. Although a little younger than Woods at the time, he, too, had "mutinied," disobeyed a British officer's order to clean his boots. But this was different. Now he was an American general leading an American army in enemy territory.

Old Hickory felt he must make an example of Woods, or risk having his army disintegrate. So, on the fatal day, the army formed a hollow square around the condemned youth, who stood blindfolded, his hands tied behind his back, an open grave behind him. The general could not bear to see the sentence carried out. Later, he explained that he had walked into the forest, out of earshot, because the execution "was a fearful ordeal for me." It was worse for poor Woods. Upon command, twelve bullets slammed into his body, pitching him backward into the grave. The execution, officers claimed, had a "most salutary effect" on the army.[23] Desertions came to a halt.

Supplies and reinforcements arrived soon afterward. Old Hickory renewed his advance, defeating the Red Sticks at places with tongue-twister names like Emukfaw and Enotachopco. Always in the thick of the action, he inspired his men, who cheered his courage. Rachel did not. "My Dearest

Life," she wrote. "I Cryed aloud and praised my god For your safety. . . . Oh Lord of heaven how Can I beare [your absence]. . . . Our Dear Little Son sayes maney things to sweet papa. . . . Your faithfull wife until Death. RACHEL JACKSON."[24]

On March 27, 1814, Jackson stood before the Red Sticks' stronghold, a town on the Horseshoe Bend of the Tallapoosa River in central Alabama. The river's loop formed a natural fortress of thick brush and clumps of trees protected on three sides by water. A breastwork, or breast-high barricade of logs and earth, stretched across the landward side. Hundreds of canoes bobbed in the water for a quick getaway if necessary. The town held a thousand warriors and their families.

Jackson planned to strike from two directions at once. While his main force hit the breastwork head-on, his Cherokee and Choctaw allies would swim across the river to cut the canoes' ropes, setting them adrift. Although he wanted victory, he did not want a massacre. So, before attacking, he allowed the Red Sticks to send their women and children to safety. At noon, the Red Sticks signaled they were ready to fight.[25]

Attacked front and rear, their escape by water blocked, the warriors broke into small groups. Twenty battles raged at once, turning Horseshoe Bend into a slaughter pen. Vowing to die fighting, "not a warrior offered to surrender," Sam Houston recalled, "even while the sword was at his breast." To learn the cost of the battle, Jackson ordered a body count of the Creek and American dead. So as not to count the enemy dead twice, Jackson's men cut off the tip of the nose of each Red Stick body they found, even though mutilation was banned by the rules of "civilized warfare" at the time. Some Tennessee soldiers carried the mutilations further, cutting long strips of skin from bodies to make into bridle reins. The Creek dead totaled 857, more than in any other single battle in the entire history of American–Indian warfare. Jackson lost 47 men. He followed up his victory with a campaign of terror. Sweeping through the remaining Red Stick towns, he burned them, their stored food, and any crops growing in the surrounding fields. Then he marched to the Hickory Ground, the Creek's holiest spot, and began building Fort Jackson. His aim, apparently, was to show that nothing, even the Great Spirit, could protect them from Sharp Knife's wrath.[26]

Surviving Red Stick leaders surrendered at Fort Jackson, among them one who had been away at the time of the Battle of Horseshoe Bend. On April 18, 1814, a light-skinned Indian found the general sitting outside his tent.

"General Jackson?"

"Yes?"

"I am Bill Weatherford."

Old Hickory glared at him with eyes that seemed to shoot sparks. Unfazed, the chief spoke with calm dignity. He explained that his only thought was for the defenseless women and children, not his own safety.

After Jackson's defeat of the Creeks at Horseshoe Bend, Chief Red Eagle promised to bury the war hatchet forever.

"General Jackson, I am not afraid of you," he said. "I fear no man, for I am a Creek warrior. I have nothing to request in behalf of myself. You can kill me if you desire. But I come to beg you to send for the women and children who are starving in the woods. . . . I exerted myself in vain to prevent the massacre of women and children at Fort Mims. I am now done fighting. . . . Send for the women and children. They never did

you any harm. But kill me, if the white people want it done. . . . Your people have destroyed my nation. You are a brave man: I rely upon your generosity."[27]

"Kill him! Kill him!" soldiers shouted.

"Silence," Old Hickory snapped.

Although a dogged enemy, he appreciated courage and dignity, qualities Red Eagle had in abundance. Besides, his appeal to Jackson's honor and generosity shows he had read his opponent's character perfectly. By offering his own life to spare the lives of innocents, he acted in a way that Jackson understood. In return for a promise to bury the war hatchet, and to ask Red Stick holdouts to surrender, Jackson did as the chief asked. Red Eagle retired to his farm and died of a heart attack in 1826, during a bear hunt.

Victory over the Creeks made Jackson a national hero. Newspapers blazed his name across the land. Admiring letters poured into The Hermitage, where he had gone to recover his health. In gratitude, the government promoted him to major general in the regular army, commanding the Seventh Military District: Tennessee, Georgia, and the Mississippi Territory. Along with the appointment came another mission. Jackson must finish with words and pens what he had begun with guns and torches.

In July 1814, he ordered all Creek chiefs, enemies and friends alike, to meet him at Fort Jackson. The government wanted him to negotiate a treaty for Creek lands equal in value to the cost of the war; that is, the Creeks should repay the full cost of the war to their enemy with their lands. Jackson, however, would not negotiate anything. Negotiating involves give-and-take, working out compromises acceptable to both parties. Jackson never negotiated with anyone, if he had the power to impose his will, least of all with Native Americans. Ten years earlier, he had claimed that only force could sway an enemy he saw as vermin. "Constantly infesting our frontiers," he wrote a federal official, "their Peace Talks are only Delusions. . . . Does not Experience teach us that Treaties answer No other Purpose than opening an Easy door for the Indians to pass through to Butcher our Citizens[?]" Like most frontier people, Jackson saw only the violent result of Indians' anger and fear, not its causes.[28]

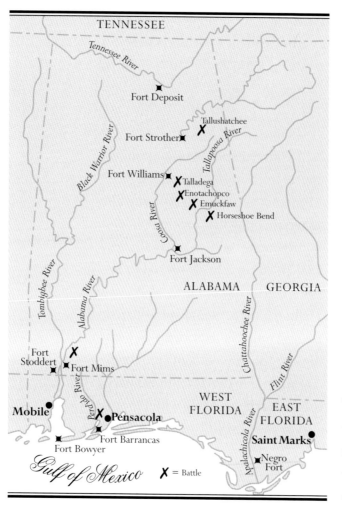

TENNESSEE

Tennessee River

Fort Deposit

Tallushatchee

Fort Strother ✗

Tallapoosa River

Black Warrior River

Fort Williams ✗ ✗ Talladega
✗ Enotachopco
✗ Emuckfaw
✗ Horseshoe Bend

Coosa River

Fort Jackson

ALABAMA   GEORGIA

Tombigbee River

Alabama River

Chattahoochee River

Fort
Stoddert ✗
✗ Fort Mims

Perdido River

WEST
FLORIDA

Flint River

Mobile

✗ Pensacola

EAST
FLORIDA

Apalachicola River

Saint Marks

Fort Barrancas
Fort Bowyer

Negro
Fort

Gulf of Mexico   ✗ = Battle

Jackson's movements and battles during the war against the Creeks.

In Jackson's view, the Creeks, both Red Sticks and his allies, should be *told* what they must do. American national security, he felt, as well the interests of settlers and land speculators, came first. To separate the Creeks completely from the Spanish in Florida, and thus their source of English weapons, Jackson wanted a huge block of Creek lands in Alabama and Georgia. He demanded 23 million acres of land, and the right to build military roads through the remaining Creek lands. This amounted to half the Creek domain, or 60 percent of today's state of Alabama and 20 percent of Georgia.

Stunned, the allied chiefs protested. This was plainly outrageous, an injustice they could barely fathom. In tribal society, one who spoke with a "forked tongue," lied or twisted the truth, was dishonorable; no self-respecting Creek would have anything to do with them.

In return for joining him against the Red Sticks, Jackson had promised to protect them. Why, then, they asked, should their people suffer after giving such loyal service? Yet they had not reckoned on Jackson's racism, or his burning desire for both himself and his country to rise in the world. That made him tough, vengeful, determined to get his way at all costs. "The United States," he growled, "would have been justified by the Great Spirit, had they taken all the lands of the [Creek] nation merely for keeping" Tecumseh's visit secret. Had they been true friends of the United States, he said, they would have handed him over to the Americans, "or have cut his throat themselves."[29]

Jackson would not change a word of the treaty. Instead, he gave the chiefs an offer they dared not refuse. If they left without putting their marks on the treaty paper, he would restart the war. They had no choice, if they wished to save their families. Food was short; so short, he told Rachel, that in some bands people were "picking up the grains of corn scattered from the mouths of the horses and trodden in the earth." Put bluntly, Jackson was holding women and children hostage. On August 9, 1814, thirty-six chiefs, only one of them a Red Stick, signed the Treaty of Fort Jackson. Thus, Old Hickory ended the Creek War by punishing his "Friends & Brothers," as he called his allies.[30]

Meanwhile, the European war ended in Napoleon's defeat. Free to concentrate on its other war in the New World, the British government decided to finish with America. It called for peace talks, and by late summer, 1814, diplomats arrived in the Belgian city of Ghent. The British, however, meant to keep fighting until both sides ratified—formally approved—the final version of the peace treaty. This strategy of talking while fighting would, the British hoped, allow them to dictate terms up to the last minute.

Britain had several war aims. Victory would remove a trade rival, particularly with the new nations of South America—Argentina, Bolivia, Venezuela, Colombia—former Spanish colonies that had won their independence during the Napoleonic wars. More importantly, Britain questioned the legality of the Louisiana Purchase. When Napoleon forced Spain to return Louisiana to France, he pledged not to sell it or give it away without Spain's consent. But Napoleon broke his word by selling it to the United States. If the British offensive succeeded before a peace treaty went into effect, the entire territory would become Spain's again. That would be a disaster for the United States, reducing its size by half, blocking its westward expansion, and closing the port of New Orleans, a vital outlet for its trade. Americans, said Lord Castlereagh, the British foreign minister, would become "little better than prisoners in their own country." They would remain forever citizens of a tiny, struggling republic with no say in world affairs.[31]

No longer needing large military forces in Europe, British leaders planned three attacks against the United States along a line running from Canada to the Gulf of Mexico. The first attack, aimed across Lake Champlain and down the Hudson Valley, would cut New England off from the rest of the country.

The burning of Washington, D.C., by the British, as seen from the Potomac River, August 1814.

The second attack would capture Washington, D.C., and Baltimore, Maryland. Finally, an army–navy task force would seize New Orleans.

The British got off to a blazing start. On August 24, in a surprise attack by Admiral Sir George Cockburn, Washington, D.C., fell. To show their contempt for America, redcoats set fire to the President's House and the U.S. Capitol, then withdrew. Only the buildings' stone walls prevented their destruction. To hide the scorch marks, President Madison ordered the walls of his house painted white—thus the name White House. Although the British failed to capture Baltimore, their victory in Washington threw the nation into a panic. Luckily, on September 11, a hastily built American fleet repelled the northern invasion at the Battle of Lake Champlain. Despite this setback, the British remained confident. Already the New Orleans strike force was assembling in the Caribbean, at Negril Bay, Jamaica.

Jackson took the burning of Washington, D.C., personally. All the hatred he had felt for Britain since childhood poured out. Touching the scar on his forehead, he vowed to take revenge. "Say to my son," he wrote Rachel, "he must never cry . . . and learn to be a soldier."[32]

Meantime, disturbing reports came from the Gulf of Mexico. British warships seemed bolder than usual. Hit-and-run raids on coastal towns were increasing. Spies reported the buildup at Negril Bay and rumors that New Orleans would be the target. Within two weeks of signing the Creek treaty, Jackson had heard enough to know the British were up to no good.

Acting on a hunch, he rushed to Mobile, Alabama, with his army. Located about 140 miles east of New Orleans, the town's deep-water harbor made it an ideal staging area for a drive into Louisiana. Upon arriving there on August 22, Jackson poured men and cannons into Fort Bowyer at the entrance to Mobile Bay, a key defense post. His hunch soon paid off. The fort's garrison defeated a British landing force, killing nearly two hundred redcoats and sinking a warship.

That victory raised another problem. Jackson learned the raiders had come from Pensacola, in Florida. With Spain's blessing, the enemy had turned it into a forward base for operations in the Gulf of Mexico. The British flag flew over Fort Barrancas, its chief fort. Two warships rode at anchor in its harbor. British soldiers gave weapons to the Red Sticks who had escaped to Florida after Horseshoe Bend. The British also sent agents into Louisiana. Disguised as merchants, they urged slaves to win their freedom by helping to overthrow the "imbecile government" of the United States.[33]

Jackson asked the War Department's permission to attack Pensacola. In reply, his instructions said he should avoid trouble; the U.S. did not need a war with Spain. Oddly enough, the instructions took six months to reach the general. When they finally arrived, the War of 1812 was over!

Urgent instructions to commanders in the field simply do not go astray for six months. Although we cannot know for sure, it seems likely that Jackson and his superiors

Admiral Sir George Cockburn, commander of the British fleet, seen against the background of Washington, D.C., in flames, as depicted in a drawing based on an 1853 portrait by J. J. Halls.

in the War Department had an unspoken understanding. Old Hickory knew that President Madison and most members of Congress, like himself and most Southerners, wanted to get Florida away from Spain. Even so, the War Department could not order an attack on the territory of a neutral country. The "missing" instructions gave the government a marvelous cover story. Without them, Jackson must act on his own responsibility. If he invaded and failed, the blame would be his alone. After all, the government wanted to avoid war; its instructions proved that. If he succeeded, nobody would remember them.

By the Eternal! Old Hickory *would* take the responsibility! Writing to Don Matteo González Manrique, the Spanish governor, he said he could not allow Britain to use Florida as a base for supplying the Red Sticks or mounting an invasion of the United States. Be warned, Jackson said, I live by a stern rule: "An Eye for an Eye, Tooth for Tooth, and Scalp for Scalp."[34]

Don Matteo ignored the warning. So Old Hickory stormed into Florida at the head of three thousand troops, reaching Pensacola on November 7. Before the garrison realized its danger, John Coffee's horsemen were whooping and shooting in the streets. The Spanish troops surrendered. The British blew up Fort Barrancas and set sail for Jamaica. Humbled, Don Matteo wrote the victor a letter in which he "kisses your hands."[35]

Another War Department message *did* reach Old Hickory in Pensacola. It confirmed what his spies in Jamaica had already reported: the British were about to attack New Orleans. There was no time to lose now. Jackson marched his army back to Mobile, pausing briefly to further strengthen its defenses. "I will hold New Orleans in spite of Urop [Europe] and all hell," he swore. Five days later, on November 27, the British fleet put to sea.

Catching the breeze, acres of canvas blossomed with a loud snap. The fleet stretched for miles across the blue Caribbean. Admiral Sir Alexander Cochrane, commanding, led in the eighty-gun *Tonnant,* followed by fifty-nine other vessels, warships and transports. The transports carried fourteen thousand redcoats, the flower of the British army. Besides those who had burned Washington, there were veteran units fresh from European battlefields.

Major General Sir Edward Michael Pakenham, thirty-seven, commanded the army. His teacher in the art of war was none other than the Duke of Wellington, his brother-in-law. "Pakenham may not be the greatest genius," said the duke, "but he is the best we have." A war hero, he followed a simple rule: Get at the enemy as fast as you can, then pound away as hard as you can until he dies, surrenders, or runs away. In keeping with that rule, Pakenham had personally led headlong charges against Napoleon's best troops. In one battle, a bullet struck him in the neck. When the wound healed, it left his head leaning to one side. In another battle, a bullet struck the same spot, restoring his head to its normal position.[36]

Pakenham's destination, New Orleans, lies on the east bank of the Mississippi River, about 120 miles north of where it empties into the Gulf of Mexico. In 1814, the surrounding country was mostly swamps teeming with alligators, snakes, and water-birds: ducks, flamingos, pelicans. A maze of narrow waterways, or bayous, twisted through the countryside. Lake Borgne, a shallow arm of the Gulf of Mexico, reaches to within six miles of the river east of the city. Even the humblest redcoat expected to make his fortune by looting New Orleans. Thanks to the Royal Navy's blockade of American seaports, it was a treasure-house heaped with unsold cotton, sugar, and other valuables.

Old Hickory reached New Orleans on December 1. At first, many people did not know what to make of him. *This* was the defender of their city, their savior?! With his sickly yellowish complexion and scrawny body, he seemed, one wrote, "more fit for the hospital than the field." Another described him as "an ugly old Kaintuck flatboatman"—that is, a savage. Ladies whispered among themselves, "What shall we do with this wild General from Tennessee?"[37]

Edward Livingston, chairman of the civilian defense committee, gave a dinner in Jackson's honor. Everyone who was anyone attended. When the guest of honor appeared, those who had seen him earlier scarcely recognized him. He wore a spotless blue uniform with gold braid and gleaming black boots. Smooth as silk and sweet as honey, he made his way around the room, speaking

Major General Sir Edward Pakenham, commander in chief of the British army during the New Orleans campaign. A brother-in-law of the "Iron Duke" of Wellington, Pakenham was a hero of the wars against Napoleon.

to all, always poised, polite, and charming. After dinner, Jackson left the house with his host. The moment the door closed behind them, guests crowded around Mrs. Livingston. "Is *this* your backwoodsman?" they asked. "Why, madam, he is a prince." However, one lady noticed something else, something menacing, about this prince. "A fierce glare [lit] his bright and hawk-like eye."[38]

All doubt that an invasion was coming vanished when lookouts along the coast sighted the British fleet. Panic swept New Orleans. In reply, Jackson declared martial law, a normal practice when generals think the city they must defend is in imminent danger of attack. New Orleans became an armed camp ruled by the military. Free travel was banned; nobody could enter or leave without a pass from his headquarters. Soldiers patrolled the streets around the clock. Those caught outdoors after 9 P.M. without a pass "shall be apprehended as spies" and shot by firing squad, an order read. Civilians began to calm down.[39]

Yet Jackson was anything but calm. An inspection of the defenses showed New Orleans open to attack. Immediately, orders issued from headquarters. Post five small gunboats on Lake Borgne to warn of the enemy's approach!

Area of Andrew Jackson's war against the British, 1814–1815.

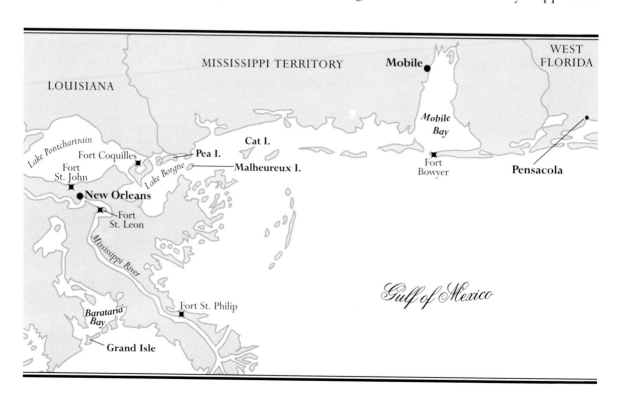

Reinforce Fort St. Leon and Fort St. Philip on the river below the city with heavy artillery! Send work details to block bayous with fallen trees! (This was a vital defensive measure, for an invader who found the right bayou open could approach the city undetected.)

The general also collected as odd an assortment of men as ever fought under the Stars and Stripes. Among them were Creoles, men of French ancestry born in Louisiana, dressed in gaudy uniforms of red, blue, and gold. Choctaw warriors led by Chief Pushmataha, a longtime ally of the whites, came, too, along with "free men of color." Over the years, Louisiana masters had allowed some slaves to buy their freedom with earnings from work outside the plantation. When it came to soldiers, Jackson was color-blind. He gladly enlisted free blacks. A paymaster received a tongue-lashing for giving them less than whites. Pay up, Old Hickory growled, "without inquiring whether the troops are white, Black, or Tea." In time, he would praise the "great bravery" of his black troops.[40]

Jackson's army even had room for pirates. The Lafitte brothers—Jean, Pierre, and Dominique You—specialized in capturing Spanish ships and smuggling. Jean, thirty-seven, was in charge, his younger brothers serving as his lieutenants. No ordinary criminal, Jean headed an organization of a thousand men and two dozen ships. British agents promised Jean money and a pardon if he joined them, but he offered his services to America instead, because he and many of his men originally hailed from France.

The general refused to deal with pirates under any conditions; "these hellish Banditti," he called them. However, he changed his tune after Jean boldly walked into headquarters and asked for a private meeting. No one knows what they said to each other. However, we do know that Jackson needed the pirate's cannons and expert gunners, some of whom had fought under Napoleon. The two men must have gotten along well,

The general and the pirate. Andrew Jackson poses next to Jean Lafitte in this crude illustration from The Pirate's Own Book, or Authentic Narratives of the Lives, Exploits, and Executions of the Most Celebrated Sea Robbers, *New York, 1842.*

because, from then on, Jackson called the pirates "my comrades in arms" and "those gentlemen." Their chief became a member of his personal staff.[41]

Yet Jackson welcomed no fighters more warmly than his own people, the backcountry men of Tennessee and Kentucky. While John Coffee rode overland with the cavalry, other officers brought the infantry down the Mississippi on flatboats. The genteel New Orléanais literally turned up their noses at them; they stank so badly that it was best to stay upwind of them. Locks of greasy hair hung around their shoulders. Tomahawks nestled in their belts beside slim hunting knives called Tennessee toothpicks. Homespun breeches and buckskin hunting shirts, dyed with berries and crawling with lice, made them seem like beggars.

Shabby as they looked, they carried themselves with pride. Their rifles gleamed. Historians would later say the effects of these weapons had been overrated. Yet those who knew best, the New Orléanais, thought differently. Jackson's men, one noted, "were all practiced marksmen, who thought nothing of bringing down a squirrel from the top of the loftiest tree with their rifles." Their rifles would be more than a match for the redcoats' muskets.[42]

Those redcoats were closer than Jackson thought. On December 14, the British fleet anchored outside Lake Borgne. Since it was too shallow for his ships, Admiral Cochrane sent forty-five barges, each with a cannon mounted in front, to destroy Jackson's five gunboats. A full day's rowing found the gunboats becalmed, unable to use their sails. In a fierce fight, Royal Marines captured them and their crews. Now no one could report the enemy's arrival. Even so, British ignorance would play into Jackson's hands. When asked about his army's strength, the prisoners lied like patriots. They swore Old Hickory had fifteen thousand men, five times the actual number he had at that time.

For the next week, British patrols explored bayou after bayou, only to turn back when they found the waterways choked by tangles of fallen trees—put there by Jackson's men. Finally, one found Bayou Mazant clear. To this day, we do not know why Jackson's work parties overlooked it. Perhaps pirates wanted to keep it open for their smuggling operations.

At dawn on December 23, Major General John Keane led an advance force of 1,800 men into Bayou Mazant in rowboats. His plan was to penetrate deep inland, as close to New Orleans as possible, without alerting the defender's secure foothold, and await the main force. Gradually, the waterway narrowed until they reached firm ground and went ashore. Moving in single file, they fanned out behind a clump of trees. Across a clearing they saw a sugar plantation owned by a Creole family named Villeré. Beyond it lay the Mississippi River, with New Orleans a few miles upstream.

Major Gabriel Villeré, of the Louisiana militia, sat on the porch of his house, quietly puffing on a cigar. Suddenly, redcoats ringed him with bayonets, as others came pouring out of the woods. Villeré understood why they had come, and what he must do. Placed under arrest, he bided his time, then, at the right moment, leaped through a window. "Catch or kill him!" an officer cried. Bullets whined past his ears, but the major kept going. Making his way to a friend's plantation, he and the owner mounted horses and rode toward New Orleans to alert Jackson.[43]

A two-hour march would have brought Keane to New Orleans. Caught off guard, Jackson would probably have been unable to mount an effective defense. Yet the British general believed the American sailors' lies about Jackson's strength. Ignoring his officers' pleas to go forward, Keane decided to await reinforcements as planned.

"The British have arrived!"

Major Villeré's words dazed Jackson, but only for a moment. "By the Eternal," he shouted, pounding his fist on a table, "they shall not sleep on our soil!" Already a plan was forming in his mind. "Gentlemen," he declared, turning to his aides, "the British are below. We must fight them tonight."[44]

Church bells clanged. Drums beat the call to arms. Red-shirted pirates with black mustaches and tattooed arms scrambled aboard the armed vessel *Carolina.* Instantly, she slipped her cable and silently glided downstream. At four o'clock in the afternoon, exactly two hours after getting Major Villeré's news, Jackson left New Orleans with an 1,800-man strike force. Before mounting his horse, an officer saw him pause for a moment. "I will smash them, so help me God!" he mumbled to himself.[45]

It was pitch-dark at 7:30 P.M. when the Americans silently took up their attack positions. A mist had settled over the river, so that the only light came from the British campfires.

The redcoats had just lain down to sleep when the dark shape of *Carolina* loomed over the riverbank. "Flash, flash, flash, came from the river," Lieutenant George Gleig, 85th British Regiment, later reported. Cannonballs rained down "like thunderbolts amongst the astounded troops." Above the roar, redcoats heard someone shout, "Give them this for the honor of America." Jackson let the bombardment continue for about twenty minutes. Then, with the enemy's attention turned toward *Carolina,* he ordered the infantry to advance.[46]

Redcoats were professional soldiers; they did not panic easily. "Fall in! Fall in!" sergeants bellowed. Bugles sounded the charge. "Push on the bayonet!" officers cried, pointing toward the advancing Americans with their swords.

A furious fight erupted in the darkness. Men shot not at one another, but at gunflashes nearby. Men rolled on the ground, hands grasping one another's throats. Tennessee toothpicks found their mark. The action swayed back and forth until midnight, when Jackson gave the signal to withdraw. American losses were 213 killed and wounded, compared to 277 for the British.

Daylight on December 24 found the British alone on the battlefield. Several hours earlier, in Belgium, British and American diplomats had signed the Treaty of Ghent. Yet, since there was no telephone or radio then, ships would have to carry the news across the Atlantic. Even had the armies known about the treaty, it would not have changed their plans. The treaty allowed fighting to continue until both governments ratified it, which would not happen for another seven weeks.

That morning of Christmas Eve, the only Americans General Keane's men saw were dead; Old Hickory had sent his wounded to New Orleans. A British officer described the awful scene. He had fought on many European battlefields, but, for sheer horror, none came close to this.

Wounds more disfiguring, or more horrible, I certainly never witnessed. A man shot through the head or heart lies as if he were in a deep slumber. . . . But of these many had met their deaths from bayonet wounds, saber cuts, or heavy blows from the butt ends of muskets; and the con-

American and British diplomats sign the Treaty of Ghent. Although the treaty ended the War of 1812, it would not go into effect until both governments ratified it. Thus, the decisive Battle of New Orleans was fought after the signing but before the United States approved of the treaty.

sequence was, that not only were the wounds themselves exceedingly frightful, but the very countenances of the dead exhibited the most savage and ghastly expression. Friends and foes lay together in small groups of four or six, nor was it difficult to tell almost the very hand by which some of them had fallen. Nay, such had been the deadly closeness of the strife, that in one or two places the English and American soldier might be seen with the bayonet of each fastened in the other's body.

The officer's best friend lay among the dead. "I threw myself on the ground beside him, and wept like a child."[47]

Old Hickory had pulled back to the Rodriguez Canal. Lying ten miles south of New Orleans, the "canal" was really a dry ditch, ten feet wide by four feet deep, that ran for nearly a mile from a cypress swamp to the eastern bank of the river. The Americans halted behind the canal and began to dig in the dark. Working in relays, they deepened it and built a breastwork of earth and cypress logs. Their commander supervised the work, making do with an hour or two of sleep each night. Fatigue and stress took their toll. "Uncle Jackson," a soldier wrote home, "looks very badly and has broken very much." Yet he had drawn the line. If the invaders wanted New Orleans, they would have to go past him here to get it.[48]

Sir Edward Pakenham arrived with reinforcements on Christmas Day. A deserter brought Jackson news of his arrival, and of his boast that he would hold a victory banquet in New Orleans. "If so," Jackson snapped, "he'll find me at the head of the table."[49]

Dawn, December 26, found Sir Edward up a tree, scanning the American position with his spyglass. He decided to ride closer with his staff to get a better view. Suddenly, some American cavalry galloped across the field to look them over, then sped away. Pakenham frowned. The Americans, he wrote, had the "appearance of snipe and rabbit hunters beating the bushes for game," like the laborers on his Irish estates. Without realizing it, he had committed a commander's worst error. By holding the enemy in contempt, he misjudged their fighting abilities.[50]

Pakenham turned to the "watery dragon," *Carolina,* and her sister ship, the recently arrived *Louisiana.* He had his gunners prepare a surprise. Working at night, they placed cannons along the riverbank. At daybreak on December 27, they lifted red-hot cannonballs out of portable furnaces with tongs and rolled them down the gun barrels. Moments later, *Carolina,* her hull drilled through with "hot shot," exploded with a roar heard ten miles away in New Orleans. Luckily, a quick-thinking officer had ordered the crew to jump overboard in time. British gunners cheered as they turned their attention to *Louisiana.* Just then the wind died down, forcing *Louisiana*'s crew to scramble into lifeboats and tow her out of range with ropes.

Despite *Carolina*'s loss, the American line grew stronger. Every man, pick, and shovel that New Orleans could spare went to the breastwork at the Rodriguez Canal. Over two thousand slaves, rented from local plantation owners, joined the white work details. When they finished, the breastwork was eight feet high by twelve feet thick, and ran from the riverbank to the swamp. Across the river, Old Hickory placed a twelve-gun battery to cover the ground in front of his position.

Pakenham did not keep him waiting. Next day, December 28, British gunners cut loose with artillery and rockets, primitive devices made of thin iron tubes filled with gunpowder ignited by fuses. Unlike today's rockets, these were impossible to aim with any accuracy. Yet the defenders grew restless, for no frontiersman had ever seen man-made "comets." Jackson, however, rode behind the line on a white horse, cheers following him as he went. "Don't mind these rockets," he called to each unit he passed. "They are mere toys to amuse children." Cheers turned to laughter as the rockets swished harmlessly overhead.[51]

Nobody laughed at the British infantry, however. These veterans advanced in long columns, as if on parade. Bugles sounded commands to quicken or slow the pace, or to move right or left. Bayonets glinted. Battle flags fluttered. The bagpipes of the 93rd Highlanders, a Scottish unit, wailed. Americans stood speechless, stunned by these moving red walls of humanity.

Suddenly, *Louisiana* opened fire on the column closest to the river. Moments later, guns on the breastwork thundered. "Scarce a ball passed over, or fell short of its mark," a British officer recalled, "but all striking full in our ranks occasioned great havoc." Cannonballs literally blew men to bits, turning teeth and bone fragments into missiles that slammed into comrades nearby. Pakenham, realizing his attack would fail, called back the columns. The British counted 152 men killed and wounded; the Americans had 17 killed and wounded.[52]

Sir Edward decided he needed more firepower to neutralize the American artillery. So, for the next few days, work crews hauled guns from the British fleet through Bayou Mazant. Unlike the smaller army guns that had destroyed *Carolina,* these were naval guns able to send twenty-four-pound iron balls a full mile. Fourteen of them arrived under cover of darkness. For protection, gunners placed them behind a breastwork of hogsheads, huge barrels filled with sugar.

Escaped slaves worked beside the gunners. These runaways understood that an American victory meant continued slavery for them, while a British victory held out hope of freedom. Some had suffered terribly; you could tell that just by looking at them. Black men had backs crisscrossed with scars from whippings. One had a collar of iron bars locked around his neck. He explained "that he had not been able to lie down since his flight, the collar being so contrived to prevent the wearer from using any other

To discipline their slaves, masters had them wear horrible torture devices like this, which prevented a person from lying down to sleep. Runaway slaves joined the British in hopes of gaining their freedom.

than an upright position." An officer had a blacksmith remove it, mocking "this ingenious symbol of a land of liberty."[53]

The morning of January 1, 1815, found the Americans preparing to celebrate the New Year with a parade. As the bands began tuning up, the British guns added their own thundering music. Terrified, Jackson's men broke ranks and ran to their posts. Jackson himself was getting dressed at his headquarters nearby, a house on the Macarty Plantation. Rushing to a top-floor window, he was met by a hail of splintering glass and falling plaster.

The British soon lost the advantage of surprise. Although they wrecked three American cannon and blew up an ammunition wagon, their gunners often aimed too high, wasting their shots. Meanwhile, Jackson's gunners began to find the enemy's range, wrecking their guns and killing their crews. Jagged splinters from hogsheads whirled through the air like immense razor blades. The unrefined sugar spilled out of the barrels and, mixing with the light rain that began to fall, became a sticky goo.

Having failed to break Jackson's line, Pakenham decided "nothing short of a grand assault at any cost" could bring victory. It would be a combined assault, aimed at punching straight through the American position. A strong detachment would cross the river downstream, capturing the guns covering Jackson's position along the Rodriguez Canal. As columns of redcoats advanced on the breastwork, their comrades would blast the Americans from across the river with the captured guns. Caught in a cross fire, Jackson would have to abandon his position, along with New Orleans. This plan was not as foolish as some critics later charged. It was a good plan badly executed because of poor timing, needless errors, and Pakenham's astonishing arrogance.[54]

To avoid further surprises, Jackson sent Choctaw scouts to watch the enemy at night. After dark, on January 7, they heard troops massing along the entire British line. Now and then they glimpsed men carrying bundles of sticks for filling ditches and ladders to scale breastworks. Work details hauled flat-bottomed boats overland, toward the river. "Oh, there is not doubt of it; they mean business; they will attack at daybreak," said Jackson before turning in for a few hours' rest.[55]

Jackson slept on a couch at headquarters. Toward midnight, an officer entered the darkened room with the latest report. He walked gingerly, threading his way among the general's aides sleeping on the floor around him. Fully dressed, all had their swords and pistols beside them. Old Hickory nodded as he listened to the whispered report. "Gentlemen," he said softly, almost apologetically, "we have slept enough."

The army was soon astir, checking weapons for the last time and eating breakfast, usually little more than corn bread and whiskey. Pirates, however, needed a bubbling brew of tar-black coffee to start their day. "That smells like better coffee than we can get," said Jackson, turning to Dominique You. "Smuggle it?" The fierce little man grinned as he filled his guest's cup. "Mebbe so, Général," he said. "I wish I had five hundred such devils," Jackson muttered as he passed on.[56]

While he visited each unit in turn, he saved his warmest greetings for the Tennesseans. As they crowded around him in the gloom, Jackson called out names by the sound of the voices.

"Joe, how are they using you? Wouldn't you rather be with Aunt Lucy than with me?" he teased Private Joseph Robertson.

"Not by a damned sight, General," came the reply.

"Stick to 'em, Joe." Jackson slapped the private on the back and moved on. Altogether he had 5,700 men. Pakenham had about 8,000 men.

At dawn on January 8, 1815, a rocket rose from the British lines and burst in a shower of bluish-silver sparks. Moments later, an answering rocket came from the riverbank. "That is their signal to advance, I believe," said Jackson.[57]

What he did not know was that a key element in Pakenham's plan had already gone wrong. The plan called for troop-carrying boats to head across the river just after nightfall. But delays had prevented their leaving until dawn. Then, after they set out, the current swept them two miles below the intended landing site, causing further delay. Even if the redcoats captured the American guns, they could not support the advancing columns in time. Knowing this, Pakenham should have canceled the attack, as his aides, in fact, advised. However, contempt for the Americans overcame sound military judgment. "I will wait my own plans no longer," he said impatiently. "Let the columns go forward!"[58]

This time the British columns came without drumbeat or bugle call. At first, the men behind the breastwork could only stare at the red waves. Then, either for joy or to relieve tension, they began to cheer. The British took up the cry, glad they were about to close with the enemy. An American band struck up "Yankee Doodle." The tune would rise above the gunfire until the battle ended.

"Give it to them, boys!" Jackson cried. "Let us finish the business today!"

The American guns fired with a deafening roar. A British officer described how cannonballs "knocked down the soldiers and tossed them in the air like old bags." Gaps opened in the ranks, but filled quickly. "Close up! Close up!" sergeants bellowed. The soldiers obeyed; they had learned on the drill field to step over the dead without breaking stride.[59]

Each American rifleman pressed his cheek against the wooden stock of his weapon and sighted down the barrel. He aimed at the spot where the white belts crossed over a redcoat's chest, or at the center of his forehead.

At the high point of the Battle of New Orleans, January 8, 1815, Old Hickory rode a white horse just behind the front line, encouraging his troops. The warships depicted here are the artist's invention; no naval vessels took part in the battle.

"They're near enough now, gentlemen," Jackson told his aides. "Fire when ready!"[60]

Seen from the British side, a "leaden torrent" spewed from the breastwork. Every rifle bullet seemed to find a mark in the densely packed columns. British officers, those who survived, agreed that Jackson's rifleman made military history that day. "Instantly," one recalled, "the whole American line . . . was ablaze. In less time than one can write it, the Forty-Fourth [Regiment] was literally swept from the face of the earth. . . . No such execution by small arms has ever been seen or heard of." Entire regiments lost their nerve, broke ranks, and ran for their lives.[61]

Pakenham was with Major General Samuel Gibbs's column on the American left when the column broke. "For shame! Recollect that you are British soldiers. *That is* the read you ought to take," he cried, pointing his sword toward the sheets of flame leaping from the breastwork. It was useless. His arm already broken by a bullet, Pakenham toppled over with bullets through the legs and stomach, dying soon afterward. Moments after, Gibbs received a mortal wound, as did General John Keane.[62]

The only British success that day came across the river, where the landing party went into action three hours late. It forced the American gun crews to retreat, but not before they made their weapons useless by "spiking"—hammering iron spikes into the firing mechanisms. Shocked by the heaps of bodies lying around him, Major General John Lambert, the highest-ranking British survivor, ordered a retreat.

Old Hickory congratulated each unit for its efforts. The soldiers cheered. The band played "Yankee Doodle" as loud as it could. Then, as the smoke began drifting away, a hush fell over the American line.

The area in front of the breastwork was a sea of red. One could have walked over British bodies for a quarter mile without setting foot on the ground. Body parts lay everywhere: arms, legs, heads, intestines. Wounded men groaned, screamed, and wept. Jackson stood speechless. The sight of the wounded stirring amid the piles of dead reminded him of the biblical account of the last days. "I never had so grand and awful idea of the resurrection as on that day," he would say later. That day's fighting cost the British 2,037 killed, wounded, and captured. Jackson reported American losses as "only seven killed & six wounded." No wonder he saw the hand of God in his victory.[63]

Jackson ordered a truce so the British could gather their wounded and bury their dead. Since there were so many wounded, he sent hundreds of them to New Orleans for treatment. On the night of January 18, the invaders returned to their ships. Pakenham's body went along, in a barrel of rum, to preserve it for burial at home. Most runaway slaves found freedom in the West Indies. Tragically, the British sold some back into slavery in the islands.

While New Orleans welcomed Jackson as a hero, the rest of the country knew nothing of his victory. News traveled slowly back then, via sea or mounted messenger, and was often outdated by the time it arrived. Within a week to ten days, Americans learned about the fight on Lake Borgne, the British advance, and Jackson's retreat to the Rodriguez Canal. Rumors of his defeat and the burning of New Orleans flew about, growing worse with each telling. "We are a lost country," newspaper editors moaned, reflecting the national mood.[64]

John Bull, the traditional symbol of England, hauled in disgrace out of a Louisiana swamp by the ears after his defeat by Old Hickory at New Orleans.

News of Jackson's victory reached Washington, D.C., on February 4. Next day, a newspaper printed the story under a headline in its largest, boldest type: ALMOST INCREDIBLE VICTORY! Although repairs had barely begun, the capital went wild with joy. Strangers shook hands and hugged one another in the

streets. At night, windows shone with candles and lanterns. From Washington, riders spread the news across the land. Before long, everyone was saying "victory" and "Jackson" in the same breath. On February 14, the Treaty of Ghent arrived in Washington. Two days later, the Senate ratified it by a vote of thirty-five to zero.

Jackson knew none of this when Rachel and Andrew Jr. joined him in New Orleans. Rachel, now forty-eight, had grown so stout that elegant Creole ladies sneered, "She shows how far skin can be stretched." Yet they could also tell by her husband's admiring eyes that he thought her beautiful. At a ball given to celebrate George Washington's birthday on February 22, they won the hearts of the New Orléanais with a display of folk dances. A guest wrote: "To see these two figures, the General, a long, haggard man, with limbs like a skeleton, and Madame la Generale, a short, fat dumpling, bobbing opposite each other like half-drunken Indians, to a wild medley of *'Possum up de Gum Tree,'* and endeavoring to make a spring into the air, was very remarkable, and far more edifying a spectacle than any European ballet could possibly have furnished."[65]

Official word of the peace treaty reached New Orleans on March 13, sixty-four days after the last battle between the Americans and the British. Aides offered Jackson their congratulations. For the first time, he told them of his childhood and of his mother, Betty. "Gentlemen," he said, "how I wish *she* could have lived to see this day." She, more than anyone, had shaped the boy who became the man.[66]

The treaty did not mention the grievances that caused the war. Diplomats saw no need to go into them. With Napoleon gone from the scene, Britain ended its blockade of France, and thus the need to search neutral ships. The treaty turned the clock back to June 1812. Neither side gained or lost terri-

PEACE.

Office of the Political and Commercial Register,
Sunday, Feb. 12th, 1815—2 o'clock, P. M.

We have the heartfelt satisfaction of announcing to our Fellow Citizens, that an express passed through Philadelphia this morning for Washington, bearing the most welcome intelligence that a Treaty of PEACE had been signed by the American and British Commissioners on the 24th of December.

Mr. Carrol, who brings the Treaty, arrived at New York in the British Sloop of War Favorite, Capt. J. Maxwell.

When the Express left New York last night at 11 o'clock, the City was brilliantly Illuminated in honor of this most grateful event.

Our Church Bells are now saluting the great occasion with a joyful peal.

The Southern Mail of this day brings nothing new.

One of the first announcements that the Treaty of Ghent had reached the United States.

tory by it. At first glance, then, the conflict proved—nothing. What is worse, Jackson's victory seemed a useless exercise in killing.

Yet the actual results, beyond the words of the treaty, are more complicated. After signing the treaty, the head of the American negotiating team, John Quincy Adams, turned to an English diplomat. "I hope," he said, "this will be the last treaty of peace between Great Britain and the United States." That wish came true. British contempt for America died with Sir Edward Pakenham and his redcoats in front of Jackson's breastwork. Gradually, peace healed old wounds, and with healing came respect and friendship. Within fifty years, the United States and Canada would share the longest demilitarized border in the world. In the twentieth century, the United States and Britain fought as allies in two world wars.[67]

Americans called the War of 1812 the "second war of independence." They believed it proved that their country was no accident of history. England's former colonies were truly an independent nation, with a rightful place in the family of nations.

Jackson's victory at New Orleans was equally important. While it could not influence the treaty makers, because the treaty was drawn up before the victory, it decided how the treaty would be applied. His victory settled the question of the Louisiana Purchase. The purchase was probably illegal, as Britain and Spain maintained, although no court would ever rule on the matter. Yet, as practical men, British and Spanish officials conceded that American possession of the Louisiana Territory was an accomplished fact, so they said nothing more of its legality. Louisiana, the first part of the territory admitted as a state, in 1812, would remain in the Union.

Now settlers could continue their westward march, with all the problems attendant upon it. On the Great Plains, settlers would come upon immense buffalo herds and the tribes that hunted them on horseback. Like their woodland cousins, tribes such as the Lakota, Cheyenne, and Comanche would fight to save their way of life. In time, Americans would cross the Rocky Mountains into Spanish California. More, Jackson's victory at New Orleans sealed the fate not only of the Creek Nation, but of every Indian tribe in the South, and also of Spanish Florida. That, in turn, would open new lands to growing cotton and the spread of slavery and, ultimately, to the Civil War.

ATTENTION.

THE committee of arrangement is authorised to state to the citizens of Nashville and its vicinity, that GENERAL JACKSON will arrive at Nashville on Monday next. Messrs. *G. M Deaderick* and *Thomas Claiborne*, members of the committee, are deputed to meet GENERAL JACKSON, with such other citizens as may be desirous of accompanying them, at Franklin on Sunday evening, and the next day to escort him from thence to Nashville.—Messrs. *James Jackson* and *John Childress*, two other members of the committee, will meet the *General* at some convenient place, a few miles south of Nashville on Monday, and in conjunction with the Franklin escort, conduct him into town. The citizens of the town and neighborhood, are *all* respectfully invited to join them on horseback, at 10 o'clock monday morning, on the public square.

May 12, 1815.

A broadside announcing Nashville's official welcome for Jackson after winning the Battle of New Orleans.

But these results lay in the future. In 1815, Old Hickory spoke of the recent war's deeper meaning. "Henceforward we shall be respected," he told his Nashville friends. "Years will continue to develop our inherent qualities, until, from being the youngest and weakest, we shall become the most powerful nation in the universe."[68]

For countless Americans, the orphan from the Waxhaws embodied that nation.

IV

ON THE BRINK OF FATE

We stand this moment on the brink of fate. . . . We are no longer to remain plain and simple republics of farmers, like New England colonists, or the Dutch settlements on the Hudson. We are fast becoming a great nation, with great commerce, manufactures, population, wealth, luxuries, and with the vices they engender.

—JUDGE JAMES KENT, NEW YORK, 1821

In the early 1800s, the tale of Rip Van Winkle fascinated Americans. In Washington Irving's famous story, the main character gets drunk and falls asleep for twenty years. Awakening at last, he finds nothing is as it used to be. His wife is dead, his daughter is married, and a Revolutionary War has ended with the creation of the United States of America.

Rip's experience mirrored real life. For those aged fifty or older in, say, 1815, the world in which they had grown up was becoming a fading memory. Change, swift and dramatic, was making itself felt. Another America, a dynamic, vigorous America, was coming into being, and Old Hickory would nourish it and help it grow.

Returning home from New Orleans, Jackson grew restless after five months. So, when the government divided the United States Army into two divisions, north and south, he agreed to head the Division of the South. Not only did the post pay $2,400 a year, a high salary in 1815, it allowed him to make his headquarters at The Hermitage.

The general's chief task was protecting the nation's border with Spanish Florida. Trouble there sprang from the treaty Jackson had forced the Creeks to accept the previous year. It was so unfair that, instead of having a calming effect, it acted as a provocation. The surviving Red Sticks, joined by Jackson's former Creek allies, grew ever more resentful. Whenever surveyors tried to map the treaty lands, Jackson had to send troops to protect them. Some warriors, the troops learned, had recently gotten guns from British traders in Florida.

The Treaty of Ghent, which ended the War of 1812, posed a different problem for Jackson. Under Article IX of the treaty, the United States promised to return all Indian lands taken since 1811, including the 23 million acres seized from the Creeks. What to do? While in command at New Orleans, Jackson had asked whether, in times of danger, "it [is] wise . . . to sacrifice the spirit of the laws to the letter, and by adhering too strictly to the letter, lose the *substance* forever?" He answered his own question, insisting that "laws must sometimes be silent when necessity speaks." In other words, the former judge believed, it was all right to break the law if "vital" interests were at stake.[1]

This idea runs counter to the American belief that a law must be obeyed until it is changed in a lawful way, that is, by the lawmaking body that created it in the first place. Jackson disagreed. He had no doubt about *his* motives; in his mind, he always did what he knew was best for the country. Treaties, of course, are the law of the nation, as valid and binding as any law passed by Congress and signed by the president. By the Eternal! Jackson would not enforce Article IX, and damn the consequences.

What followed was even more shocking than his defiance of the law. Nothing happened. Nobody—not President James Monroe, elected in 1816; not the cabinet, the heads of the main government departments; not Congress, the national legislature—challenged him. The administration, like the public at large, wanted to keep the Indian lands, and take more. Besides, the administration thought, why challenge the greatest war hero since George Washington just to please the Indians and Great Britain? His Majesty's government knew Jackson was flouting the treaty. However, to protect its territory in the north, Canada, it sacrificed the Indians of the South.[2]

Between 1816 and 1820, the Monroe administration gave Jackson a free hand in dealing with the Cherokee as well as his former allies, the Chickasaw and Choctaw. "Look around and recollect what happened to our brothers the Creeks," Jackson told a gathering of chiefs. Fearing the man they called Sharp Knife, and tempted by his offers of trade goods, they signed away another 2 million acres of land in Tennessee, Alabama, Georgia, and Mississippi.[3]

Next, Jackson turned to Florida, which Southerners especially wanted for cotton growing. Southerners also saw Florida as a threat to their "Peculiar Institution," slavery. The Spanish territory had become a haven for blacks escaping slavery in Georgia and South Carolina. Jackson had enlisted "free blacks" to fight the British, but these were runaways fleeing to foreign territory. According to state laws, they were property, and remained so wherever they happened to be. Over time, the fugitives had cleared land and planted crops. A few intermarried with local Indians. Knowing slaves' value, however, Indians often collected rewards for returning runaways to plantation owners or kept them for themselves.

The British, allied with the Seminole Indians, had built a fort on the Apalachicola River sixty miles south of the Georgia border. When Jackson drove the British from Florida in 1814, a band of blacks drove the Seminole from the fort. Mauricio de Zúñiga, governor of Florida, did not consider the blacks free people, let alone citizens of Spain. "Negro Fort," as Spaniards called it, became a serious problem. A magnet for runaways, it was a base for blacks' raids into Georgia; blacks raided for revenge against former masters, to free enslaved family members, and for loot. Blacks even attacked Spanish outposts and Seminole villages. Señor Zúñiga wanted Negro Fort destroyed, but lacking soldiers, he wrote the "esteemed" General "Andres" Jackson, saying he "would be proud" to serve under him against the blacks.[4]

Jackson did not need Spanish help. In the spring of 1816, he ordered General Edmund P. Gaines to destroy Negro Fort. As two American supply boats approached the fort, they drew fire from its cannons. Blacks also captured a sailor named Daniels, covered him with tar, and burned him alive; burning alive was a punishment Southerners meted out to rebellious slaves or slaves who had killed white people.[5]

Joined by Seminole warriors, Gaines advanced on Negro Fort by land, supported by two gunboats on the river. On July 27, a cannonball heated in a boat's cook oven struck a shed filled with gunpowder. Some 270 men, women, and children died in the blast. Gaines returned sixty survivors to slavery in Georgia; he gave three black leaders, captured alive, to the Seminoles for execution. Before long, however, the Seminole themselves became the enemy.[6]

The Seminoles, or Wanderers, were a mixture of Florida Indians and Creeks who had drifted south during the 1700s. All Seminole villages lay in Florida, except Fowltown, just across the border in Georgia. Fowltown was on land surrendered by the Creeks in the Treaty of Fort Jackson. Villagers in Fowltown, encouraged by Alexander Arbuthnot, an elderly Scottish trader who had befriended the Indians, refused to leave. The treaty, villagers said, did not apply to them; they had not fought the United States or signed away anything. Ordered by Jackson to expel the villagers, on November 21, 1817, Gaines destroyed Fowltown, driving the inhabitants away. So began the First Seminole War.[7]

To avenge what Gaines did to Fowltown, Seminole warriors stormed out of Florida to ravage frontier Georgia. On one occasion, they ambushed an open boat with forty soldiers, seven women, and four children on the Apalachicola River. Only four soldiers and a woman escaped by swimming ashore. Furious, the warriors grabbed the children by their feet and bashed their heads against the sides of the boat. It was Fort Mims again, the press howled. Again Indians had massacred "innocent" whites. Journalists, however, never mentioned the connection between the injustices of the Fort Jackson Treaty, white land hunger, and Indian violence. For most Americans at that time, it seems, justice lay all on one side—their own.[8]

To safeguard frontier Georgia, Secretary of War John C. Calhoun, once a leading War Hawk, ordered Jackson to stop the Seminole raids at all costs. The general, however, wanted to use the Seminole troubles as a pretext for conquering Florida for the United States. The conquest would accomplish three things at once. It would secure Georgia's southern border, deprive European enemies of a possible base in any future war, and open more land to American settlers. Already some Southerners, anticipating the seizure, had illegally cleared small plots for farming and brought enslaved blacks into areas of northern Florida. The Spanish authorities were too weak to stop them. Seizing all of Florida, Jackson told President Monroe in a private letter, "can be done without implicating the government." All the president had to do was give him some hint of approval "and in sixty days it will be accomplished."[9]

Critics called President Monroe "a dull, sleepy, insignificant-looking man [who] hasn't got brains enough to hold his hat on." But although the president might have sometimes seemed inept, he was a shrewd politician skilled at avoiding blame. Monroe wanted to take Florida; that is clear from his letters. Jackson had asked him to consent to an invasion of the colony of a nation at peace with the United States. Now, under the Constitution, Congress alone may declare war. Yet nobody had asked Congress to declare war on Spain. In effect, then, Jackson was asking the president to play dumb while he launched an illegal war. Monroe did not answer his letter. Later, during the uproar following the invasion, the president said he did not remember reading Jackson's letter. Since he was ill when it arrived, he simply put it aside and forgot it, he said.[10]

Although we have no written proof, it is hard to believe that Monroe did not understand the general perfectly. When Jackson got no response to his letter, he took Monroe's silence as permission for an invasion. After the invasion began, war secretary Calhoun may have let the secret out. He wrote Governor William Bibb of Alabama: "General Jackson is vested with full power to conduct the war as he may best judge." What war? The Seminole War? The war to seize Florida? Probably both.[11]

On March 15, 1818, Jackson invaded Florida with three thousand regular troops, Georgia militia, and Indian allies who joined at his insistence. Moving swiftly, Jackson waged a campaign of terror, burning every Seminole village where warriors offered resistance. On April 6, he captured St. Marks on the Gulf of Mexico, a Spanish fort where reports said Seminole warriors had gone for guns. Finding no warriors, he headed toward a Seminole stronghold, the villages of Chief Boleck—Billy Bowlegs to whites. After a grueling march through swamps, he found the villages deserted. Two misses in a row. Had someone tipped off the enemy?[12]

Along the way, a naval officer captured two important Red Stick fugitives, Hillis Hadjo and Himollemico, by an old pirate trick. To get close to its prey, a pirate ship would fly the flag of a friendly country, then show its "true colors," the black skull and crossbones, at the last moment. The officer flew a British flag from his ship's mast. Upon searching his prisoners, he found that one carried an official document dating from the War of 1812 naming him a British officer. Although these men were not charged with any specific

Capture of the Red Stick leaders Hillis Hadjo and Himollemico during Jackson's invasion of Florida in 1818. Jackson had them hanged, even though they had not been charged with any specific crime.

crime, to break the Indians' will to resist, Jackson had them hung from the ship's mast. He justified his action by insisting, "it is all important that these men be . . . made examples of." According to the laws of war, as defined in Jackson's day, a commander may punish crimes committed in a war zone after conviction by a court-martial; the law said nothing about executing prisoners without trial to make "examples."[13]

Jackson's men also arrested Alexander Arbuthnot, the trader who had befriended the Fowltown villagers, and Robert Ambrister, a former lieutenant in the Royal Marines, both British subjects. Meanwhile, a soldier captured a black man carrying a letter from Arbuthnot to his son, who happened to be visiting Chief Boleck. In the letter, he told his son of the American advance and advised him to leave.

Jackson ordered the prisoners court-martialed. Arbuthnot defended himself by saying that, yes, he had denounced American aggression against Indians, but he had not urged Chief Boleck to escape. Ambrister, a freelance adventurer, admitted to having armed and sent a party of Seminoles to attack the invaders. A panel of officers convicted Arbuthnot of aiding Chief Boleck and sentenced him to hang. Next, it sentenced Ambrister to be shot for waging war against the United States. Ambrister threw himself on the court's mercy. Without explaining why, it reduced his sentence to fifty lashes "on his bare back" and a year's hard labor. Jackson was in no mood to show mercy. Declaring Ambrister "an outlaw and a pirate," he overruled the court. On April 29, both men died.[14]

Robert Remini, Jackson's leading modern biographer, believes that the general's behavior toward his prisoners reveals an ugly picture of frontier fears, racism, and violence. Moreover, executing two British subjects on *Spanish* soil showed not just a willingness to take responsibility, but a recklessness that raised the fear of a "Napoleon," a military dictator, in America. Indeed, Spaniards called Jackson "the Napoleon of the woods."[15]

Jackson continued his advance, storming Pensacola on May 24. After token resistance, he arrested the governor, imprisoned the Spanish garrison, and set up a military government. On June 2, he declared the war over and left for Tennessee. Having caused so much misery, his campaign, in turn, had made him a physical wreck. "I am at present worn down with fatigue and by a bad cough with a pain in my left side which produced a spitting of blood, have reduced me to a skeleton. I must have rest," he wrote President Monroe.[16]

News of Jackson's Florida campaign outraged people on both sides of the Atlantic. In England, an American diplomat wrote from London, the deaths of Arbuthnot and Ambrister led to mass protests. "WAR MIGHT HAVE BEEN PRODUCED BY HOLDING UP A FINGER." That is, the government could have declared war with the eager support of the people. In Washington, Don Luis de Onís, the Spanish minister, demanded "satisfaction," a polite term for Pensacola's return, an American apology, and a court-martial for Jackson.[17]

Official Washington wanted to put the blame on Jackson alone. House Speaker Henry Clay claimed, correctly, that the Seminole War had originated with the harsh Treaty of Fort Jackson. "A more dictatorial spirit I have never seen displayed in any instrument," Clay said. "It spared to the poor Indians neither their homes [nor] their property." Worse, Clay warned, the general's actions threatened "a triumph over the constitution of the land . . . a triumph over the liberties of the people." Nothing personal, Clay added, but Jackson could not be allowed to become the American Napoleon. Jackson, however, always took criticism personally. When he read Clay's words, he snapped, "I despise the villain." Clay had made a lifelong enemy.[18]

In their meetings, Monroe and his cabinet ganged up on the absent general. They accused Jackson of illegally invading Spanish Florida, executing British subjects on foreign territory, and provoking Britain—all of which he had actually done. Soon afterward, Jackson learned of what may be the first attempted government cover-up in American history. Monroe suggested that he allow him to "correct"—change—embarrassing parts of his reports from Florida. Since those reports described Jackson's actions in detail, Monroe could not say he did not know what was going on. The general indignantly refused to allow anyone to doctor his reports.[19]

Jackson had one defender. As the chief negotiator of the Treaty of Ghent and a legal scholar, Secretary of State John Quincy Adams carried great weight in Washington. Like all cabinet members, Adams wanted to make Florida American, but believed that punishing Jackson would encourage Spain to hold on to it more tightly. In his diary Adams noted, "everything that [Jackson] did was *defensive,* that as such it was neither against Spain nor [in] violation of the Constitution." The execution of Arbuthnot and Ambrister, he added, were "acts of retributive justice"—punishment for real offenses. Later, in words close to Jackson's own, Adams told the cabinet that Jackson's actions in Florida had been "justified by necessity." Rather than punish him, the government should praise him for his "most eminent services to the nation."[20]

Adams asked the president to calm things down by ordering U.S. troops out of Florida. Then, in a document widely circulated in Europe, he justified America's "defensive acts of hostility." In scathing language, he recalled Britain's long history of stirring up "Indian and Negro War" against the United States. Had Britain not allowed its subjects to make trouble in Florida, Adams said, Arbuthnot and Ambrister would still be alive. As for Spain, he addressed King Ferdinand's "profound indignation" at the invasion. For years, Indians had killed Americans in cross-border raids from Florida. "Where was His Majesty's profound indignation at that?" Spain must decide. Let it police Florida properly, or sell it to the United States. If it could do neither, let force decide the issue.[21]

Adams's message had an immediate effect. The surviving ex-presidents— John Adams, Thomas Jefferson, James Madison—approved the secretary of state's position. Criticism of Jackson in Washington vanished like air from a punctured balloon. Britain backed down, His Majesty's government deciding it preferred to trade with America rather than go to war over the "unauthorized practices" by the two men Jackson had executed. Unable to fight without British aid, Spain gave in.[22]

On February 22, 1819, Secretary Adams and Minister Onís signed the Transcontinental Treaty. For $5 million, Spain sold Florida to the United States and recognized the legality of the Louisiana Purchase. Adams gave credit where it was due. Jackson's invasion of Florida, he said, "had been among the most immediate and prominent causes that produced the treaty." Jackson's popularity soared to new heights. Not only had he defeated the British at New Orleans, he had opened millions of acres of Indian lands to settlers and played the key role in adding Spanish Florida to the United States. Most Americans, apparently, were so impressed by his achievements that they overlooked his rough-and-ready methods.[23]

Meanwhile, Old Hickory looked toward the future. One day in the spring of 1819, Jackson's friend and neighbor Major William Lewis came to The Hermitage for a visit. The two men went for a stroll, winding up near the log house the Jacksons had lived in for fifteen years. Pausing, Jackson stuck his cane into the ground. We have outgrown that old place, he said. Now that he could afford better, he wanted to build another, grander house—a mansion. Rachel deserved it. "Mrs. Jackson chose this spot, and she shall have her wish. I am going to build this house for *her*," he said. "I don't expect to live in it myself." Although his health had improved, at age fifty-two he doubted he had much time left.[24]

The result was a two-story brick mansion, probably of Jackson's design, built by slaves working under a white supervisor hired for the job. Two parlors, a dining room, and the couple's bedroom led off a central hallway on the first floor; the second floor had six bedrooms for guests. Jackson spared no expense to make The Hermitage a showplace. Furniture, carpets, chandeliers, wallpaper, tableware—he filled it with the best money could buy.

While grand by American standards, the Jacksons' home did not impress European visitors. "The first thing that struck me was the simplicity of his house," a French guest wrote. "I asked myself if this could really be the dwelling of the most popular man in the United States." In Europe, minor officials "would think themselves dishonored, and would not dare to receive anyone in their houses, if they only possessed a residence as this of Jackson's." Then again, George Washington's stately Mount Vernon, and Thomas Jeffer-

The Hermitage as portrayed in an 1856 lithograph by Samuel B. Jones.

son's Monticello, also inspired "contempt and disgust" in wealthy Europeans.[25]

As always, the Jacksons kept an open house. Friends found a warm welcome, plenty to eat, and good conversation. John Overton, by now a leading state judge, came often. The years had left their mark on him. A guest described Overton as a "queer-looking little old man," bald as an egg, who had "lost his teeth and swallowed his lips." A younger man, Sam Houston, spent several weeks there, training for an upcoming duel under Jackson's expert eye. Ralph E. W. Earl came for a few days and stayed seventeen years. A wanderer who made his living by painting portraits, Earl married a niece of Rachel's. When she died soon after the wedding, Rachel asked him to live at The Hermitage, the first real home he had ever known. Earl painted dozens of pictures of the general and his family, for which he received fifty dollars each.[26]

To supervise Spain's handover of Florida, in 1821 the president appointed Jackson governor of the territory. Jackson would have preferred to stay in Tennessee to pay off his debts, the result of a recent economic downturn. Yet the post paid well and did not involve fighting. He had seen enough of war to hate it. While nations may have to fight at times, he wrote his favorite nephew, Jack Donelson, "war is a great evil . . . and a curse to any nation." Old Hickory resigned from the army, arriving in Florida in July. After completing his job, in November he resigned as governor of the territory and went home.[27]

He returned a physical wreck. Florida's tropical heat and humidity, combined with his generally poor health, nearly killed him. Recovering slowly, Jackson said he wished to live out his days quietly, with Rachel, at The Hermitage. Yet that was not to be. His actions since 1813 had important results. Thanks in part to him, an America far different from the one he and Rip Van Winkle had known as children back in the 1700s was emerging. For eight years, 1829 to 1837, Old Hickory would guide the nation as its president. We cannot understand what he did without first understanding the nation he led.

In the mid-nineteenth century, foreigners used the term "American Multiplication Table" for a population increase that rose more steeply than any previously known. In 1790, the first U.S. Census counted 3.9 million people, white and black, up from roughly 2.7 million a decade earlier. After that, population grew by a third every ten years, nearly doubling every twenty years: 5.3 million (1800), 7.2 million (1810), 9.6 million (1820), 12.8 million (1830), 17.1 million (1840).

Tens of thousands of European immigrants arrived each year, but the bulk of the increase was from American-born children. Moreover, these were more likely to reach adulthood than children born elsewhere, and so America's population growth astounded the rest of the world. With land cheap and food plentiful, families with four or five children were common, and those with eight or ten not unusual even in cities. Children provided valuable farm labor even from an early age. As they became adults and their parents grew infirm, children cared for them. Thus, most parents assumed that the more children they had, the better.

Visitors noted that American society differed from that of Europe in key ways. Coming from lands ruled by monarchs and nobles, where ordinary people had almost no chance of rising above their "station," Europeans saw a more just society in America. There, all free white men were equal in the eyes of the law. Americans tended to accept only social divisions based on personal achievement, not on titles or ancestry. As the saying went, "kin and kin-in-law don't count a cuss." Equality released free men's creative energies, encouraging them to strive harder to improve their lives.

Note: free (and white) men, not free women. In America, as in Europe, not only could women not vote, they had little control over their own lives. Popular belief held that women were inferior to men. Men were supposedly logical, practical, and scientific, while women were sensitive, impractical, and emotional. Thus, the law put unmarried women under the control of male relatives: fathers, brothers, uncles, cousins. In effect, it regarded single adult women as children and lunatics; that is, unfit to make important decisions. As for wives, an old legal rule from England put it bluntly: "The wife is dead in law." Upon marrying, a woman promised to love, honor, and obey her husband. In return, he must cherish, protect, and guide her. Any property she had belonged to him. Their children belonged to him. If she worked outside the home, she must give him her earnings. She could not make contracts, nor sue or be sued in court.[28]

At the same time, the wife was popularly called "the angel of the house," "the center and lawgiver in the home." The home was her husband's refuge from the hubbub of the outside world. The wife made it a loving place ruled by the highest morality. Society expected her to speak, think, and act properly. Modesty dictated that she avoid certain words, like "leg." Leg was a dirty word—in 1820. *Limb* was the proper word to use. A young woman once walked away limping from a fall. When Captain Frederick Marryat, an English visitor, asked if she had twisted a leg, she blushed. No, she said; she twisted a limb. Tables and pianos had limbs, too. In some households, ladies covered them with little trousers decorated with lace frills. These rules applied only to the so-called better people, who enjoyed a higher standard of living, not to poor whites, let alone Native Americans and blacks, whether enslaved or free.[29]

America between 1812 and 1835 experienced three changes as important as the founding of the nation itself. These were the industrial revolution, the transportation revolution, and the rise of the market economy. Like stones tossed into pools of still water, each sent ripples throughout society, changing the way people earned their living, thought, and conducted politics.

The industrial revolution began in England in the eighteenth century. By the 1760s, about the time of Jackson's birth, machinery began to be used to manufacture all sorts of things. "Manufacture," in its original meaning (from

An early factory scene showing a young woman operating a weaving machine. Factories often employed women and children at lower wages than adult males.

manus, Latin for hand), was the making of an object by hand. Crafting items by hand changed with the coming of machines that were driven by running water or steam. Gathering machines at central points, called factories, made possible large-scale production of many kinds of goods.

At first, England's chief industry was textiles, the making of cloth, a basic human necessity. To safeguard trade secrets, laws forbade "mechanics," expert textile workers, from leaving the country. Nevertheless, a man named Samuel Slater did just that. In 1789, he memorized the plans of spinning and weaving machines, put on a disguise, and sailed for America. At Pawtucket, Rhode Island, he set up a small textile factory, America's first.

Factories spread slowly, until the War of 1812 halted shipments of English goods to America. As shortages grew, prices soared, encouraging others to copy Slater's methods. After the war, English goods flooded American seaports. Some Americans saw renewed trade with England as a threat to liberty. "Never shall we be a truly free people," an American manufacturer said, "till we are independent commercially of England as we are politically." Congress responded to the feelings of its manufacturing class by passing the Tariff of 1816, that is, a duty, or tax, on various foreign imports. By making these imports more expensive than the same American-made goods, the tariff gave American producers a protected market, stimulating American industry.[30]

Textile manufacturers preferred cotton for everything from clothing to bedsheets. Cotton is a marvelous fiber—lightweight, cool, and easy to dye in attractive colors. England got its cotton from Egypt, India, and the West Indies. However, as the demand for cotton grew, it had to find other sources of this raw material.

The Southern states in America had grown cotton since the 1780s, but never enough to meet manufacturers' needs. The problem was that it took a slave ten hours, working by hand, to separate a pound of cotton fiber from its seeds. That changed in 1793. While visiting a friend's plantation, Eli Whitney, a Connecticut inventor, saw a cat claw a chicken until only feathers remained in its claws. This gave him the idea for the cotton gin, or engine—a box with a hand crank that turned a cylinder with iron "claws" to comb out the seeds from the cotton. Now a single gin could yield a thousand pounds of fiber a day.

Eli Whitney, inventor of the cotton gin

To supply cotton to manufacturers, it is not enough to remove seeds easily; you need enough cotton to remove them from. That requires land. Cotton did not grow well in the soil of the Old South, where Virginia, Georgia, and the Carolinas specialized in raising tobacco. Worse, cotton was a "soil killer." Constant replanting used up vital nutrients and exhausted the soil, leading to the need for new land.

Here is where Andrew Jackson came in. He had not forced

the Indians to give up millions of acres of land for nothing. Tennessee and the states created from his land grabs had the ideal soil and climate for growing cotton on a vast scale. Alabama became a state in 1817. Mississippi joined the Union in 1819, naming its capital Jackson in his honor. Thus, Old Hickory was the founder of the Cotton Kingdom, as Americans called the cotton-growing region. Louisiana, Arkansas, and Texas would later join the Cotton Kingdom, too.

Slaves operating a cotton gin on a Southern plantation. More than anything else, Whitney's invention created the "Cotton Kingdom," the economic motor that for generations powered America's foreign trade. From a drawing in Harper's Weekly, *1869.*

When the government sold newly acquired Indian lands, those people close to Jackson cashed in on his contacts and influence. John Coffee became surveyor general of Alabama, a post that allowed him to select prime farmland before anyone else, and then buy it cheaply at a government auction. John Overton and John Donelson, Rachel's brother, also made fortunes speculating in Indian lands. In Florida, Jackson's inside knowledge allowed his nephew Jack Donelson to buy thousands of acres near Pensacola. Old Hickory bought Indian lands, too. When he bid for a valuable plot, nobody bid against him out of respect (or fear?). Yet this did not happen often, nor did it make him rich.[31]

These lands attracted settlers from across the Old South. Each family brought its livestock—and its slaves. Had you ridden along Southern roads in the 1820s, you would have seen lines of black men, women, and children trudging along, driven by armed guards on horseback. Most went barefoot. Men wore handcuffs and some were bound together by chains slipped through iron collars. They were valuable "property," for it was slavery that made large-scale cotton growing possible. By 1830, three out of every four Southern slaves were employed growing cotton. Production soared, nearly doubling every decade: 400,000 bales in 1820, 750,000 bales in 1830, 1.3 million bales in 1840. By 1850, seven-eighths of the world's "white gold" came from the Cotton Kingdom, accounting for over half the exports of the United States.[32]

An English traveler, Captain Basil Hall, thought Southerners suffered from a disease, cotton on the brain. Wherever he turned, he heard cotton, cotton, cotton. "At every dock or wharf we encountered it in huge piles or pyramids of bales, and our decks were soon choked with it. All day, and almost all night long, the captain, pilot, crew, and passengers were talking of nothing else."[33]

Cotton had become king, the dynamo driving the American economy. In the North, where states had abolished slavery after the Revolution, cotton and slavery still had a colossal impact. Manufacturers' profits, workers' wages, and merchants' sales depended on them. Aided by the tariff, Northern factories made tools for Southern farms and wove cheap cloth for slave clothing. Northern forges made the handcuffs, chains, and collars used to control unruly slaves. Northern shipyards built vessels to carry the cotton to English mills. Northern companies insured those cargoes, and the lives of the slaves who grew them.

None of this could have happened without new technologies also arising in transportation. These brought changes that amazed old-timers like Old Hickory. Within a generation, they saw the cost of moving people and things tumble, while the speed and volume of what could be moved grew beyond anything ever thought possible. We call these changes the transportation revolution.

In Jackson's youth, around the time of the American Revolution, transportation had been slow and expensive. Stagecoaches, the favorite form of long-distance travel, averaged four miles an hour and cost a traveler five cents a mile. For that, you got to squeeze into a springless vehicle with eleven other people and ride over rutted dirt roads. Now and then you got "stumped," when the coach hit a tree stump and overturned.

Corduroy roads, built of logs set side by side, offered fewer upsets, but the ride was still a jolting, bruising, teeth-jarring, stomach-churning ordeal. "For two days and two nights," a traveler recalled, "my body was exposed to the thumps of this horrid road, and when I got to

A stagecoach stops to allow passengers to stay overnight at a country inn around 1825. Before the railroad, overland travel was slow and expensive.

A side-wheel steamboat, 1835. With vessels such as this, it became possible to carry passengers and freight up rivers, moving swiftly against the current on their own power.

Philadelphia [from New York City] . . . my body was a perfect *jelly*—without one sound spot upon it, too *tired* to stand, too *sore* to sit." Although corduroy roads made travel easier, they were not suited for bulky cargoes like grain. In 1800, it cost as much to send a ton of grain thirty miles by road as to ship it by sea to Europe.[34]

That changed with the coming of the steamboat, the most important advance in transportation since ancient people invented the sailing ship. On August 9, 1807, Robert Fulton tested his *Clermont* on the Hudson River at New York City. Onlookers called the steam-powered vessel "Fulton's Folly," expecting it to burst into flames the moment it got under way. Despite its strange appearance, *Clermont* went the 150 miles to Albany in thirty-two hours, compared with three days by road.

Within eight years, steamboats had replaced flatboats on America's rivers, especially on the Mississippi. Since colonial times, each year thousands of flatboats had drifted down the "Father of Waters" to New Orleans, a journey of at least two months. Since it was impossible to float upstream, against the powerful current, after delivering their produce owners sold the flatboats for firewood. Steamboats made two-way river travel possible. Just two years after Jackson's victory over the British, a vessel called the *Enterprise* covered the 1,350 miles from New Orleans to Louisville, Kentucky, in a week. The cost of sending a hundred pounds of freight up to Louisville dropped from five dollars to twenty-five cents. Not surprisingly, the *Andrew Jackson* was the first steamboat to dock at Nashville.

Well-heeled passengers slept in cabins and relaxed in lounges, called saloons, featuring crystal chandeliers, velvet-covered furniture, and gambling tables. The majority, however, slept on a bale of cotton, if they were quick enough to get one, or curled up on the deck floor. Rich or poor, few had any understanding of hygiene. That amazed Charles Dickens, the famous novelist, who visited the United States. Fellow passengers could not imagine why Dickens was so fussy about cleanliness. He recalled:

> The washing and dressing apparatus for the passengers generally consists of two towels, three small wooden basins, a keg of water and a ladle to serve it out with, six square inches of looking-glass, two [pieces] of yellow soap, a comb and brush for the head, and nothing for the teeth. Everyone uses the comb and brush except myself. Everybody stares to see me using my own; and two or three gentlemen are strongly disposed to banter me on my prejudices, but don't. . . . In all modes of traveling, the American customs, with reference to the means of personal cleanliness . . . are extremely negligent and filthy; and I strongly incline to the belief that a considerable amount of illness is referable to this cause.[35]

Charles Dickens, the famed English novelist, wrote American Notes, *a classic travel account of the 1830s.*

Dickens was right. Poor washing habits led to a host of skin diseases, which created a huge market for phony medicines called "miracle powders."

Passengers might need a miracle to survive a steamboat journey. By 1850, accidents had destroyed nearly a thousand vessels. Submerged rocks and tree trunks cracked their hulls, sending them to the bottom and drowning passengers. Sparks from smokestacks ignited cargoes of cotton and hay, burning passengers. Boiler explosions were common, since engineers knew little about how metals behaved under the stress of heat and steam pressure. Between 1825 and 1850, boiler explosions killed no fewer than 1,400 people. Flying wreckage and scalding steam injured countless others.[36]

Steamboats also hurt the environment. In Jackson's day, they used wood, not coal, as fuel. Western forests often grew right down to the rivers' banks. A large Mississippi steamboat burned more than seven thousand cubic feet of wood each day, having to "wood up" twice daily. Wood yards, piled with logs cut to fit into boilers, lined the river, as gas stations today line highways. With over two hundred steamboats in service by 1830, forests along the Mississippi and its tributaries lost about seventy square miles of trees each day![37]

Steamboats had another drawback: they required a good river system. Yet many areas, like western New York State, were far from such systems. To reach these, Americans built artificial rivers, or canals. European cities like Amsterdam and Venice had built canals to help their trade centuries before. However, as late as 1816 the United States had only a hundred miles of canals. The following year, Governor DeWitt Clinton of New York decided to build the Erie Canal. It would be the longest in the world.

Four engineers, who had never seen a canal, designed it "by guess and by God." Under their direction, laborers, chiefly three thousand Irish immigrants, used picks, shovels, and primitive wooden cranes to dig out millions of tons of soil. As if that were not enough, they built three hundred bridges and

A picture based on a watercolor by John William Hill, from his book The Erie Canal, *published in 1831. Note the primitive wooden cranes used to move rocks and soil.*

eighty-four locks, devices for raising and lowering water level and thus boats where the land was not level. Completed in 1825, the canal stretched 364 miles from Buffalo on Lake Erie to Albany on the Hudson River. Flat-bottomed barges of fifty tons moved along the canal at five miles an hour. Their power came not from wind or steam or flowing water, but from two horses, harnessed to ropes, walking on a path beside the waterway.

A town on the Erie Canal. The building of the canal produced fantastic growth in towns already along its route and caused new towns to spring up. Notice the horses pulling the boats on the right bank.

The canal linked the entire Midwest, via Lake Erie and the Hudson River, to New York City's splendid harbor on the Atlantic coast. It reduced the travel time from New York to Buffalo from twenty days to six, and the cost of moving a ton of freight from one hundred to five dollars. Farm produce moved east from Ohio and Indiana, while American textiles and European imports moved west. As Governor Clinton predicted, the canal made New York "the greatest commercial city in the world." Its success encouraged other states to build canals. By 1830, the country had 1,277 miles of canals, rising to 3,326 miles by 1840.[38]

Steam and canal boats needed waterways; railroads went overland. Originally, "railroad trains" were lines (trains) of attached wagons drawn by horses along lines of parallel wooden beams called rail roads. In 1804, English inventors replaced the horses with a steam locomotive. The locomotive's ability to draw goods, wagons, and passenger coaches attracted the attention of Peter Cooper, a New York engineer. In May 1830, Cooper tested his *Tom Thumb,* a small locomotive with boiler tubes made of gun barrels, on thirteen miles of track near Baltimore, becoming the first American to combine the railroad with steam power.

A "railroad mania" swept the country, as business leaders pooled their money to lay tracks and build locomotives. By 1840, America had 3,328 miles of railroad track. By 1860, it had 30,636 miles, nearly as much as Britain, France, and Germany combined. Speed increased along with track mileage. *Tom Thumb* had gone ten miles an hour. Locomotives soon reached top speeds of thirty miles an hour, until then thought impossible on land. "I can only judge of the speed," said Davy Crockett, "by putting my head out to spit, which I did, and it overtook so quick, that it hit me smack in the face."[39]

Not everyone appreciated the railroad. Speeding trains scared cows into giving less milk and killed any that strayed onto the tracks. People resented trains, clanking and clattering at all hours of the day and night. Yet the railroad had come to stay. It was changing the world—changing even the way people spoke. We say to think logically is to follow "a train of thought." Railroads carried people and freight faster and farther than ever, and in all weather, except the worst snowstorms. "The Americans," Captain Marryat noted, "are a restless, locomotive people: whether for business or pleasure, they are ever on the move in their own country, and they move in masses." Why, Americans thought nothing of moving a thousand miles from home![40]

View of the interior of a passenger car about the year 1842. Early railroad travel was dangerous, with wrecks and fires claiming scores of lives each year. Yet it was fast and inexpensive.

Yet trains could be more dangerous than even steamboats. Until solid-iron rails appeared in the 1840s, passengers had "snakeheads" to fear. Vibrations caused the sheet-iron covering of wooden rails to come loose and curl up, stabbing through the floor of a car as fast as a snake strikes its prey. Wheels broke, trains ran off the tracks, and bridges collapsed. Overheated wood-burning boilers exploded. Showers of sparks from smokestacks ignited forests and wheat fields. Open coach windows admitted sparks, burning holes in seat upholstery and in people's clothing.

Despite these drawbacks, the new technology gave rise to new industries. Machinery for factories, locomotives, railroad cars, and tracks demanded ever more iron. These demands, in turn, led to advances in metalworking. Improved blast furnaces separated iron from the rock that contains it. Engineers developed machines for shaping molten iron into railroad tracks and for casting machine parts. Canals, steamboats, and railroads opened the country to settlement faster than ever before. Towns rose along their routes—as they do today, wherever cement highways allow automobiles to go.

Finally, technology spurred the market economy.

Wooden railroad bridges were often hastily built of flimsy materials, with the result shown in this print from about the year 1848.

In 1790, as lawyer Andrew Jackson settled in Nashville, most Americans—95 percent—lived on farms. Farm families mainly produced food for their own needs. Although they did not buy things very often, when they needed tools fixed or horseshoes and nails made, they visited a local blacksmith. For items like leather shoes, saddles, and tin tableware, they went to other artisans. Assisted by an apprentice or two, the artisan was his own boss. He (most artisans were men) worked in a small shop, often out of his own home. Artisans and apprentices related to one another as equals, calling one another by their first names. Working at a leisurely pace, they took frequent breaks for eating, resting, and sometimes just horsing around.

Things began to change around 1820. Wherever the transportation revolution reached, it brought the products of the industrial revolution. Many farm families came to prefer factory-made shoes, candles, soap, and furniture to those made locally. New England factories produced cloth more colorful and durable than what could be spun at home. Fire-glazed dishes were prettier and easier to clean than wooden utensils. Factory-made window glass let in more light than the paper greased with hog fat—what many farmers used in their windows. In other words, goods from far away, made by people they would never meet, enriched farmers' lives.

Yet every step forward brought problems, too. The industrial revolution forced local artisans out of business. More important, it tied country people to the market system. Farm families seldom saw cash. Normally, whatever they bought locally, they "paid" for with their own produce. Neighbors exchanged services, working to raise one another's barns and round up stray cattle. However, manufactured goods cost money. To pay for these, farmers specialized in a single "cash" crop: wheat, corn, rice, tobacco, cotton—a crop for which there was a large demand, or market. After selling a crop, they used the money to buy whatever they wanted. By growing crops for a national market, they became dependent on the same transportation network that brought them manufactured goods.

In the market system, people had to rely on forces beyond their direct control, often beyond their understanding. Always changing, the market might ruin even the best farmers. Growing more of a crop than the market needed, or a sudden economic downturn, would make the price of farm goods fall. Some families dealt with their lowered income by buying less. Many others borrowed from banks to make ends meet. If they could not repay the debt, bankers took their land or asked a court to send them to debtors' prison until relatives made good on the money they owed. Small wonder that Americans hated banks! "Horse leeches," a Nashville newspaper called them, since they "drained every drop of blood they could suck from a suffering community." Old Hickory shared this hatred. When he became president, he would turn it into a crusade.[41] More, he thought banks corrupted the political system by using the money entrusted to them to influence government policies.

To take advantage of water power, manufacturers had built the first factories along rural rivers. With the introduction of steam power, however, they found it easier to concentrate factories in towns and cities. Hoping to improve themselves, country folk flocked to the factories. Thus, the number of towns and cities with over 2,500 people more than doubled from 58 in 1820, to 126 in 1840.

Unlike the artisan workshop, the factory meant inequality. Factory labor became a commodity valued not according to the worker's skill, but by supply and demand. The less there is of a commodity and the more people want it, the higher the price. When a commodity is more plentiful than needed, consumers are not willing to pay so much, and its price falls. Words like *employer, employee, boss, supervisor, manager,* and *foreman* described the changed relationship. Worse, most factories were firetraps where even young children worked fourteen-hour days around machinery lacking safety devices. If you got hurt, you were on your own; benefits for injured workers would not exist until the twentieth century.

Thanks to technology, Americans began to see the world differently than their grandparents had. In Jackson's youth, for example, farmers and craftsmen felt no urgency about being "on time." Seconds, minutes, and hours meant little, provided the task got done within a reasonable period. Clocks were scarce and richly decorated, kept by those who could afford them for display. In 1807, Eli Terry, of Connecticut, began to produce cheap, reliable clocks. Terry's clocks allowed employers, and schoolteachers, to demand punctuality. Stagecoaches, canal boats, steamboats, and railroads had schedules to keep, so passengers had to line up on time. We still say "time is money."

Technology put people in touch as never before. Since colonial times, letters were carried by stagecoach, taking weeks to reach their destination.

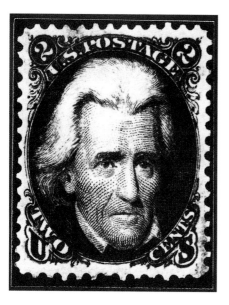

The two-cent "Black Jack" postage stamp of 1863 is today a valuable collector's item.

When a letter arrived, the recipient, not the sender, paid the postage, an expensive six cents per sheet of paper. People wrote only when necessary; many put coded messages on the back of the envelope so that the recipient could read the message and then refuse to pay the postage. All that changed in the 1840s. As transportation costs fell, the Post Office Department issued the first prepaid postage stamps. The famous two-cent "Black Jack" stamp of 1863 had Jackson's picture.

Newspapers also changed. In the 1790s, fewer than ninety newspapers existed in the entire country. These were expensive, costing up to a dollar, because each page was printed separately on a hand-operated press. By

1820, there were five hundred newspapers in the United States, sixty-five of them printed daily in cities and sold for between a penny and a nickel. Steam-driven presses reduced the cost of printing, while improved transportation made it possible to deliver newspapers faster, often to places hundreds of miles away within a few days. To attract customers, shopkeepers allowed anyone to read a newspaper free of charge. So did liquor-store owners. An English visitor, Frances Trollope, once asked a man if he thought going to the liquor store to read newspapers a "patriotic" duty. "To be sure it is," he said. "I don't say that the father of a family should always be after liquor, but I do say that I'd rather have my son drunk three times a week, than not to look after the affairs of his country."[42]

Getting the news. Thanks to improvements in printing technology, newspaper circulation skyrocketed in the 1840s. As shown here, enslaved people might also get the latest news, even though most Southern states made it illegal to teach them to read.

For countless Americans, technology represented the march of progress, allowing them to enjoy better lives than their ancestors had. "'Go ahead,' is the motto of the country," Captain Marryat observed; "both sexes join in the cry; and they do go ahead—that's a fact!" Americans were a go-ahead people. Americans were optimistic, looking to the future with hope, not despair.[43]

Most Americans measured success in money. Foreign visitors agreed that Americans loved the "Almighty Dollar," even worshiped it as a god. A young Frenchman, Michael Chevalier, observed that the motto of the American is "Victory or death! But to him, victory is to make money, to get dollars, to make a fortune out of nothing. . . . At the bottom, then, of all that an American does, is money; beneath every word, money."[44]

In Europe, society valued wealthy people of humble birth far less than lazy, pampered nobles born to title and privilege. Americans believed achievement and not birth revealed one's true qualities. Ordinary people who rose through their own efforts were nature's real nobility, Americans thought—intelligent,

As industrialization spread, cities expanded, along with cultural facilities like museums, concert halls, and public libraries. The ornate library shown in this anonymous 1855 wood engraving is the Boston Athenaeum.

disciplined, creative, and ambitious. If the reward was money, well, that not only allowed them to buy more things, but earn respect and social influence, as Andrew Jackson had. Wealth also allowed ordinary people to give to charity—more so than any other people on earth. In the cities, private wealth translated into public hospitals, libraries, museums, and parks. Not everyone, of course, believed in the virtues of moneymaking. Critics believed "a too urgent love of worldly gain" bred materialism, the idea that the chief goal in life is the accumulation of possessions.[45]

Visitors noticed ever fewer Americans speaking the "King's English." By Jackson's day, thousands of English words had taken on new meanings. For example, *ugly* came to mean angry, as in "I did feel so *ugly* when he said that." *Great* meant not only big, but fine, as in "She's the *greatest* girl in the whole world." More, the country had become a linguistic melting pot. To suit their needs, Americans borrowed words from the French like *depot, prairie, chute,* and *shanty. Mustang, bronco, lariat, ranch, adobe, canyon, plaza,* and *stampede* came from Spanish. German contributed *loaf, bum, dunk, delicatessen, kindergarten, pretzel,* and *ouch*—to mention just a few.[46]

Americans coined their own expressions, too. For example, when people are *under the weather,* they might show no *horse sense* and go *flying off the handle.* To *drive home* a point, they used outlandish words like *absquatulate* (leave in a hurry), *rambunctious, squiggle, skedaddle,* and *hornswoggle.* A *go-a-headitive* person strove to *make a pile,* then *splurge* during *a night on the town.* In describing a homely woman to Captain Marryat, a man said: "Why, sir, when she yawns, you can see down to her garters."[47]

Old Hickory may have coined the most American expression, *O.K.,* as shorthand for *oll korrect*—"all correct." Some scholars think the term came from *Oke,* Cherokee for "it is so." Jackson's name became part of the American language. People used it for anything grand and glorious. "Well," said one fellow, "I reckon that from his teeth to his toe-nail there's not a human of more conquering nature than General Jackson." The expression *go whole hog* came from a political slogan: "JACKSON FOREVER. GO THE WHOLE HOG!"[48]

Grub was a popular term for food. Free white Americans enjoyed incredible abundance. They probably had more meat in their diet than any others, except full-time hunters. Travelers wrote that they could always find inexpensive meals of pork, beef, poultry, and fish. Bread and potatoes were standbys at every meal, with vegetables and salads far less popular. Everyone had "a sweet tooth." An English traveler called ice cream the "one great luxury in America."[49]

Americans ate a lot, if not always wisely. Without refrigeration, only smoking meat over a wood fire or heavy salting kept it from spoiling. Cooks prepared pork, the national favorite, by boiling out most of the salt, then tossing it into a frying pan awash in grease. Even Americans admitted that eating "the eternal hog meat" could be tiresome, something they did as quickly as possible. "The Americans are the grossest feeders of any civilized nation known," novelist James Fenimore Cooper said of his countrymen's eating habits. "As a nation, their food is heavy, coarse, ill-prepared and indigestible. . . . The predominance of grease in the American kitchen, coupled with the habits of hasty eating and expectoration are the causes of the diseases of the stomach so common in America."[50]

Beverages were costly in several ways. Coffee and tea were safe to drink but expensive. Cow's milk could kill, if it carried the "milk sick." Water, particularly city water, might be equally deadly. Cities often took their water

Drinking whiskey. Alcohol was cheap, and alcoholism widespread in Jacksonian America.

from rivers that doubled as sewers. At best, river water had a muddy taste. At worst, it reeked of garbage and animal wastes. Visitors to New York complained of the "laxative" powers of Hudson River water; that is, drinking it gave them the "runs." That left *grog,* slang for strong drink—because it made you "groggy."[51]

Nearly every community, in some areas nearly every household, had a distillery for turning grain into alcohol. Americans adopted whiskey as their national beverage. From 1800 to 1830, they drank more whiskey than ever before or since—on average five gallons per person per year. (Today, the figure is an average of one gallon per person per year.)

Americans drank whiskey anywhere, anytime. They drank at meals, on the job, and at barn raisings. Whiskey flowed freely at gatherings: dances, graduations, weddings, christenings, funerals. Those attending political meetings, horse races, and boxing matches constantly passed the bottle around. Lawyers and judges often drank in court, becoming groggy. So did witnesses. Some ministers drank before, during, and after services. Children drank, too. In taverns, fathers proudly showed off their sons' ability to hold their liquor.[52]

Why? In part, people drank to be sociable. To refuse a "friendly" drink was deemed an insult. "Stranger, will you drink or fight?" a man once asked Captain Marryat. Another reason was that whiskey masked the taste of heavy, greasy foods. A song of the 1820s, sung to the tune of "Home, Sweet Home," said it best:

> Mid plenty of bacon and bread tho' we jog,
> Be it ever so strong, there's nothing like grog.
> A shot from the jug sends such joy to the heart,
> No eating on earth could such pleasure impart.

Grog, grog, sweet, sweet grog.

There's nothing like grog, there's nothing like grog.

The song failed to mention that drunkenness caused work accidents, unemployment, child abuse, mental illness, broken homes, and poverty.[53]

By 1820, when Jackson was fifty-three, over half the urban population lived in six cities: New York, Philadelphia, Baltimore, Boston, New Orleans, Charleston. If you were to take a walk in any of these, the smell of decay would greet you at every turn, for none had proper sanitation. You would not want to trip in the gutter. Unpaved gutters were open sewers soggy with mud, trash, slaughterhouse wastes, horse manure, and the contents of chamber pots emptied from windows. In New York, hordes of squealing pigs roamed major thoroughfares like Wall Street and Broadway at will. Pedestrians ignored them, even welcomed them, since they acted as scavengers. No self-respecting New York pig, residents said, would eat less than its own weight in garbage each week.[54]

Nowadays, most of us never think twice about the dogs we see. That was not so in Old Hickory's day. Packs of wild dogs terrorized city residents. Horror stories told of their carrying off small children to eat. Some dogs carried rabies, their bite transmitting this painful and always fatal disease. The sight of a dog foaming at the mouth would start a panic. Clanging church bells sounded the alarm. Pedestrians ran for their lives. Parents scooted their children indoors. After a small girl died of rabies in New York, the city fathers offered a dollar for each wild dog killed. "The result," Philip Hone recorded in his diary, "was a general massacre, every loafer setting out to exterminate stray dogs." Armed with clubs, gangs of dog hunters roamed the streets.[55]

In the early nineteenth century, medical science was still in its "dark ages." Not even the best doctors saw a connection between dirt, germs, and disease. Poor hygiene was normal. Historians estimate that fewer than one person in ten bathed more than once a year. Add to this the lack of proper sanitation and drinking water, and it is easy to see why cities dreaded epidemics. Typhoid, yellow fever, measles, scarlet fever, diphtheria, smallpox: the cause of each was unknown, and each took its annual toll. From time to time, cholera, carried in polluted water, swept across the world. With growing fear, Philip Hone followed the cholera epidemic of 1832 in the newspapers. It traveled from India to Europe to the Americas. When it reached New York, brought by infected ship passengers, it killed over 3,500 people during the summer.[56]

Spitting also spread disease. In Jackson's day, tobacco chewing was wildly popular with American men. Chewing, however, produces large amounts of saliva. Swallowing saliva tainted with tobacco juice is like swallowing liquid fire. Thus, men were constantly spitting. Polite men spat into sand-filled "spit boxes" or into spittoons, widemouthed brass bowls. Others spat streams of brown gunk anywhere they pleased, even in church pews.

The spitting habit was an American thing; Europeans preferred to smoke their tobacco or shove it up their nostrils in powdered form, called snuff. Spitting disgusted foreign visitors, as it did countless American women and men who did not chew tobacco. "This spitting is universal," Charles Dickens noted:

> In the courts of law, the judge has his spittoon on the bench, the counsel have theirs, the witness has his, the prisoner his, and the crier his. The jury are accommodated at the rate of three men to a spittoon, and the spectators in the gallery are provided for [also]. . . . There are spit-boxes in every steamboat . . . public dining-room . . . and place of general resort, no matter what it be. In the hospitals, the students are requested, by [printed signs], to use the boxes provided for them, and not to spit upon the stairs. I have twice seen gentlemen, at evening parties in New York, turn aside when they were not engaged in conversation, and spit upon the drawing room carpet. And in every barroom and hotel passage the stone floor looks as if it were paved with open oysters—from the quantity of this kind of deposit which [covers] it all over.[57]

Fires were as dangerous to life as disease. American cities were built almost entirely of wood, meaning that any candle, oil lamp, or fireplace could ignite an inferno. Unlike today, cities had no fire departments. Firefighters were volunteers who belonged to a neighborhood fire company, each having its own fire station and fire engine. Fire engines were water-pumping carts, which the volunteers pulled. At the scene of the fire, they put the end of a leather hose into

Racing to a Philadelphia fire in 1845

a river, if they were lucky enough to have one nearby. If not, they attached it to a hydrant, the spout of a wooden water pipe buried under the street. Men stood on either side of the cart, pushing a long handle up and down. As suction forced water into the cart, then into a second hose, other men turned it on the fire.

Fire watchers were posted in church steeples. The instant they saw a fire, they set the bells clanging. Hearing the alarm, nearby fire companies raced to the scene. For the honor of getting there first, they let nothing slow them down. An English traveler, Alexander Marjoribanks, described the routine in New York:

> The competition to be first is so ardent, that ambitious young men sleep as if a part of the brain were left awake to watch for the word 'fire'. . . . In rushing along the streets, sometimes blowing horns and ringing the large bells attached to the engines . . . they often run down and severely injure [pedestrians] who are in their way; or if one of themselves fall, the rest drag on the engine, regardless of his fate, and occasionally break his legs or arms with the wheels. . . . When two engines arrive at the fire, at the same time, the companies frequently fight for the first place, and then a desperate and bloody battle will rage for a considerable time, while the flames are making an unchecked progress.

Hardly a week passed without a serious fire in the city. On December 6, 1835, a monstrous blaze claimed nearly a thousand buildings.[58]

Every city had its poor areas, miserable places ordinary people avoided without having first made out their wills, if they were wise. Broadway, New Yorkers said, "leads to death, and worse." It led to the Five Points section, a maze of winding, trash-filled alleys where danger lurked at every turn. Gangs like the Plug Uglies, Slaughter House Boys, and Forty Thieves killed one another and terrorized law-abiding citizens. Anything might spark a riot lasting a week. "At the slightest provocation," a New Yorker said, "knives are brought out, dreadful wounds inflicted, and sometimes horrid murder committed."[59]

In Jackson's day, city taxpayers objected to paying for large police forces. Professional police were also thought to be "undemocratic," Napoleon having used them to crush opposition to his dictatorship. While the odds against a criminal being caught were high, the law dealt harshly with those convicted of a crime. It allowed prison guards to discipline prisoners by whipping them, chaining them to cell walls, and making them wear a heavy iron ball and chain on their legs. Executions took place in public, before large crowds, sending a grisly message to would-be criminals. Nevertheless, executions often became public holidays where families brought their lunches and their children to see the spectacle.

Despite the many hardships, visitors saw that Americans were proud of their country. "It's a free country," children said, as if claiming a sacred right to misbehave. Yet they had a point. White Americans, but not Native Americans or enslaved blacks, believed their country was the best place on earth, the shining example of a free people living under the rule of democratic law, not a tyrant's whims. It was a land where anything seemed possible if you set your mind to it and worked for it. "Why," one fellow bragged, "our people can turn their hands to almost anything, from whipping the universe to stuffing a mosquito."[60]

This explains why Americans celebrated the Fourth of July, commemorating the Declaration of Independence, as the high holiday of liberty. From sunrise to midnight, it was a grand patriotic festival of parades, bells, bands, fireworks, cannon salutes, whiskey, "and all America tipsy." In New York, merrymakers helped themselves, free of charge, to the "six miles of roast pig" set out on tables along Broadway. It was a day of rousing speeches about "Our Land of Heroes."[61]

And, for so many, none was more heroic than the master of The Hermitage. Those giants of the revolution had left the scene, or soon would. George Washington and Benjamin Franklin, John Adams and Thomas Jefferson had created a nation out of thirteen colonies. It would be for Andrew Jackson—hard, dynamic, angry Andrew Jackson—to lead that nation into difficult and changing times.

V

THE GREAT RACE

GREAT RACING!!! The prize to be run is the Presidential Chair! There have already [sic] four states sent their nags in. Why not Tennessee put in her stud [sic]? And if so, let it be called Old Hickory.

—*Nashville Whig, July 17, 1822*

When Jackson returned home to Tennessee from Florida in 1821, he did not think only of regaining his health and growing his cotton. Former staff officers saw their commander as a candidate for the presidency. Old Hickory was a sure vote getter. During a time of frantic social change, they thought, Americans would leap at the chance to have a president of Jackson's proven courage and ability. But he would have none of it—at least that was what he said at first. When a New York newspaper reported that some Nashville people thought he should run for president of the United States, he snapped, "Do they think I am such a damned fool? No sir; I know what I am fit for. I can command a body of men in a rough way, but I am not fit to be President."[1]

Did he mean it, or was he playing hard to get? We will never know for sure. We have only Jackson's word that he thought himself unfit for the presidency. Yet we do know that his friend and neighbor Major William Lewis, sometimes called "Jackson's other self," believed Jackson had a patriotic duty to run for the highest office in the land.[2]

The newspapers strewn across Jackson's library floor seemed to support the major's case. The industrial revolution was putting down deep roots, and these sometimes had harmful effects. What we call today "special interests" existed in the 1820s, too. Old Hickory, after all, had used his influence to help relatives in land deals. Yet if we can trust the surviving written record, he never sold influence or took a bribe. Other politicians did both.

Historians have described James Monroe's two administrations, from

1817 to 1825, as among "the most corrupt in the early history of the United States." Then, as now, superambitious people tried to further their private interests with government favors. In looking to do so, they found politicians willing to betray their public trust. Payoffs disguised as loans and salaries began at the top. President Monroe "borrowed" five thousand dollars from John Jacob Astor, America's richest man, repaying it without interest fifteen years later. Meanwhile, on "further information," Monroe canceled an order limiting fur trapping on certain federal lands that would have cost an Astor company dearly. In a clear "conflict of interest," Massachusetts senior senator Daniel Webster drew salaries from several firms while serving on Senate committees that handled their business. This practice is illegal today.[3]

Corruption also took another, equally dangerous, form. Americans still debate what limits, if any, there are or ought to be to the powers of the central government. When government under the Constitution began in 1789, the debate led to the formation of two political parties, the Federalists led by Alexander Hamilton and Thomas Jefferson's Republicans.

Hamilton was born to an unmarried woman in the West Indies in 1755. Sent to Columbia College in New York City by a kindly employer, he joined George Washington's staff at the start of the Revolutionary War, becoming a trusted aide. No believer in democracy, he said "the people are turbulent and changing; they seldom judge or determine right." Hamilton saw the common people as ignorant, violent, and unstable, unfit for self-government. Government, he insisted, must be strong. More, it must be left to "the rich and the well-born"; that is, to the successful and the wealthy, who would keep the masses in line. Hamilton's ideas became the basis of the Federalist Party. Although President Washington did not believe in political parties, thinking they led to corruption and division, he supported Federalist policies, particularly those encouraging overseas trade. His successor, John Adams, proudly called himself a Federalist.[4]

Jefferson disagreed with the Federalists on many issues. Although a wealthy slaveholder, he despised kings and nobles as idiots who fought silly wars with others' blood. He also despised "money men," those who grew rich in business, and he disliked cities, which he considered sewers of evil where mobs went about "eating one another." In Jefferson's vision of America, citizens would be neither rich nor poor, but would have enough to live comfortably.

VENERATE THE PLOUGH

Thomas Jefferson's ideal for America was a democracy based on small-scale, independent farmers, not cities with their dirt, poverty, and violent mobs.

That meant having a democracy of small-town people and independent farmers. As for the central government, he had a simple rule: Less is best. Government must stay out of people's everyday lives. Since Jefferson hoped to keep government close to the people, he favored states' rights, limiting federal power to allow the greatest possible self-rule by the states.[5]

Both Hamilton's distrust of the common people and Jefferson's desire for self-rule by the states are reflected in the way Americans elected state and national officials. The Constitution left it to the states to decide voting qualifications; at first, that resulted in only white male property owners being allowed to vote. Most states also had "stand-up" voting; that is, voting by voice, not secret ballot. Since one voted in public, a "wrong" vote invited reprisal by wealthy landowners and employers. In many states, a person had to own several hundred acres of land to qualify for holding public office. State legislatures also chose senators, and would until the year 1913.

No American president has ever been elected by direct popular vote—that is, the combined vote of all the voters in all the states. Instead, the framers of the Constitution adopted a complicated system called the Electoral College. The college is not a school; it has no buildings, no professors, no students. Instead, it is the collective name for the whole body of electors chosen by the states to elect the president. According to the Constitution (Article II, section 1), the numbers of electors from each state must be equal to the number of representatives it sends to Congress, but the electors cannot be members of Congress themselves.

The Constitution allows each state to choose its presidential electors as it pleases. Originally, some states chose them by popular vote statewide; or by voting for an elector in each congressional election district; or by the legislature, without a popular vote. Electors were men of property, supposedly chosen for their wisdom, not because they favored a particular candidate. However they were chosen, the electors met in their state capital, and there they cast ballots for two candidates, usually the leading national figures of the day, for president and vice president. The winners received *all* the state's electoral votes, regardless of how narrow their margin of victory. The winners' names were then certified and sent to the president of the U.S. Senate. When the electoral votes of all the states were counted, the person with the most votes became president, the runner-up vice president.

With the rise of political parties after 1800, electors were chosen from "slates" or "tickets"—lists of men printed on the ballot under the names of party candidates. Today, electors' names seldom appear on the ballot. Instead, the phrase "Electors for" usually appears in small print on the ballot in front of each party's set of candidates for president and vice president.

The Federalists controlled the central government until 1800, when the Republicans took over the presidency with the election of Thomas Jefferson. Although they remained strong in Congress, the Federalists never regained the presidency. During the War of 1812, the party self-destructed. With disaster following disaster, in December 1814, delegates from all the New England states met at Hartford, Connecticut, to decide what to do. Some delegates to this Hartford Convention wanted their states to secede, or leave the Union, if the war continued. But before they could get the others to take action, news of the Treaty of Ghent reached America. By demanding peace at any price, even secession, the Federalists lost the nation's confidence. That left only the Republicans. Through the caucus, a meeting of party members within a legislature, congressional Republicans nominated their candidate for president. In 1820, James Monroe ran without opposition. In effect, the United States had fallen under one-party rule. Monroe got 231 electoral votes. One elector from New Hampshire voted for John Quincy Adams, who had not run in the election. The elector voted for Adams not because he opposed Monroe, but because he did not think anyone but George Washington should ever receive a unanimous electoral victory.

Yet important changes were underway. The expanding economy led to an outcry against special interests. Throughout the 1820s, states rewrote their constitutions, abolishing property qualifications for voting and for office holding. Although women, Native Americans, and enslaved people still could not vote, free white men could. Written ballots replaced stand-up voting. Voters won the right to choose the presidential electors in all but six states, where the legislatures still picked electors.

While Jackson welcomed these changes, he felt they had not gone far enough. A wealthy man himself, he nevertheless feared the corrupting power of money upon America more than he feared any foreign invasions. Many Americans still do; in our day, there are demands for campaign finance reform, limiting the ability of special interests to buy influence and decide elections. The nation had proven its ability to resist foreign enemies, Old Hickory said. Corruption was another matter. He saw it as a disease, a cancer eating away at the system of free representative government under the Constitution.

To check corruption, Jackson believed, as did Jefferson, that the government had to be kept close to the people. Yet his idea of "the people" went beyond Jefferson's notion of small-town folks like self-employed merchants, craftspeople, and independent farmers. Jackson defined the people as "the humble members of society." These included free white factory workers and city dwellers "who earn their living by the sweat of their brow"—landless people who work for wages.[6]

Yet Jackson never had a program to improve common people's living conditions, nor apparently did most Americans expect him to have one. Until the early twentieth century, American political leaders and the courts had a very limited view of the duties of the national government. Basically, it was supposed to keep the peace at home, defend the country from foreign enemies, and make certain "internal improvements"—mostly build roads—things that private citizens could not afford to do on their own. The government had not yet accepted responsibility for addressing the often disastrous effects of old age, sickness, accidents, or unemployment upon the wage earner's life. The central government had limited funds. It got its money from tariffs on imported goods, the sale of federal lands, and borrowing to cover short-term expenses. There was no tax on income, no tax on inheritance, to allow the government to help large numbers of people. Private charity was expected to do that.

Good government, Old Hickory felt, was honest government—rooting out corruption and special interests, thus enabling the common people to help themselves. Jackson trusted the common people. He believed in their goodness, intelligence, and ability to govern themselves. "The people are sovereign," he insisted, the supreme authority in the nation. "Their will is absolute." Thus he opposed anything that prevented their wishes from becoming the law of the land. Given his way, he would abolish the Electoral College and also have senators elected by the people directly. So that politicians would not use their offices for personal gain, he favored term limits; Jackson thought even the president should serve no more than a single term of four or six years. The president was the whole people's true guardian, he said. Congressmen and senators were elected locally, by their districts and state legislatures, but the nation as a whole chose the president. Jackson's point was that the president represents *all* the people. As head of the executive branch of the government, the president and not Congress, Jackson believed, should set the nation's goals and direct government activities.[7]

Jackson's Nashville friends argued that only he, if president, could root out corruption. To defeat the caucus system, they intended to have the Tennessee legislature nominate him, thus sparking similar movements in other states. When told of their plan, Old Hickory did not say yes or no. Yet, as a patriot, he felt he must obey when the people called. "I have never been a candidate for any office. I never will," he told an ally. "But the people have a right to choose whom they will to perform their constitutional duties, and when the people call, the citizen is bound to render the service required." Should the Tennessee legislature nominate him, he could not refuse.[8]

That was just what his friends wanted to hear. Major Lewis, Judge Overton, Sam Houston, and Senator John Eaton, a close aide in the War of 1812, began to mobilize their political allies in Tennessee. In July 1822, the state legislature nominated Old Hickory for president. The following year, to bolster his candidacy, it sent him back to the Senate.

Everyone in Nashville was thrilled—everyone, that is, but Rachel. She had no patience for politics or politicians. "They come here to talk, talk everlastingly about his being President," she said of her husband's backers. "In this as all else I can say only, the Lord's will be done." Jackson had second thoughts as well. He did not care to leave his wife alone for long periods. But he was now a senator, and felt he could not turn back. So, in November 1823, he set out for the nation's capital.[9]

In 1823, Washington, D.C., bore little resemblance to the city we now know. When Thomas Jefferson dubbed it "that Indian swamp in the wilderness," few challenged his description. Although it had thirty-nine thousand inhabitants, enslaved people included, in many ways it was still just a frontier town set in the marshes along the Potomac River. The unfinished Capitol sat on a hilltop, in a clearing hemmed in by trees and brush. Bored congressmen would slip away to shoot birds, rabbits, and squirrels on its grounds. In the distance, the shaft of the Washington Monument, also unfinished, rose amid a jumble of storage sheds and marble blocks.[10]

Wide avenues nearly empty of houses stretched to the horizon. In the heat of summer, their unpaved gutters turned to deserts of swirling sand and powdered horse manure. In winter, gutters became muddy streams. "The mud," a visitor noted in 1819, "is so frightful that one sinks down above the ankles." Fine carriages let elegant ladies out in quagmires; many walked barefoot to keep from soiling their shoes. Mosquitoes rose in clouds from the foul marshes, and cockroaches scurried about. Mounds of trash stank to high heaven, food for the pigs roaming Pennsylvania Avenue. Known simply as "The Avenue," it was the city's main thoroughfare, connecting the Capitol and the White House. A brick sidewalk ran along its west side. A stream—really an open sewer—flowed down Capitol Hill and ran along its east side, right past the White House.[11]

Most government officials lived in boardinghouses on or near The Avenue. Usually they "messed"—ate and drank—together for companionship and to share expenses. Washington was a drinker's town, alcohol coming in endless varieties from raw corn whiskey to the finest French champagne. At night, men gathered around silver punch bowls described by a visitor as being "large as a Roman bathing tub," discussing the day's events. At the boardinghouse where the justices of the Supreme Court stayed, boarders voted to drink only in wet weather, to preserve their health. Chief Justice John Marshall, hardly a wild lad, could not do without his wine. Informed that the sun was shining brightly, Marshall would say, "All the better; for . . . it [is] certain that it must be raining somewhere." Fill the glasses![12]

Senator Jackson took in the sights. He had not been to Washington since the fall of 1819, when Congress debated his invasion of Florida. Again he visited the Capitol, the nerve center of government. Besides the House of Representatives and Senate, this building held the Library of Congress and the

Supreme Court chamber—in the basement. In the House, representatives sat at their desks answering letters, dozing, or chatting with neighbors. Now and then someone called out "Mr. Speaker! Mr. Speaker!" to raise a question or ask permission to reply to a speech. Yet the acoustics were so bad that hardly anyone heard anything clearly. No matter. Speakers droned on, chiefly to have their words printed, at public expense, and sent home, also at public expense, to show voters what a fine job they were doing. Captain Marryat recalled "long-winded speeches about nothing," chock-full of "eagles, star-spangled banners . . . clap-trap, flattery, and humbug."[13]

The Senate was more formal. Senators did not wear their hats, toss their legs over their desks, and slouch in their seats. The chamber itself was an elegant room, thickly carpeted, with polished brass spittoons gleaming in the candlelight. Both houses had a spittoon near each desk. It made no difference. The floors oozed with spit. Charles Dickens's stomach churned at the sight of tobacco juice "squirted and dabbled . . . in every direction." He added, "I strongly recommend all strangers not to look at the floor; and if they happen to drop anything, though it be their purse, not to pick it up with an ungloved hand on any account."[14]

Senator Jackson did not overwork himself. He spoke four times in six months, for a total of less than twenty minutes, always on military matters. While he framed no laws, he supported a protective tariff and internal improvements, particularly roads, vital to commerce and national defense. Mostly, he worked at making a good impression. Those who knew his reputation as a frontier soldier and general expected to see a savage with a tomahawk in one hand and a scalping knife in the other, he said. Yet people found him quite the opposite. "General Jackson's manners are more presidential than those of any of the candidates," Daniel Webster wrote his brother. "He is grave, mild and reserved. My wife is decidedly for him." The would-be president knew how to control his temper when it suited his interests.[15]

Old Hickory also mended fences with an enemy. After their gunfight in 1813, Thomas Hart Benton had settled in Missouri. There he rose steadily in politics, becoming a senator in 1812. A big, burly fellow with a booming voice, he was a skilled deal maker who knew how to get what he wanted. Benton saw Jackson as the coming man, whom he needed for his own ends. Jackson saw Benton as a politician he would rather have as an ally than an enemy. Making up with him would be a brilliant political move, too. How, then, could anyone accuse Jackson of being an unforgiving brute?

Both sat on the Senate Military Affairs Committee. One day, as a meeting broke up, Benton made the first move. How is Rachel's health? he asked. Benton had been a favorite of hers, and Jackson knew their feud hurt her. Just fine, he replied, clearly pleased. A few days later, Benton and his wife met Jackson at a White House reception. Benton bowed, respectfully, and they shook hands. With that handshake, the bitterness of ten years began to melt away. Near the end of his life, Benton told a friend, "Yes I had a fight with Jackson. A fellow was hardly in the fashion then who hadn't. But mine was different from his other fights. It wasn't about Aunt Rachel. . . . If it had been, he would never have forgiven me." The senator became Jackson's leading supporter in Congress and a loyal friend as well. However, Thomas's brother, Jesse, never forgave the senator for making peace with their old enemy.[16]

John Quincy Adams, from an 1847 daguerreotype by Mathew Brady.

Besides Jackson, four other candidates for president came forward in 1823, nominated by state legislatures or by various state party organizations. They all ran as Republicans. Secretary of State John Quincy Adams was New England's favorite son. Kentucky's Henry Clay, the speaker of the house, had his power base in the West. Secretary of War John C. Calhoun, of South Carolina, represented Southern interests. The Republican Party's congressional leaders backed Secretary of the Treasury William Crawford, a Georgian. No candidate ran in every state, as presidential contenders do today. This was because backers in certain states lacked enough support to get their man on the ballot, or because they felt their man did not have a chance of winning. Jackson's name was not on the ballot anywhere in New England. Adams's name did not appear on the ballot in Kentucky or North Carolina. In total, Crawford and Clay were on the ballot in only five states. Sensing defeat, Calhoun withdrew from the presidential contest to run unopposed for vice president.

Jackson and Adams, the front-runners, had always respected each other. Jackson was grateful for Adams's support during his invasion of Florida. Adams admired Old Hickory's patriotism, his courage and willingness to take personal risks for the country's sake.

Yet Jackson had a clear advantage. Apart from a few appearances, he did little campaigning. Nor did he have to. With more people voting than ever before, his Nashville friends knew they had to form an emotional bond between their candidate and the "common man." That did not mean discussing serious issues, Major Lewis argued; these are often complicated and lack simple solutions. Instead, they had supporters portray Jackson as simply the people's best friend. According to one slogan, the race was between men from different worlds:

> John Quincy Adams
> Who can write,
> Andrew Jackson
> Who can fight.

While Adams had served his country with devotion as a diplomat and secretary of state, he could not match his opponent's war record. It seemed that all Jackson's allies had to do, he said, was shout "8th of January and battle of New Orleans," and people went wild over him.[17]

Unlike today, when federal elections are held on the first Tuesday in November, in 1824 the whole nation did not go to the polls on one specific day. Each of the twenty-four states had its own rules, and men voted for presidential electors between October 29 and November 22. Each legislature then tallied the results and named its state's electors. Mounted messengers, steamboats, and stagecoaches then brought the results to the capital. The results did not all arrive in Washington until mid-December.

More Americans voted for Jackson than any of the other candidates. However, under the electoral college system it is not the popular vote but the electoral vote that decides the next president. Jackson won eleven states with a total of ninety-nine electoral votes. Adams came in second, with eight states and eighty-four electoral votes; Crawford had two states with forty-one electoral votes, and Clay had three states with thirty-seven electoral votes. Under the Twelfth Amendment to the Constitution, in effect since 1804, a candidate needs an absolute majority—at least one more than half the total—of the electoral votes to become president. Should nobody win that majority, the House of Representatives must choose from among the three leading candidates. In the House, each state delegation votes separately; the state then casts a single ballot for the winner. The person who gets the majority of state votes becomes president. Thus, the candidate with more popular votes but without a majority of state electoral votes can lose the election. Nationwide, the popular vote was: Jackson, 151,271; Adams, 113,122; Clay, 47,531; Crawford, 40,856.

Clay, with the fewest electoral votes, dropped out of the race. Crawford, partially paralyzed by a recent stroke, could not serve even if elected. That left Jackson and Adams. Yet, in the contest that followed, Clay would name the next president.

Born in 1777, Henry Clay, nicknamed "Harry of the West," came from a well-to-do Kentucky family owning twenty-one slaves. Like Jackson, he was six feet tall and rail thin. Unlike Jackson, he had an extremely wide mouth; friends called it the "finest kissing instrument" this side of the Atlantic Ocean. Brilliant and arrogant, Clay fought duels, drank whiskey, gambled, and danced. Once he leaped onto a banquet table, sixty feet in length, dancing from end to end to the sound of breaking glass and crashing china. Nevertheless, he was a serious politician with big plans for the growing nation. Dubbed the "American System," his plans called for the federal government to promote economic development. It would carry out internal improvements in the form of a vast network of canals and roads to speed Western farm products to Eastern cities. Protected by high tariffs, American industry would grow quickly, providing the money to pay for the improvements.

A man of many nicknames, including the "Great Compromiser," Henry Clay was a brilliant speaker and an astute politician. Old Hickory hated him.

There was no love lost between Clay and Jackson. Old Hickory never forgave Clay for wanting him punished for invading Florida. In turn, Clay called Jackson "a military chieftain," an indirect reference to the dictator Napoleon. Jackson's worst offense, however, was that he stood between the Kentuckian and his heart's desire: the presidency. Clay and John Quincy Adams met privately at least once. There is no record of what they said; Adams's usually detailed diary is silent about their meeting. What we do know is that Clay wanted to see Adams become president. If Adams won through his influence, Clay stood to become secretary of state, a stepping-stone to the presidency after Adams left office; every secretary of state since 1800 had gone on to become the next president.

Expecting victory, Jackson and Rachel had come to Washington for the vote in the House of Representatives. The general, at fifty-seven, was as striking a figure as ever. Henry A. Wise, a future Democratic governor of Virginia, saw him up close. Wise was especially taken with Jackson's long hair; each strand stood straight up as if it had a will of its own. Years later, Wise recalled:

> His presence immediately struck us by its majestic, commanding mien. He was about six feet high, slender in form, long and straight in limb, a little rounded in the shoulders, but stood gracefully erect. His hair, not then white, but venerably gray, stood more erect than his person; not long but evenly cut, and each hair stood forth for itself a radius from a high, full-orbed head, chiseled with every mark of massive strength. . . . His cheek-bones were strong, and his jaw was rather "lantern" [thin, almost transparent]; the nose was straight, long, and Grecian, the upper lip the only heavy feature of his face. . . . His teeth were long . . . and were loose, and gave an ugly, ghastly expression to his nasal muscle. His chest was flat and broad. He was very unreserved in conversation, talked volubly, and with animation, somewhat vehement and declamatory, though with perfect dignity and self-possession.[18]

On February 9, 1825, the House met as the Constitution directed. Each delegation then sent a member to slip its state's ballot into a box. Tellers opened the box, counted the ballots, and gave the result to Clay. The speaker cleared his throat and announced that seven states had gone for Jackson, four for Crawford, and thirteen for Adams. Thanks to the speaker, Adams won the presidency on the first ballot. Clay had delivered "his" three states—Kentucky, Ohio, Missouri—to Adams, while persuading Maryland, Illinois, and Louisiana to switch from Jackson to the New Englander. For a moment, everyone sat stunned, unable to believe their ears. Suddenly, Adams supporters burst into applause, instantly drowned out by hissing.

The next day, at noon, Adams received official word that he was the president-elect. Those who saw him realized that he was not a happy man. Sweat rolled down his face as someone read the notice. He shook from head to foot, too upset even to speak. "It was not a triumph to be proud of," a modern biographer has written, explaining Adams's reaction. For Adams knew that the politicians, not the people, had made him president.[19]

Old Hickory seemed to take his defeat calmly. That evening, he attended Monroe's regular Wednesday reception at the White House, where the president met foreign diplomats, politicians, and influential visitors. He found the

A reception held in honor of president-elect John Quincy Adams. Standing from left to right are John C. Calhoun, Daniel Webster, Andrew Jackson, and Henry Clay. Adams stands on the extreme right. Jackson accused him of "stealing" the election of 1824 by making a deal with Clay for votes in the electoral college.

East Room crowded—so much so that a pickpocket got away with the general's wallet. Harry of the West strutted around the room, greatly pleased with himself. "The villain!" guests murmured as he passed. Adams had supporters there, too, but for a while he stood alone in a corner, as if trying to melt into the woodwork—with good reason. From across the room men pointed toward him and sneered, "There is our *Clay President.*" All eyes were on Jackson as he crossed the room, shook the president-elect's hand, and asked how he was. An eyewitness, a lady, noted Jackson's good humor and Adams's coldness.[20]

Four days later, it was announced that Adams had named Clay secretary of state. The news came as a shock. "Corrupt bargain!" cried Jackson and his supporters. Yet they did not invent the outcry, nor were they alone in using it. It arose from the country. Clay's appointment, people felt, was the payoff for a dirty deal to make Adams president. It is not known if there ever was such a deal. If not, it still looked that way.

Our system of government depends on leaders obeying the rules. Perhaps the most basic rule is that leaders cannot defy the people's decision as given in a free election. Kentucky's electoral vote for Adams was a glaring example of just such defiance. As we saw earlier, Adams had not run in Kentucky, and so got no votes there. Moreover, the Kentucky legislature had directed the state's delegation to vote for Jackson in the House of Representatives. But Clay persuaded them to ignore the order, putting his own wishes above those of the people of Kentucky. In effect, Clay treated the state's votes as his personal property, to use as he pleased.

Jackson said he feared the worst. "This, to my mind, is the most open, daring corruption that has ever shown itself under our government," he wrote Major Lewis. "I look forward and shudder for the liberty of my country. If . . . men are found base and corrupt enough to barter the rights of the people for . . . office, what may we not expect from the spread of this corruption hereafter?" The outright sale of public office, perhaps? Paying judges for favorable decisions? Old Hickory believed Clay and Adams had stolen the election, and with it the government. So did countless others. Still, for Jackson, the "corrupt bargain" became a political weapon, allowing him to paint his opponents as enemies of American liberty.[21]

Old Hickory resigned from the Senate and left Washington. As expected, the Tennessee legislature nominated him again for the presidency, nearly four years before the next election. Such a thing had never happened before, nor would it happen again.

Now there were two Andrew Jacksons. The public Jackson was calm, charming, and good-natured. By not making a ruckus over his defeat, he disarmed critics. Yet the private Jackson seethed with anger, hating with all the hatred he could muster. Just the sound of Clay's name made his eyes blaze. He called the Kentuckian "the Judas of the West," the monster who had betrayed the American people, as a false disciple had betrayed Jesus Christ. "That arch fiend, J. Q. Adams," he called the man he had once respected.[22]

John Quincy Adams in 1843. Adams was not known for his sunny disposition.

Yet John Quincy Adams, not Andrew Jackson, moved into the White House. The sixth president was a fascinating character. Born the same year as Jackson, this eldest son of John Adams (the second president) was short and squat, with a massive bald head and watery eyes. A book lover, he owned a library worth more than his house in Quincy, Massachusetts. Deeply religious, he read Bible passages three times a day— first in English, then in German, and finally in French. He also read Greek and Latin.

Adams was not a person you could warm up to easily. Like his father, he was cold and distant; even followers called him a "chip off the old iceberg." He agreed. "I am a man of reserved, cold, austere, and forbidding manners, an unsocial savage," he wrote. Would-be allies he turned away with biting criticism and a face that seemed frozen in a scowl. Distrusting others, he kept lists of enemies. A know-it-all, he enjoyed putting down opponents; Henry Clay said, mockingly, that he doubted if Adams had ever been wrong in his life. Yet he loved his country as fiercely as he loved his own children.[23]

Adams was also a free spirit, one who did as he pleased, whatever others might think. Back then, the president had no bodyguards. Adams would leave the White House before dawn, alone, for a brisk four-mile walk through the trash-filled streets. During the blistering Washington summers, he attended church barefoot. Whenever possible, he swam nude in the Potomac River. One day, he and a servant, Antoine Guista, set out in a leaky rowboat, intending to swim in the shallows along the Virginia shore. When the boat overturned, they lost their clothing and shoes. Adams made it to shore with only his shirt and pantaloons. Guista wrung them out, put them on, and left to find a carriage to take them to the White House. Passersby saw the president sitting on a rock beside the river, naked, deep in thought.[24]

Jackson was also deep in thought—about vengeance. Vowing to avenge his defeat, he decided that, rather than sling political mud himself, he would let others do it for him. He had plenty of help. The Republicans had split into two factions after the election. Adams and Clay led the National Republicans. Jackson led the Democratic Republicans, a name soon shortened to the Democrats. So began the Democratic Party, the world's oldest, continuously existing political party.

Democratic Party branches formed throughout the country. As they did, some fifty newspapers lined up behind them. With each issue, they lambasted President Adams as "the assassin." In Congress, Democrats attacked his administration at every turn. Irritating, provocative remarks kept the corrupt-bargain charge alive. Things got so bad that Speaker Clay challenged Virginia senator John Randolph to a duel; they exchanged shots, missed, and called it a day. Adams, however, was the Democrats' chief target. This pitiful creature could do nothing right, they said. In keeping with Clay's American System, he had proposed canal-building projects, a national university, and an observatory to study the heavens. Though it was a sensible program, Democrats attacked it as a scheme to waste public money on "lighthouses in the sky."[25]

Adams himself made things worse. Public officials must choose their words carefully. If they do not, they risk giving offense and spreading confusion. The president did both. In his first message to Congress, he warned of the danger of becoming "palsied by the will of our constituents." Most likely, he meant the government must always act as it thought best, that it must show leadership and exercise wise and forward-looking judgment. If the voters disagreed, they would throw it out at the next election. Democrats pounced on Adams's words. Aha! They had been right all along! By inviting Congress to ignore the people's wishes, he proved their charge of the corrupt bargain. Ultimately, these tactics paid off. In the congressional elections of 1827, the Democrats won control of both houses of Congress. Ahead lay the most important contest of all—the next presidential election.[26]

Although Martin Van Buren looked like a dandy, he was a tough politician skilled at using his personal charm as a political tool.

Andrew Jackson's ablest political ally was Senator Martin Van Buren of New York. Van Buren came from a long line of Dutch farmers in Columbia County, the land of the fictional Rip Van Winkle. Fifteen years younger than Jackson, Van Buren also had risen from humble beginnings. Lacking formal education, he read law on his own and took part in local politics, slowly gaining respect and influence. Short and fair-skinned, with sandy hair and blue eyes, he was a dandy's dandy. Van Buren went about in dainty leather shoes, an orange tie, a pearl-colored vest, white linen pants, and yellow kid gloves. Vain about his appearance, he scrunched his ample figure into a corset. Davy Crockett, no admirer, said Van Buren "struts and swaggers like a crow in the gutter. He is laced up in corsets, such as women in a town wear, and, if possible, tighter than the best of them."[27]

Behind the finery lurked a wily politician. Shrewd and tough, Van Buren knew how to use charm. He never had a quarrel, much less a duel, in his life. Yet, said fellow politicians, he could slip a knife between your ribs without you ever feeling it. Nicknamed the "Little Magician" and the "Sly Fox," he built a powerful political machine, an organization that obeyed his commands. "Patronage," by which the party in power gives government jobs to those who have helped it, kept the machine running smoothly. Jackson admired Van Buren's skill. "I am no politician," he would say, a faint smile crossing his lips. "But if I were a politician, I would be a New York politician."[28]

The New Yorker became Jackson's closest political adviser and campaign manager. Acting in his first role, Van Buren gave him sound guidance. Act the statesman. Appeal to the largest number of voters possible. Never go into details, but speak in broad terms—about the people, patriotism, prosperity, democracy, equality. Should opponents attack you personally, on your marriage or hot temper, stay calm. By getting you to lose your temper, they aim to show that you are hotheaded and unstable, unfit to lead the nation.

Controlling his temper grew harder as the campaign advanced. Historian Samuel Eliot Morison has described the election of 1828 as "the first presidential one that really smelled." It did smell—to high heaven. A vicious, disgraceful affair, it mocked the principles of democracy and insulted common decency.[29]

The National Republicans gave Jackson a smearing as no candidate for the presidency has had to endure before or since. The so-called Hero of New Orleans, they charged, was really a drunken, gambling, ignorant boor. Opposition speakers played up Jackson's duel with Charles Dickinson, the gunfight with the Benton brothers, and the executions of Arbuthnot and Ambrister. All showed his ungovernable temper and thirst for human blood, they said. So did the Coffin Handbill, a small poster depicting the coffins of six militiamen

The Coffin Handbill was used by Old Hickory's enemies to discredit him in the presidential election of 1828.

critics accused Jackson of "murdering" on phony desertion charges after the Battle of New Orleans. These and similar charges stuck. In New England, a Sunday-school pupil, asked to name the killer of Cain's brother Abel, from the Bible, replied, "General JACKSON, ma'am."[30]

Such attacks stung, but as Van Buren advised, Old Hickory shrugged them off as "politics." However, he could not ignore attacks on the two people he worshiped, his mother and his wife. Betty had been in her grave forty-three years. Yet that did not prevent her son's opponents from insulting her memory. A Washington newspaper, the *National Journal,* announced:

— General Jackson's mother was a COMMON PROSTITUTE, brought to this country by the British soldiers! She afterwards married a MULATTO MAN, with whom she had several children, of which number General JACKSON IS ONE!!![31]

Doubly insulting, this lie accused an Irish woman of selling her body to the hated British, then marrying a mulatto, a man of mixed white and black heritage. One day, Rachel found her husband sitting on a chair in stunned silence. "Myself I can defend," he finally said, pointing to the article. "You I can defend; but now they have assailed even the memory of my mother." Then Old Hickory burst into tears.[32]

Yet this was just the beginning. Word came of a private detective nosing about Nashville, asking questions about Rachel and her marriage to Jackson. The detective's employer was Charles Hammond, editor of the Cincinnati, Ohio, *Gazette,* another Republican newspaper. A few weeks later, Hammond struck. In a blistering article, he accused Jackson of using force on another man, Lewis Robards, to steal his wife. The article portrayed Rachel as an adulteress, a wicked woman who broke her solemn marriage vows. Hammond followed the article with a pamphlet, which Adams's supporters in Congress sent through the mail at public expense. It asked: "Ought a convicted adulteress and her paramour husband to be placed in the highest office of this free and Christian land?"[33]

Jackson was outraged, and the object of his outrage was Henry Clay. Without offering any proof, he accused the Kentuckian of being behind the insults to Rachel's "sacred name," threatening Clay's "actual destruction." Perhaps Jackson was just letting off steam. Perhaps he really intended Clay to come to a violent end. Clay thought so. Friends warned that Jackson men were gunning for him. Whatever Jackson's intentions, Van Buren warned him against losing his temper in public; it was exactly what his opponents wanted and, besides, would hurt Rachel further. Seldom leaving The Hermitage, she knew little of the campaign raging outside. Jackson hid the foul pamphlet from her.

Democrats fought fire with fire. In a barrage of newspaper articles, they portrayed Adams as an educated fool who knew about books but lacked common sense. Cartoons depicted him with a horsewhip, driving away a crippled war veteran for daring to ask for a penny. The president had a "crown on the brain," critics said; given the chance, he would make himself King John of America. He had outfitted the White House as a royal palace, at taxpayer expense, with an ivory chess set and a billiard table, a "gambling instrument" favored by European rulers. An immoral man, while ambassador to Russia he had forced an American girl to submit to the "lusts" of the emperor. Editors also said Adams's wife's parents had not been married, and that she had slept with her future husband before their marriage.

At that, Old Hickory put his foot down. If those who attacked Louisa Adams hoped to win his favor, they were mistaken. *"I never war against females,"* he wrote, "and it is only the base and cowardly that do." From then on, nobody said a word against the first lady. Her husband could have done the same for Rachel. Although Adams did not personally spread vile charges against her, he knew about them. Yet he never raised a finger to stop them, and Jackson never forgave him for it.[34]

Van Buren's greatest contribution to Jackson's cause was as his campaign manager. No detail was too small for the New Yorker to attend to. Eager to draw first-time voters to the Democrats, he organized America's first modern election campaign. Since then, all campaigns are variations, increasingly expensive, on the model he created.

Jackson's supporters distributed handbills such as this to portray their candidate as "The Man of the People" in the campaign of 1828.

Jackson Forever!
The Hero of Two Wars and of Orleans!
The Man of the People!
HE WHO COULD NOT BARTER NOR BARGAIN FOR THE
PRESIDENCY!

Who, although "*A Military Chieftain*," valued the purity of Elections and of the Electors, MORE than the Office of PRESIDENT itself! Although the greatest in the gift of his countrymen, and the highest in point of dignity of any in the world,

BECAUSE
It should be derived from the
PEOPLE!

No Gag Laws! No Black Cockades! No Reign of Terror! No Standing Army or Navy Officers, when under the pay of Government, to browbeat, or

KNOCK DOWN

Old Revolutionary Characters, or our Representatives while in the discharge of their duty. To the Polls then, and vote for those who will support

OLD HICKORY
AND THE ELECTORAL LAW.

Van Buren began by forming central party committees in each state. These committees then assembled teams of writers to make the case for Jackson. Talented writers like novelist James Fenimore Cooper and historian George Bancroft eagerly joined the effort. The general's friend John Eaton wrote *The Life of Jackson,* the first biography in American history explicitly designed to get a candidate elected.

Van Buren's central committees directed the countless activities of local—town, city, or county—committees. To get out the vote, they held mass meetings, veterans' reunions, and rallies featuring speeches and fireworks. No gathering was complete without a few thirty-gallon barrels of whiskey with ANDREW JACKSON painted on them, and an invitation for all to drink up. The name Old Hickory became a political symbol. Democrats planted hickory trees and slapped posters on walls that proclaimed: OLD HICKORY, LAST OF THE REVOLUTIONARY PATRIOTS. Men wore hickory buttons with his picture, proudly carrying hickory canes and hickory sticks. Hickory clubs held nighttime parades. In the glare of torches, squads of "hurrah boys" shouted, "Hurrah for Jackson." Crowds bellowed America's first campaign song, "The Hunters of Kentucky," telling of Jackson and his boys, each "half a horse and half an alligator," a combination of speed and ferocity, and how they trounced the British at New Orleans.

All this ballyhoo had the desired effect. In Spencer County, Indiana, a lanky nineteen-year-old, Abraham Lincoln by name, marveled at how one person could so dazzle a nation. Inspired to try his hand at poetry, Lincoln wrote:

> Let auld acquaintance be forgot
> And never brought to mind;
> May Jackson be our president,
> And Adams left behind.[35]

So it was.

Nobody could doubt the outcome this time. Old Hickory won a sweeping victory, with 56 percent of the popular vote and 178 electoral votes, more than twice Adams's 83 electoral votes. Even Clay's home state went for him by a wide margin. Jackson was the first president elected from the West, indeed from any state other than Virginia and Massachusetts. In some frontier towns, he took every vote. His vice president was John C. Calhoun, who had held that office under Adams, but had broken with the president's policies.[36]

Nevertheless, victory proved more bitter than sweet. For in winning the presidency, Jackson lost the love of his life.

When Major Lewis brought the election results to The Hermitage, Rachel took the news hard. Yes, for her husband's sake, she was glad. For her part, however, she had never wanted him to be president. Rachel did not see herself as a first lady. She was a plantation mistress, a homebody, who liked nothing better than smoking her pipe with relatives and friends. The idea of being first lady, of having strangers snicker at her plain dress and country manners, terrified her. "I assure you," she told a Nashville lady, "I had rather be a doorkeeper in the house of God than to live in that palace in Washington." She never got the chance.[37]

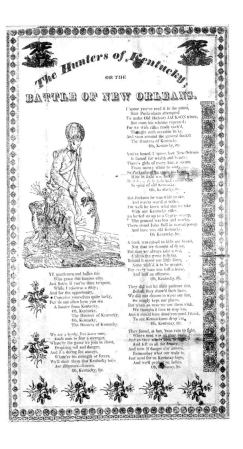

A song, "The Hunters of Kentucky," popularized Old Hickory's image as a war hero. A lithograph by James Ballie from the Library of Congress.

Sixty-one at the time of Jackson's election, Rachel had aged rapidly, and not well. She tired easily. For some time, she had complained of shortness of breath and wheezing, signs of asthma. She had chest pains and heart palpitations. To make matters worse, the couple's Creek son, Lyncoya, had died of tuberculosis just before the election. Rachel had nursed him to the end, but the shock of his passing left her stricken with grief.

Nashville planned to celebrate Jackson's victory with a banquet. Rachel had to go to town to buy her outfit and the clothes she would need as hostess in "that palace," the White House. In going from store to store, she grew tired and stopped at the office of a relative, a newspaper editor. While resting, she picked up a pamphlet written by her husband's friends. It contained detailed references to the dirty campaign charges he had tried to hide from her. In it, the authors defended her behavior before their marriage. Now, for the first time, she realized that Jackson's enemies had wanted to discredit him by accusing her of adultery and bigamy. Losing her self-control, she crouched in a corner and cried for hours.[38]

She caught a severe cold soon afterward; a few days later, she felt a stabbing pain in her chest and left arm—signs of a heart attack. Beside himself with worry, Jackson called in local doctors. They opened a vein in her arm; "bleeding" was then a standard treatment for any ailment, meant to expel "poisons" from the body. After they left, Jackson sat by her bedside all night. Slowly, the pain eased as she seemed to recover. Yet it was not to be. Three days later, on December 22, while sitting in a chair smoking her pipe, Rachel collapsed and died.

Jackson refused to believe it. He felt her heart, took her pulse, and looked into her face, desperately searching for any sign of life. Finally, he admitted the truth. John Coffee was with him. Grasping the giant's hand, he said, "John, can you realize she's dead? I certainly can't."[39]

On December 24, Christmas Eve, Rachel went to her rest in The Hermitage garden. Nashville had never seen such an outpouring of grief. Ten thousand people came—rich and poor, white and black, free and slave. For miles around, they streamed toward the big house on foot, on horseback, and by farm wagon. Many took shortcuts across the fields to avoid the traffic-choked roads. Why? Not for show. Not even out of respect for the president-elect. They came out of love for Aunt Rachel, who had touched all their lives with her gentleness and kindness. "She was a truly good woman," one said, speaking for all.[40]

Sam Houston, teary but stone-faced, led the pallbearers. Jackson followed, supported by John Coffee and another officer. There was no hickory in him now. The toughness had vanished. In its place stood a frail old man. "I shall never forget his look of grief," said an onlooker. Jackson seemed to have aged two years in one night.[41]

His grief soon gave way to hatred. A few days later, as he sat with visitors, they could almost touch his raw fury. His political enemies had made his love die of a broken heart. "May God Almighty forgive her murderers as I know she forgave them," Jackson said, adding, "I never can."[42]

VI

THAT MOST AMERICAN
OF AMERICANS

*. . . he was the most American of Americans—an embodied Declaration of Independence—
the Fourth of July incarnate!*

—JAMES PARTON

*They were his blood relations, the only blood relations he had. To labor for the good of the
masses was a special mission assigned to him by his Creator, and no man had ever better disposed to work in his vocation in season and out of season.*

—MARTIN VAN BUREN

Saturday, January 18, 1829. A carriage waited to take the president-elect
on the first leg of his three-week journey to Washington. Andrew Jackson Jr.
would go along to keep his father company. Major William Lewis would serve
as an adviser, and Jack Donelson as private secretary. Jack's young wife, Emily,
twenty, would take Rachel's place as White House hostess.

Visiting Rachel's grave one more time, Jackson stood silently before the
raw earth mound for several minutes. Then he turned and slowly walked away.
Yet, he might have said, his wife's spirit went with him. A black mourning
band encircled his arm, and a "weeper," or black silk ribbon, trailed down the
back of his hat. A miniature portrait of Rachel hung on a black cord around
his neck, over his heart. He would wear the weeper and the miniature all the
rest of his days.

Stepping into the carriage, he turned and tipped his hat to The Hermitage
in farewell, as if to a living person. A black servant, called Uncle Alfred by
everyone living on the plantation, noticed him sobbing as the carriage rolled
away. It halted at The Hermitage landing, a dock where slaves loaded cotton

bales for shipment to New Orleans. The steamboat *Pennsylvania* waited there, smoke billowing from its tall stacks. The vessel had two hickory brooms tied to its bow, symbolizing the clean sweep Old Hickory intended to make in Washington. As he went aboard, its whistle tooted and he murmured, "My heart is nearly broke."[1]

Pennsylvania sailed down the Cumberland River to the Ohio River, then upstream to Pittsburgh, from where the presidential party traveled overland by road. People hailed it at every stopping place along the way. They crowded around, eager to cheer their hero and shake his hand. He had a good word, if not a smile, for everyone. At Cincinnati, Ohio, "a greasy fellow" hit an all-time low for bad manners. Standing just inches away, he fairly spit his questions into Jackson's face:

"General Jackson, I guess?"

Jackson nodded.

"Why, they told me you was dead."

"No! Providence has hitherto preserved my life."

"And is your wife alive, too?"

Jackson shook his head, wincing.

"Aye, I thought it was one or t'other of ye."[2]

Reaching Washington, he found the Potomac River a sheet of ice, the streets pools of slush and mud. Yet people from everywhere—the common people—jammed the city. Backcountry folks and war veterans, farm families and factory workers: all came to see the inauguration. They packed hotels and boardinghouses, the "lucky" ones glad to sleep five and six to a bed with strangers. The unlucky ones slept on billiard tables and tavern floors, under staircases, even in doorways. Food grew scarce. Some places ran out of whiskey, which people guzzled to stay warm and, as they said, "spread good cheer." At least one drunk froze to death in the open; another fell facedown in a gutter and nearly drowned in the mud. These outsiders reminded some Washingtonians of stories they had heard of the riotous mobs in Paris before the French Revolution.

Jackson stayed at the National Hotel on the corner of Pennsylvania Avenue and Sixth Street. There he greeted well-wishers, met with political allies, and chose his cabinet. Henry Clay was not on his list of must-see people. Nor was

John Quincy Adams. Normally, the president-elect pays a courtesy call on the outgoing president. Not this time. After the attacks on Rachel, Jackson had no intention of being polite to "J. Q. Adams." Adams repaid the snub by refusing to attend Jackson's inauguration.

On Tuesday, March 4, 1829, Inauguration Day, Jackson appeared at the front door of his hotel at 11 A. M. sharp. He wore a black suit, black tie, and a long black coat. Since he was still in mourning, there would be no parade, but a "patriotic walk" to the swearing-in ceremony. A troop of veterans of the Revolutionary War and of the Battle of New Orleans escorted him along Pennsylvania Avenue. Even at a distance, there was no mistaking the president-elect. Ever the soldier, tall and erect, he towered over the escort. Only he wore no hat, out of respect for the people, because he was their servant, not their master. Onlookers understood the silent tribute and loved him for it.

Reaching the Capitol, Jackson entered by a basement door. After witnessing the swearing-in ceremony of Vice President Calhoun in the Senate cham-

President-elect Jackson speaks to the people while on his way to his inauguration in Washington, D.C. Rachel had recently died, leaving him heartbroken. From an engraving in Harper's Weekly, *1881, done many years after the event.*

ber, he made his way to a platform built outside. Below, at the foot of the steps, fifteen to twenty thousand people saw him and broke into cheers. Margaret Bayard Smith, the wife of a Maryland senator, watched the scene from a window.

"There, there, that is he," people cried.

"Which?"

"He with the white head!"

"Ah, there is the old man and his gray hair, there is the old veteran, there is Jackson."[3]

He wore two pairs of spectacles, one in front of his eyes, the other resting on top of his forehead; bifocals had not been invented yet, so he needed different eyeglasses for reading and for looking into the distance. Unlike modern inaugurations, Jackson delivered his address before taking the oath of office. Among the shortest on record, it lasted ten minutes. He read it in a low voice, barely heard by anyone. In it, he outlined his reform program: ending corruption, paying off the national debt (the money the government borrowed over the years to pay expenses and fund public improvements), increasing the size of the navy, and "a just and liberal policy" toward Native Americans.

When he finished, Chief Justice Marshall held out a Bible. Placing his right hand on it, Jackson repeated the oath taken by every president since George Washington: "I solemnly swear that I will faithfully execute the office of President of the United States and will, to the best of my ability, preserve, protect, and defend the Constitution of the United States." President Jackson then raised the Bible to his lips and kissed it. Cannons fired a salute. The crowd cheered again, only louder. Jackson bowed. As he did, hundreds dashed up the steps to congratulate him in person. Rather than be mobbed, he charged down the steps, his friends running interference, to a waiting horse.

The president rode down The Avenue to the White House, followed by the crowd. There was not a police officer in

After Jackson's inauguration on March 4, 1829, joyous well-wishers stormed the White House. (A contemporary print by Robert Cruickshank from the Library of Congress.)

sight; the capital had few police, and besides, the authorities did not expect trouble. The White House staff had prepared a small reception for the Washington elite. In the East Room were tables set with bread, roast chicken, cakes, ice cream, and orange punch laced with whiskey. What happened next surprised everyone.

Jackson entered the room with the crowd close behind, following him in. Anxious to get a glimpse of him, men in muddy boots stood on satin-covered chairs. Tables tipped over, sending crystal glasses and chinaware crashing to the floor. Ladies fainted. Men's fists flew and elbows jabbed, leaving black eyes and bloody noses. A guest stood laughing hysterically as a "stout black wench" sat alone "eating in this free country a jelly with a gold spoon in the President's House." Across the room, a proud mother watched as her daughter jumped up and down on a sofa. "Just think, mama!" the little Democrat shouted. "This sofa is a millionth part mine!"[4]

Jackson, the fearless war hero, stood helpless, pinned against a wall by well-wishers. For a moment, Margaret Bayard Smith feared for his life. "After [he had] been *literally* nearly pressed to death and almost suffocated and torn to bits by the people in their eagerness to shake hands with Old Hickory," some men came to his rescue. Linking arms, they formed a human shield around him and got him out through an open window. Still, people continued to pour into the East Room. To coax them outside, servants carried buckets of orange punch and trays of sweet goodies to the lawn. Following their appetite, the "rabble" surged after them through the door and windows.[5]

The day's events shocked polite society. "The reign of KING MOB seemed triumphant," huffed Joseph Story, an associate justice of the Supreme Court and an Adams man. Amos Kendall, a Kentucky newspaperman and Jackson supporter, disagreed. "It was a proud day for the people," he wrote of the inauguration. "General Jackson is *their own* president." Kendall was right. Despite the near riot, the inauguration symbolized an advance in American democracy. For the first time, the common people had chosen a president with a clear majority of both the popular and the electoral vote.[6]

Meanwhile, Jackson settled into his new home. The White House had few of the conveniences found in the "better" houses of the day. For example, there

View of the White House in Andrew Jackson's time.

was no running water; all its water came from wells, brought in buckets and barrels. Since factories manufactured cast-iron pipe for indoor plumbing, Jackson had pipes connected to an outdoor pump to carry water to two "water closets," or toilets. A "bathing room" had a shower and bathtub that used water heated in a boiler in the basement. To improve the building's appearance, the president refurnished the East Room and placed twenty brass spittoons around the vast room. He also planted magnolia trees in his wife's memory and added a portico, a walkway with a roof supported by columns, to the north side of the building.

Yet nothing could rid the White House of vermin. Rats ran around the basement and rummaged in the walls. At night, their squealing and scraping made life miserable for light sleepers. Poisoning them made matters worse; rats returned to their hiding places and died, their rotting bodies smelling awful. Cockroaches scurried about the floors. Horseflies with steel-blue bodies flew in from nearby stables. The sleeping quarters crawled with bedbugs, wingless, smelly insects with flat, reddish bodies that feed on human blood. Bedbugs made the president miserable. While away from Washington, he wrote Major Lewis to "say to the chamber maid to have all our beds clear of bed bugges."[7]

Poor health dogged Jackson's White House years. He was ill most of the time; his letters read like a catalog of sicknesses. Bouts of malaria, a result of his Florida campaigns, tormented him for weeks on end. The nicotine from smoking and chewing tobacco gave him splitting headaches. Carelessness about dental hygiene cost him nearly all his teeth. Jackson had dentures made, heavy metal ones with springs, but they never fit properly, making him miserable. He suffered from "inflammation in the rectum"—hemorrhoids—which made it agony to sit for any length of time. Bouts of diarrhea, he wrote a friend, "weakened me very much." An English visitor reported a private interview with the president: "The conversation of the first quarter of an hour was about the state of his bowels. . . . We then got on to European politics."[8]

Jackson was his own doctor, not necessarily a bad thing, given the state of medical science then. He treated himself with massive doses of laxatives, drugs to loosen the bowels, and emetics, drugs to induce vomiting. Calomel, a mixture of mercury and lead, was his favorite medicine, used for nearly all afflictions. This he swallowed, bathed in, even squirted into his eyes. Since mercury and lead are poisons, he was slowly poisoning himself without realizing it. Doctors routinely prescribed these drugs for their patients, but Old Hickory went overboard in using them on himself.[9]

The bullet Charles Dickinson fired into his chest in 1806 tormented him endlessly. Every month or so, it produced abscesses, swollen infection-filled areas, near his left lung. These triggered violent coughing and hemorrhages, severe bleeding from torn blood vessels. When Jackson felt a hemorrhage coming on, he bled himself to reduce its severity—or so he thought. He would "lay bare his arm, bandage it, take his penknife from his pocket, call his servant to hold the bowl, and bleed himself freely. Often, indeed, during his presidency, he performed the operation in the middle of the night without any assistance."[10]

The president's workday began early. As a soldier and a plantation owner, he was used to getting up long before daybreak. Although he sometimes took an afternoon walk or rode horseback to neighboring Georgetown, he worked as hard as any president before or after him. Even when ill, he worked intensely for hours, often sitting up in bed surrounded by papers. Jackson simply refused to let pain dictate how he would live his life. Somehow he managed to get past it, focusing on the task before him. "He could not be kept from work," said Nicholas Trist, an aide. If pain kept him from working with his hands, "he wore himself out with thinking." We would call him a workaholic today.[11]

Jackson read a lot. Apart from the Bible, which he read from every day, he seldom opened a book. Mostly, he read newspapers, reports, and letters. The president wrote a lot, too—as many as twenty letters a day to his family, friends, politicians, and replies to citizens' letters. In preparing an official message, he would scribble ideas on scraps of paper and in the margins of newspapers. These he tossed into a tall hat. Someone else, usually Amos Kendall, later organized them into a speech. A Kentuckian, Kendall was a walking skeleton with a deep-lined face and a high-pitched voice; friends said he "looked like death on a pale horse." Constantly suffering from chills, even on the hottest days Kendall wore a heavy overcoat buttoned up to his neck. Yet Jackson trusted him to put his scribbles into polished sentences.[12]

Like every president, Jackson held cabinet meetings. Today, the cabinet has fifteen members. In the 1830s, it had six members: the secretary of state, of war, of the treasury, and of the navy, the postmaster general, and the attorney general, the nation's chief law officer. Everyone, even critics, admired Secretary of State Van Buren. Opposition journalists, however, called the Little Magician's fellow cabinet members "minnows," small men with small abilities.[13]

Modern presidents use the cabinet to help them set government policy. Old Hickory, however, used it merely as a source of ideas and opinions. A good listener, he let his cabinet discuss an issue from every angle. Members argued back and forth, encouraged by the president to speak their minds. Yet, in the end, he made up his own mind, alone. Once he did, nothing could change it. Warnings and difficulties could not weaken his resolve. "I care nothing about clamors, sir," he told Nicholas Trist. "I do precisely what I think right."[14]

Not only is the president the nation's highest official, he is also its chief host. Jackson took the job of entertaining guests seriously. He spent almost his entire salary of twenty-five thousand dollars a year on private dinner parties for friends, political bigwigs, and well-connected foreign visitors. Meals consisted of elaborate dishes like oyster pie, duck, ham, a "monster salmon in waves of meat jelly," and desserts, all served with whiskey, wine, and punch. Alcoholic beverages often cost more than the meal itself.[15]

Calling the White House the "People's House," Jackson reserved Thursday evenings for public receptions, or levees. Other presidents had had levees, but chiefly for higher-class people. Anyone could attend a Jackson levee. Business leaders introduced their wives and daughters to the president. A bearded frontiersman came "in all his dirt" to pat Old Hickory on the back with one hand while holding a horsewhip in the other. A drunken canal worker squeezed his hand with a great callused paw. An English visitor stood beside factory workers, "men begrimed with all the sweat and filth accumulated in their day's—perhaps their week's—labor." Americans wanted to meet their president, tell him their troubles, seek his advice, and ask for favors. Although always polite, Jackson had no time for those who tried to ask for improper favors. His blazing see-through-you eyes would send them scooting to the nearest exit.[16]

Even among crowds, Jackson felt lonely. Missing Rachel, he thought of her constantly. Her image was the last thing he saw upon closing his eyes at night. It filled the emptiness he felt deep down, bringing him close to her. Late one night, Nicholas Trist returned to the White House with some letters he had forgotten to have him sign. "Come in," Jackson said as Trist knocked on his bedroom door. Trist recalled:

> He was undressed, but not in bed, as I had supposed he must be by that time. He was sitting at the little table with his wife's miniature [portrait] before him, propped up on some books; and between him and the picture lay an open book, which bore the mark of long use. This book, as I learned afterward, was *her* prayer-book. The miniature was always next to his heart, suspended around his neck by a strong, black cord. The last thing he did at night, before lying down to rest, was to read in that book with that picture under his eyes.[17]

Yet Jackson did not always sleep through the night. No guards protected the White House. A servant simply locked the front door at sundown and unlocked it at daybreak. Sometimes an intruder climbed through a window to steal a silver spoon or a candlestick. One found himself in Jackson's bedroom. A light sleeper, the president awakened with a start, demanding to know what the man was doing there. The fellow said he had lost his way in the dark, had blundered into the White House, and was trying to get out. Deciding he was a thief, Jackson had him locked in a stable until lawmen took him away next morning. Morning came, but the stable was empty. The incident was soon forgotten.[18]

This might seem strange today, but Jackson's world was a different world from ours. Back then, nobody feared an assault on the president, least of all the president himself. This had nothing to do with Jackson's reputation with a pistol. Violence against leaders was not unusual in Europe, with its crowned heads, ancient injustices, and simmering family and class hatreds. Americans, however, prided themselves on being different from other nations. Violence against leaders was unpatriotic. It was natural, people said, for the oppressed to want to harm their oppressors. Americans, however, had no reason to harm bad leaders, since they could vote them out of office. No president had ever suffered physical attack. None, that is, until Old Hickory.

The first attack came in 1833, after his election to a second term. Jackson had boarded a steamboat at Alexandria, Virginia, and was sitting on a deck chair, reading a newspaper. The boat had not left its dock when, suddenly, Robert B. Randolph came up to him. A former naval officer, he blamed the president for his dismissal for theft. As Old Hickory looked up, Randolph slapped his face and ran ashore. Arrested later and charged with assault, he was lucky. The long-ago advice Jackson's mother had given him never to take a man to court for an injury or an insult, but to settle the matter by himself, now played a role. As president, Jackson could not break the law by dueling; besides, he was too old for that sort of thing. So he refused to testify at Randolph's trial, and his attacker went free.

In his two terms as president, Jackson received more than five hundred letters threatening his life. These came from all sorts of people with "grievances." The best-known letter writer was Junius Brutus Booth. A famous actor, Booth was half crazy and fully alcoholic. Locked in his room by his manager, he would bribe servants to bring whiskey, which he sipped with a straw through the keyhole. On July 4, 1835, he wrote Jackson: "You damn'd old Scoundrel . . . I will cut your throat whilst you are sleeping." Nothing came of the threat. However, the actor's son, John Wilkes Booth, was a chip off the old block. Also a famous actor, in April 1865, he assassinated President Abraham Lincoln.[19]

Jackson ignored death threats. If he let them bother him, he felt, he could not go anywhere or do anything. On January 30, 1835, he attended funeral services for a congressman. As he left the House chamber, a man stepped from the crowd just six feet from him. Without warning, he drew a pistol and "fired" at Jackson's heart. The loud noise startled everyone. Unharmed yet

In the first assassination attempt on an American president, in January 1835, Richard Lawrence tried to shoot Andrew Jackson. Luckily, both his pistols misfired. Notice his first pistol on the ground.

"boiling with rage," the president did what came naturally. He lunged toward the gunman with his cane, but missed. The fellow drew a second pistol and "fired." Again Jackson lunged with his cane, missing again. A navy lieutenant knocked the gunman down; someone else brought a pair of handcuffs.[20]

The failed assassin was Richard Lawrence, an unemployed housepainter. Lawrence fantasized that Jackson had blocked his claim to the British throne. Resolving to kill him for that, he loaded his pistols with the best gunpowder, the kind used in dueling pistols. When fired afterward, each pistol sent its bullet through an inch-thick board at a distance of thirty feet. Good luck had spared Jackson's life. For some reason, the firing caps Lawrence used were defective. When struck by the pistol's hammer, they had made a loud crack without igniting the gunpowder charge. A court found Lawrence insane and sent him to an asylum. Jackson took the shooting in stride. Afterward, he returned to the White House, where Van Buren found him with one of Jack and Emily Donelson's children sitting on his lap.[21]

Having "family" around made life bearable for Jackson. Ralph Earl, the painter, moved into the White House, as did Major Lewis. The Donelsons lived there with their three children. The president loved them as his own. When they came down with measles at the same time, he fussed over them as much as their parents. Often, in the dead of night, he peeked into their room to check on his "little pets," as he called them.

Jackson had a simple rule: the more children, the better. Visitors knew how happy it made him when they brought their youngsters. Then, at presidential order, the Oval Room—later made into the Oval Office—became a wonderland of ice cream, cake, lemonade, toys, and gifts. Children threw cotton snowballs and played blindman's buff. Afterward, the little guests lined up by the door. Boys bowed and girls curtsied, saying, "Good night, General," as they left the room. One Christmas Eve, Jackson mentioned that Santa Claus had never visited him when he was their age. Feeling sorry for him, they begged him to hang up his stocking. Next morning, a visitor found him in tears over the pipe and other gifts that the children had stuffed into the stocking.[22]

In November 1831, Andrew Jackson Jr. married Sarah Yorke of Philadelphia. Even before meeting her, the president loved her. Tell Sarah, he wrote his son, "that I shall receive her as a daughter, and cherish her as my child." He meant it. When the newlyweds reached the White House, he hugged his new daughter at the front door.[23]

Young Andrew's marriage to Sarah was the best thing he ever did for his father. She was his joy, calling him "dear father" and giving him grandchildren: Rachel and Andrew III. Sadly, Andrew Jr. could not seem to grow up. He never learned the value of money, because he never had to earn any himself. Life was too easy for him. Given the job of running The Hermitage, he spent most of his time hunting, gambling, and piling up debt. Andrew Jr. died in 1865, at the age of fifty-six, having accidentally shot himself while hunting.

In the same year that his son married, Jackson had The Hermitage enlarged and remodeled. Three years later, in 1834, a fire nearly destroyed it. Although servants saved some furniture, nearly all of Rachel's letters went up in flames. Not only was this a great loss to Jackson, it leaves a huge gap in our understanding of their lives together.

Old Hickory decided to rebuild the place as quickly as possible. When his plan became known, a drive began to pay for the project with money collected from the public. Jackson, a proud man used to earning his way, rejected the offer. If supporters wished to collect money in his name, very well, but let it go "to some charitable institution." His attitude may seem odd to us nowadays, when private donations to presidential libraries can seem like payoffs for past services to special interests.[24]

Jackson believed in democracy, in bringing the government close to the people, and the people into the government. But for that to happen, he felt he must first eliminate corruption.

In our modern civil service system, a person must pass a competitive examination to qualify for most government jobs. It was different in Jackson's day. Back then, department heads appointed workers as needed, and as Congress budgeted the money for their salaries. Normally, men of "good family," with political contacts, got these jobs. Jobholders saw their positions as a form of property, a lifetime post belonging to them. Whatever their ability or character, they quickly felt that the job existed to serve their needs, not the public's.

Most government workers were decent, honest men. A few were incompetent through no fault of their own. Since there was no set retirement age, some elderly men became forgetful, unable to do a day's work. Moreover, every department had its share of drunkards—no surprise, given the way Americans abused alcohol. Then there were the outright crooks. For example, during the Monroe and Adams administrations, treasury officials stole over $300,000 in gold, an amount equal to about $30 million in today's money.

The six presidents who served between 1789 and 1829 fired a total of seventy-three jobholders. Then along came Old Hickory with what critics called his "dangerous ideas" about democracy. All "offices are created solely for the benefit of the people," he insisted. Thus, "no one man has any more intrinsic right to official station than another." His inauguration set off a panic. Expecting a "Reign of Terror" as in the bloodiest days of the French Revolution, men in government went to work each day as if it were their last. Some went insane, cracking under the nervous strain. Three committed suicide out of fear of being dismissed.[25]

Although Jackson might feel sorry for them, he also felt they had profited from an undemocratic system. Every free white man, he said, deserved a chance to share in running the government. So it would be best if jobholders appointed by the last administration left when a new one took over. He called it "rotation of office," opening the way for newcomers.

What about ability? It did not take a genius to do government work, Jackson insisted. The work was "so plain and simple," he said, that any intelligent person could do it. The president had a point. In the 1820s, most professions still required little, if any, formal training. Surgeons did not go to medical school but lived with an experienced man and watched him work. Law students read law and observed attorneys in action, as Jackson had done. Generals learned on the job, as he and George Washington had done. Unlike today, no colleges had schools of public administration.[26]

Jackson's opponents disagreed, however. Rotation of office—nonsense! It was a say-nothing term for rewarding Democratic Party workers with government jobs. They used another phrase, borrowed from Senator William Marcy, a New York Democrat. Marcy claimed politicians "see nothing wrong in the rule that to the victor belongs the spoils of the enemy." Before long, critics shortened "the spoils of the enemy" to the "spoils system." The name stuck.[27]

Jackson never used the term "spoils system." He did, however, use rotation of office to fight corruption *and* reward loyal Democrats. Yet there was no "bloodbath," as critics charged. In his first eighteen months in office, Jackson "rotated" 919 out of 10,093 federal jobholders; over the entire eight years of his presidency, the total amounted to only one-tenth of all jobholders. Yet he tried to be humane even if that meant going against his own stated principles. When an aide suggested that he get rid of a supporter of John Quincy Adams, a village postmaster barely able to write his name, Jackson leaped from his chair. "By the Eternal!" he cried. "I will not remove the old man. Do you know that he carries a pound of British lead in his body?" Another time, Jackson dismissed a treasury clerk for incompetence, a man with a young wife and six children. He felt so terrible he raised money to aid the family.[28]

Rotation of office or the spoils system—whatever we call it—had clear benefits. It allowed the new president to choose his own team. The government, in turn, reflected public opinion as expressed through the ballot box. Under Jackson, it provided able, honest government.

However, no system is foolproof. Occasionally, a real thief got a government job under Jackson. Samuel Swartwout, collector of customs at the Port of New York, was the worst of them. Since the opening of the Erie Canal, the port had grown into the nation's busiest. Swartwout cashed in, becoming the first American ever to steal a million dollars. He pocketed $1.2 million in customs fees before fleeing to Europe. Jackson, flabbergasted, never imagined that a person could be so dishonest. "Can he live after this," the president asked, "or will he cut his throat?"[29]

In the end, the spoils system did the nation more harm than good. Critics rightly accused Jackson of making government service a tool of the Democratic Party. Yet his opponents quickly followed suit, because the practice was too tempting to ignore. Handing out jobs after a successful election enabled leaders of all parties to strengthen their local organizations, reward loyalty, and attract the workers needed to get out the vote. People worked hard for a candidate, expecting to receive a job in appreciation for their efforts, if the candidate was elected. Despite the creation of a modern civil service in 1883, not all government jobs fall under its rules. Thus, the spoils system still continues in a few federal offices, even more in state and local governments. Now we call it "patronage," politicians giving out jobs to increase political power and reward past services.[30]

Margaret "Peggy" Eaton in her later years. Known as a "loose" woman, the scandal she caused nearly wrecked Jackson's presidency.

A scandal, not the spoils system, nearly destroyed Jackson's presidency at its outset. The scandal swirled around a woman. Born Margaret O'Neale in 1799, she was the daughter of a Washington boardinghouse owner. Known to everyone as Peggy, she was a beauty, with a "peach-pink complexion," dark eyes, and fun-loving nature. As a child, Peggy had joked with her father's guests, chiefly politicians, and played the piano for them. As a teenager, she worked as a barmaid and talked politics with them as an equal. Never shy, she flirted and danced wildly, baring her ankles![31]

Eventually Peggy married a naval officer. But during his long absences at sea, she took up with her father's star boarder. The boarder was Senator John Eaton, thirty-nine, Old Hickory's friend, aide, and choice for secretary of war. Soon afterward, her husband, John Timberlake, committed suicide for reasons that remain a mystery. Two months later, on New Year's Day, 1829, Peggy and Eaton married with the blessings of the president-elect.

Gossip flew thick as Washington mosquitoes in July. "The hussy!" society ladies hissed. Peggy, they said, was everything "a lady" should not be: "bold," "uncouth," "pushy," "fast," "uppity." She "brazenly" violated the ideals of womanhood. Unfaithful to her husband, she lacked the decency to mourn him properly, they claimed. A widow was supposed to wear "weeds"—that is, black from head to toe. She must not attend social events, or even think of re-marrying for at least two years. Peggy had her own mind. She remarried quickly, wore the latest fashions, and went to parties. Worst of all, gossips said, she had slept with "eleven doz. others" before marrying Eaton. We do not know if this charge was true. We do know that nobody ever stepped forward to name even one of her "lovers."[32]

Vice President Calhoun's wife, Floridé, came from one of South Carolina's "best" families. Outraged at Peggy's behavior, she persuaded three other cabinet wives to refuse to be in the same room with Peggy or receive her in their homes. Visiting was serious business in nineteenth-century America. Well-born women had engraved calling cards with their names printed in raised letters. When a woman visited, she left her card as a show of respect, whether the lady of the house was in or not. Being received in someone's home showed the visitor's acceptance by polite society. Not being received, or failure to return a visit, meant rejection. Men were powerless here. Although women had few rights, in "proper" families, by custom the wife had the last word on social matters.[33]

The Peggy Eaton scandal touched Jackson deeply. He rated friendship above nearly everything else. "I never *desert a friend, without cause; I never will, a friend in distress,*" he wrote a Nashville lady. He meant it. John Eaton was his friend. The old soldier would stand by him no matter what happened. It was the same with Peggy, whom Rachel had met during a visit to Washington. Rachel liked her, which was enough for Jackson. Apparently, Rachel and Peggy became linked together in Jackson's mind. Enemies had hounded his beloved into the grave with disgusting lies, as they were now hounding Peggy. Jackson could not stand for that.[34]

Politics further complicated things. Martin Van Buren knew that he wanted eventually to succeed Old Hickory as president. Having made that decision, the Little Magician began working overtime. A keen student of human nature, he had "read" Jackson perfectly, and knew the value the president placed on friendship. It was, Van Buren thought, the key to his personality. A widower, Van Buren could run his private life as he pleased. He befriended Peggy, took her for carriage rides, and gave dinners in her honor. This made him the president's friend, too, and not just his secretary of state.

John C. Calhoun also wanted to succeed Jackson when he finally left the presidency. There were no term limits back then, but George Washington had served two terms, thus setting a precedent that would be broken only in the twentieth century, when Franklin D. Roosevelt was elected to four terms. However, only Calhoun's wife, Floride, not he, decided whom she would receive. By refusing to receive Peggy or visit her at home, Floride undercut her husband's influence with the president. Jackson told the vice president that his wife *must* receive Peggy. When Calhoun said he dared not ask that of her, Jackson decided to deliver the message in person. Floride listened, silently. When he finished, she rang for the butler. "Show this gentleman to the door," she ordered. Throwing the president out of her house did not endear her husband to him. Nor did Jackson like Calhoun any better when, as we will see

This anonymous print of 1829, titled She's Chaste as a Virgin, *has Peggy Eaton dancing before Jackson and his cabinet. It never happened. Although Jackson defended her in a cabinet meeting, she was not present.*

later, the South Carolinian defended a state's right to ignore federal laws. In any case, the Eaton affair aroused Jackson's suspicions. He began to think, quite wrongly, that the couple's critics were really using his friendship with them to humiliate him, thus eventually securing the presidential nomination for Calhoun. Now he began to see Calhoun as an enemy.[35]

On September 10, 1829, Jackson called what may be the strangest, if not the craziest, cabinet meeting in American history. It was devoted not to important government matters, but to a sex scandal that was increasingly preying on the president's mind. All cabinet members except Eaton attended. After bitter debate, Jackson roared: "She is as chaste as a virgin!" Despite his claim, the meeting settled nothing. It did, however, nearly draw blood. Eaton learned that Treasury Secretary Samuel Ingham had said unkind things about his wife. When Peggy learned of this, too, she demanded that her husband challenge Ingham to a duel. However, Ingham obeyed the law against dueling; he ignored the challenge. Eaton, hounded by his wife and determined to defend his honor, then arranged to have Ingham waylaid in the streets and beaten up by thugs. After a narrow escape, the treasury secretary begged the president for help. Jackson refused to interfere, so the poor fellow, fearing for his life, skipped town, resigning soon afterward. The whole business was absurd. And dangerous, too.[36]

As members resigned from Jackson's cabinet over the Peggy Eaton affair, this cartoon, titled "The Rats Leaving a Falling House," depicted the expected collapse of the administration.

What Van Buren called "the Eaton Malaria" was tearing the Democratic Party apart, and with it the administration. By making support for Peggy a test of loyalty to himself, Jackson had turned the scandal into political dynamite. By choosing sides for and against their wives' stand on Peggy, cabinet members were, in effect, supporting Van Buren or Calhoun for the presidency later. If things continued this way, a hundred Democratic congressmen warned, they would break away from Jackson. The president stood firm. "Let them come on—let the whole hundred come on," he roared. "I would resign the Presidency or lose my life sooner than I would desert my friend Eaton." Meanwhile, newspapers printed hundreds of cartoons about the affair, none favorable to the Democrats.[37]

What to do? Van Buren decided he had to save the administration by saving Jackson from the results of his own actions. He planned a brilliant move, one worthy of the Little Magician. He would resign as secretary of state, persuading Eaton to leave his post of secretary of war as well. With Jackson's best men gone from the cabinet, he supposed the president would feel free to demand the others' resignation. The plan worked. In April 1831, for the only time in American history, the cabinet left office. With it went Calhoun's friends, whom Jackson distrusted and Van Buren wanted to get out of his way. The New Yorker became minister to Great Britain. Eaton became minister to Spain, taking Peggy with him. Jackson named another cabinet at once.

Still, he did not go to it when he needed advice on important matters. For this, Jackson had used a small group of outside advisers even before his cabinet resignations. This informal circle met in the back rooms of the White House, thus its nickname, the "Kitchen Cabinet." Members included Van Buren (before he left for London), Major Lewis, and Jack Donelson. There were also several newspaper editors, loyal supporters tuned to public opinion. Besides Amos Kendall, Jackson sought advice from Francis P. Blair, Duff Green, and Isaac Hill, whom he also appointed to a high treasury post. Another trusted Kitchen Cabinet member was Roger B. Taney, a brilliant Maryland lawyer.[38]

Later presidents would have their own versions of the Kitchen Cabinet. Theodore Roosevelt's was

President Jackson's Kitchen Cabinet shows his unofficial advisers quarreling. Jackson did not formally meet with members as a group, but privately sought their advice, as presidents still do from trusted individuals. Kitchen Cabinet members might have disagreed, but not to the point of violence.

called the "tennis cabinet," because its members met in the clubhouse. War-ren G. Harding had his "poker cabinet," since it discussed business around the card table. Herbert Hoover, a physical fitness fan, went to his "medicine ball cabinet" for advice.[39]

Recovery from the "Eaton Malaria" freed Jackson to turn to matters of true importance. Three issues would shape both his terms in the White House, and the rest of this book will be devoted to them. These issues played out at the same time, creating a complex, at times confusing picture. Two issues—preserving the Union and Indian removal—are large enough to require sepa-rate chapters. The third issue was the struggle against the Bank of the United States, or the Bank War, for short. In it, Jackson resisted what he saw as a grave threat to democracy. Let us consider it first.

To understand the Bank War, we must understand the money system in the early nineteenth century. It was a system quite different from the one we are familiar with today. Back then, the federal government issued only small amounts of gold and silver coins called specie, or hard money. It issued no pa-per currency until the advent of the "greenbacks," called so because they were printed in green ink, during the Civil War in the 1860s. Mostly, Americans bought and sold goods with notes issued by banks chartered, or licensed, by their home states. Each bank had a board of directors and stockholders, who owned shares in it. That is, they shared ownership in the bank. As backing for its notes, the bank held small amounts of specie (issued by the government) in its vaults. In theory, at the issuing bank anyone could exchange a note for specie. In practice, banks, always eager to make loans, issued more notes than they had specie to back them up. By 1830, there were 330 state-chartered banks.

Let's say you needed five hundred dollars to buy a farm. Since you did not have that amount of money saved, you asked a banker to lend it to you. If he agreed, you received his bank's notes, which you spent on the farm. Each note was really the bank's written promise to exchange that note for its value in specie. Each bank's notes looked different. Varying in color and size, they had printed on them the issuing bank's name, a picture of a famous person, and a value. Over time, from your earnings, you repaid the bank's loan—with interest, an additional amount the banker charged for lending you his money—for taking the risk that you might not pay it back.

Banknotes varied in value. A note from a trustworthy local bank might be worth its face value, or close to it. Yet if it came from a faraway bank, or one with a shaky reputation, people would be careful about accepting it. For example, a shopkeeper might consider a twenty-dollar note from a faraway bank worth seventeen dollars, giving only that amount in goods in return. Worse, if too many people tried to exchange their notes for specie at the same time, the issuing bank could not pay them all. It "crashed," ruining stockholders and leaving note holders with worthless paper. Several large banks crashing at once might plunge the entire country into a depression, that is, a sharp economic downturn that could last for years.

To avoid such disasters, in 1816 Congress chartered the second Bank of the United States. Eastern stockholders owned and controlled the bank, which also acted as the federal government's financial agent. Back then, as we saw earlier, there was no income tax, so the government raised cash from land sales, duties on imports, and the tax on whiskey. The bank held these funds for safekeeping in its Philadelphia headquarters, paying no interest on them. It also issued notes and made loans, even to the federal government. Finally, if a state bank made too many risky loans, the Bank of the United States bought up its notes through its twenty-nine branches. By demanding hard money—specie—for these notes, it curbed risky loans, keeping the economy on an even keel by controlling the money supply.[40] The charter of the first Bank of the United States, founded by Alexander Hamilton in 1790, when he was the first secretary of the treasury, had expired in 1811.

Led by its president, Nicholas Biddle, the Bank of the United States played a key role in American life. The social opposite of Jackson, Biddle was born to a wealthy Philadelphia family in 1786, graduating from Princeton University at the age of fifteen. Witty and cultured, he spoke French, German, and Latin, studied painting and architecture, and wrote beautifully. His history of the Lewis and Clark expedition became an American classic. Even his enemies thought him one of the handsomest men alive.

For Biddle, the Bank of the United States came first. He always put its interests above the nation's. To advance those interests, he used its vast financial

Old Hickory's war against the Bank of the United States, portrayed here as a many-headed monster, with director Nicholas Biddle at the center. The bank used its tremendous political power to buy influence in Congress, benefiting its directors and stockholders at the public's expense.

power to buy political influence. Biddle backed bank-friendly politicians with cash and lent money to friendly newspapers in hard-fought election districts. To tide them over until Congress passed the yearly appropriation bill, the bank paid congressmen's salaries in advance. It also gave them interest-free loans. The bank's influence even reached top congressional leaders. Henry Clay was on its payroll as a "legal adviser." It supplied Daniel Webster, a member of its legal team, with loans totaling $111,166.[41]

Jackson despised the bank. "Money is power," the president said, meaning that it gave a wealthy minority power beyond what it should have in a democracy. He denounced the "monied aristocracy," the bank's stockholders, who thought themselves born to rule. In truth, he said, they were the "money predators," wolves preying upon the public by corrupting its elected representatives. How come? Because they dealt in paper "trash," not "full-blooded money,"—hard money—gold and silver. Government exists to protect the people's God-given rights, Jackson argued. The Declaration of Independence says so. It cannot do this by handing out monopolies, privileges, and special favors to the rich. Whatever it does, it must do for all. To save democracy, then, Old Hickory felt he must crush "the Monster."[42]

Henry Clay gave him the chance to do just that. Now a senator, Clay was the Republican presidential candidate in 1832. He needed an issue, a club to beat Jackson over the head with in the campaign. That club would be the bank's charter, due for renewal by Congress in 1836. Rather than wait until then, Clay pressed for early renewal. Everyone knew of Jackson's hatred for the bank. Signing the renewal bill would brand Jackson a hypocrite who traded principle for political advantage. Vetoing it, however, would be worse. "Should Jackson veto it," Clay boasted, "I'll veto him!" A veto might cost Jackson the bank's home state, Pennsylvania, and probably the election.[43]

The renewal bill sailed through Congress. Jackson vetoed the bill. Now, it seemed, he had fallen into Clay's trap. Yet Clay had not imagined that Jackson would defend his action in an eloquent plea for democracy against special interests. Although the words were Amos Kendall's and Roger B. Taney's, the ideas were pure Jackson. Dated Washington, July 10, 1832, his veto message focused on the corrupting influence of money in politics.

> . . . the rich and powerful too often bend the acts of government to their selfish purposes. Distinctions in society will always exist under every just government. Equality of talents . . . or of wealth cannot be produced by human institutions. In the full enjoyment of the fruits of Heaven and the fruits of superior industry, economy and virtue, every man is equally entitled to protection by the law. But when the laws undertake to add to these natural and just advantages artificial distinctions, to grant . . . exclusive privileges, to make the rich richer and the potent more powerful, the humble members of society—the farmers, mechanics, and laborers—who have neither the time nor the means of securing like favors to themselves, have a right to complain of the injustice to their Government. There are no necessary evils in government. Its evils exist only in its abuses. If it would confine itself to equal protec-

BORN TO COMMAND.

OF VETO MEMORY.

HAD I BEEN CONSULTED.

KING ANDREW THE FIRST.

During Jackson's second campaign for the presidency in 1832, opponents used this famous cartoon, "King Andrew the First," showing him as a dictator stepping all over the Constitution.

tion, and, as Heaven does its rains, shower its favors alike upon the high and the low, the rich and the poor, it would be an unqualified blessing. In the act before me there seems to be a wide and unnecessary departure from these just principles.[44]

The spirit of Jackson's message has echoed down through the years. Money's influence in politics is a never-ending threat to democracy. Our greatest twentieth-century presidents feared the ability of the few, controlling vast wealth, to become a law unto themselves. In 1907, Theodore Roosevelt denounced "malefactors of great wealth," rich evildoers ready to sacrifice liberty to profit. In the 1920s and 1930s, his cousin Franklin D. Roosevelt condemned such people as "economic royalists." FDR admired Jackson's stance in the Bank War. He praised his "earnest determination to keep control of the government out of the hands of the professional moneymakers and . . . in the hands of the people themselves."[45]

Jackson's veto message gave voters a real choice in the election. Biddle, the bank, and its backers poured money into Clay's campaign. Their actions made the old soldier even more determined to win. "Mr. Van Buren," he told his running mate, back from England, "the Bank is trying to kill me, *but I will kill it!*" He spoke calmly, without visible anger. Still, his eyes told a different story. For him, as for the nation, the election of 1832 was about one question: Should the Bank have its charter renewed?[46]

Led by the Little Magician, Jackson's campaign team presented the veto as a courageous act. They encouraged people to see the election as a struggle between good and evil, between the people and the money power. Democratic speakers pounded away at the "Monster Bank," vowing to kill it and plant a hickory tree on its grave. Marchers chanted "Clay and rag money! Jackson and gold!" The Clay people, in turn, called Jackson a would-be dictator. A famous cartoon, titled "King Andrew the First," showed the president, pinch-faced, wearing a crown and royal robes, trampling on the Constitution. In one hand he holds a scroll labeled VETO, in the other a king's scepter.[47]

Jackson won in a landslide; even Pennsylvania went for him. He took 55 percent of the popular vote, and 219 electoral votes to 49 for Clay. Soon afterward, a new party replaced the Republicans. A grab bag of politicians united chiefly by their opposition to Jackson, they called themselves the Whigs, after the English party that had sympathized with America during the Revolutionary War. The country now had a working two-party system.[48]

Old Hickory had never been more popular. After the inauguration, he boarded a train, his first, for a victory tour of Northern cities. Cannon salutes, steam whistles, and cheering crowds greeted him everywhere. New York City went wild. Those who remembered George Washington's inauguration there in 1789 hardly believed their eyes—or their ears. George Washington, said Philip Hone, was "too dignified, too grave." Jackson, however, had a good word for everyone. "Talk of him as the second Washington! It won't do now; Washington was only the first Jackson."[49]

In Cambridge, Massachusetts, Harvard University gave Jackson an honorary doctor-of-laws degree. John Quincy Adams sputtered with rage. What a disgrace, he said, that the school he loved should honor "a barbarian who could not write a sentence of grammar and hardly spell his own name." By then, Adams hated Jackson as bitterly as Jackson hated him. Soon afterward, a lung hemorrhage forced the president to cancel the rest of the tour. While recovering in the White House, he prepared for his next ordeal.[50]

Jackson saw his reelection in 1832 as a signal to continue the Bank War. To break the bank, he decided to remove all federal deposits, placing them in twenty-three selected state banks, dubbed "pet banks" by opposition newspapers. When Treasury Secretary William Duane refused to obey the removal order, Jackson fired him and gave Roger B. Taney the post. Taney saw that the money went to the pet banks.[51]

Biddle struck back by raising interest charges and calling in loans before their due dates. Acting on his orders, the bank returned piles of notes to state banks, even sound ones, demanding payment in specie. With fewer notes in circulation, and thus fewer notes to loan or to borrow, credit tightened. Business activity slowed, and unemployment rose. A depression threatened to wreck the American economy—exactly what Biddle wanted. To force the return of federal deposits to the bank, he meant to take the nation hostage.

Worried businessmen urged the president to return the deposits or risk national ruin. Old Hickory stood his ground. He would rather cut off his right hand, he said, than yield to Biddle's bullying. "Andrew Jackson will never restore the deposits!" he told a group from Philadelphia. "Andrew Jackson will never recharter that monster of corruption! Sooner than live in a country where such a power prevails, I would seek asylum in the wilds of Arabia."

A few days later, a Baltimore delegation came to ask Jackson for relief from the tight money supply. People needed to borrow money, to get loans, in order to conduct business.

"Relief, sir!" the president snapped. "Come not to me, sir! Go to the monster!"

"The people, sir—"

In The Downfall of Mother Bank, *Old Hickory watches the collapse of the Bank of the United States while a workingman cheers.*

He never got to finish the sentence. "The people!" Jackson interrupted, "The people, sir, are with *me.*"[52]

Most people *were* with him. The Senate was not. Led by Henry Clay, Biddle's allies moved to censure—officially condemn—Jackson for removing the deposits. Despite Senator Benton's efforts to defeat the motion, it passed.

Gossips expected Jackson to challenge censure supporters to a duel. Yet Biddle's arrogance, not a presidential bullet, defeated him. The public realized he would gladly sacrifice the country's well-being to save his bank. As outrage swept the country, the banker retreated, restoring the flow of credit. Too late. In April 1834, the House upheld Jackson's veto, voting against renewing the bank's charter or restoring federal deposits. Jackson had slain the monster. Several months earlier, he kept another promise. In July 1835, he declared that the national debt had been paid off. Never before—or since—had the United States owed a cent to no one. Ironically, the face of the man who hated paper money would later grace first the five-, then the twenty-dollar bill.

Historian Robert Remini has called the bank veto "the most important veto ever issued by a President." Perhaps it was. Yet it is just part of a larger picture. Previous presidents had used the veto a grand total of nine times. In each case, they rejected a bill because they thought it violated the Constitution. Jackson vetoed twelve bills. He believed the president could kill any bill, for any reason, if he thought it might harm the nation. Since the president represented the *entire* nation, as Jackson saw it, he had a duty to shape the legislation that affected it, even though the official legislative branch was the Congress. So began the tradition of bold, dynamic presidential leadership. From Jackson's time onward, Congress would have to consider the president's wishes *before* passing laws. No wonder so many Americans loved the old soldier. Despite his faults, he appealed to their sense of justice by safeguarding their equality.[53]

VII

THE SUPREME LAW:
PRESERVING THE UNION

The preservation of the Union is the supreme law.
—ANDREW JACKSON, 1832

Throughout its history, the United States has only lived under two forms of national government. The first was a dismal failure lasting eight years. The second, perhaps humanity's finest achievement in self-government, has lasted to this day.

In 1781, the original thirteen states adopted the Articles of Confederation. These gave a national Congress authority over military and foreign affairs, but no power over the states or taxation. Since the country lacked a strong central government, each state did as it pleased. States fought over boundaries, charged out-of-staters for using their waterways, and taxed goods passing through their territory. The states squabbled so and differed so much that Americans wondered whether the states could survive *united,* and if the struggle for independence had been for nothing.

In 1787, delegates from every state except Rhode Island gathered at the Constitutional Convention in Philadelphia to work out a better system, the United States Constitution. Its preamble says, "We the people of the United States" devised the Constitution "in order to form a more perfect union" than existed under the Articles. By aiming to create a unified country, or union, the Constitution promised effective government to "establish the blessings of liberty to ourselves and our posterity." With the states' approval, the Constitution went into effect in 1789.

Yet it left certain questions unanswered. What is the Union, *really?* Once a state joined, must it stay in forever? Or did the Union consist of separate countries called states, free to secede—leave—if they wished?

Was a bill passed by Congress and signed into law by the president binding if it harmed a state's "vital" interests, as the state saw them? Or could a state nullify a federal law—declare it invalid and refuse to obey it—defying the will of the majority that had been expressed through their representatives in Congress?

Today, most Americans do not actively think about these questions, because we usually take the answers for granted. The Union is a reality; we accept it as natural, like sunrise and sunset. It was not like that in Andrew Jackson's day. Back then, quarrels over the nature of the Union carried the threat of civil war.

For Old Hickory, the threat first arose over what might seem an unlikely issue, the tariff, the instrument by which the federal government raised money for its own expenses and to protect American industry from foreign competition.

Yet tariffs did not benefit all sections of the Union equally. With the industrial revolution going full blast in the North, tariffs raised prices on manufactures sold elsewhere, particularly in the Cotton Kingdom. Short of cash, planters had to borrow from Yankee "moneymen" to pay for what they needed. That, in turn, bred resentment. Southerners saw Yankees as money-mad misers who would sell their souls for a dollar. "We have always been taught," said Davy Crockett, "to look upon the people of New England as a selfish, cunning set of fellows . . . that made money by their wits, and held on to it by nature; that called cheatery mother-wit . . . [and] raised up manufactures to keep down the South and West."[1]

In 1828, the Democrat-controlled Congress raised the tariff on various items. Although Southerners opposed it loudly, Jackson's advisers thought people in the South would vote for him anyhow. Better yet, by saying he favored a "judicious tariff," whatever *that* meant, he would also do well in the industrial states. Although their gamble paid off, Jackson's victory did not end the matter. Overseas demand for raw cotton had recently slowed, sending cotton prices tumbling. Lower profits and the higher cost of imports hit Southerners hard. Charleston's once bustling port lay deserted. Wagons rolled through deserted streets lined with empty warehouses and rotting wharves.

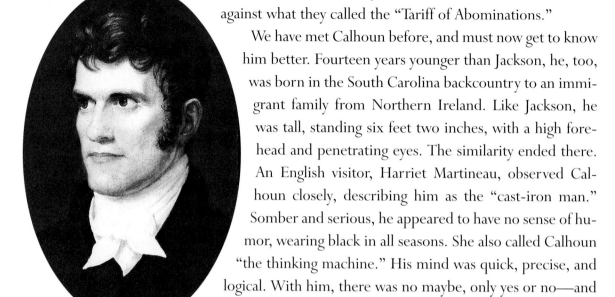

John C. Calhoun was a champion of states' rights. This picture is an etching based on a painting by Charles Bird King from the National Portrait Gallery.

Meanwhile, Vice President John C. Calhoun rallied Southerners against what they called the "Tariff of Abominations."

We have met Calhoun before, and must now get to know him better. Fourteen years younger than Jackson, he, too, was born in the South Carolina backcountry to an immigrant family from Northern Ireland. Like Jackson, he was tall, standing six feet two inches, with a high forehead and penetrating eyes. The similarity ended there. An English visitor, Harriet Martineau, observed Calhoun closely, describing him as the "cast-iron man." Somber and serious, he appeared to have no sense of humor, wearing black in all seasons. She also called Calhoun "the thinking machine." His mind was quick, precise, and logical. With him, there was no maybe, only yes or no—and he always knew which.[2]

The Tariff of Abominations set Calhoun's quick mind racing. Soon after the 1828 election, he wrote an essay, "South Carolina's Exposition and Protest," printed by the state legislature at public expense. The Constitution, he argued, was a compact—an agreement—among sovereign states. To be sovereign is to have absolute power, with responsibility to no higher authority. States did not surrender their sovereignty by joining the Union, said Calhoun. Should the majority of states gang up on the minority, passing a "harmful" law in Congress, the minority could defend itself. A state need not obey a "tyrannical majority." It could call a convention to nullify that law. If Congress refused to repeal it, the state could secede from the Union. In effect, nullification and secession, for Calhoun, meant a state could choose what federal laws it would or would not obey.

Could the United States survive such picking and choosing? That question led to a verbal showdown in the Senate. January 21, 1830, was not a normal business day on Capitol Hill. The House stood empty, its members gathered in the Senate chamber. The chamber was full; visitors jammed the two galleries, many sitting on the floor and steps, amid splashes of tobacco-tainted spit. About three hundred society women attended in all their finery, though "crowded to suffocation."[3]

When Vice President Calhoun took his seat as president of the Senate, the debate began. It would last two days, one speaker addressing the Senate each day.

Senator Robert Y. Hayne of South Carolina led off. Hayne could have lifted his speech from Calhoun's essay, so closely did he follow its defense of nullification. As he spoke, Calhoun glowed with pleasure. His eyes "shone approvingly," a senator recalled; occasionally a smile even crossed his tight-pressed lips. When Hayne finished, Southerners thought he had said the last word on the subject. Nobody, they imagined, could challenge the logic of nullification. Yet they had not reckoned on Daniel Webster. After Hayne stepped down, the Massachusetts senator snorted, "I will grind him as fine as a pinch of snuff."[4]

Born in 1782, Webster began life poor, but quickly left poverty behind. After teaching school for a short time, he became a lawyer, supposedly the highest paid in America. A devoted servant of Mr. Biddle's bank, he hungered after money "as an addict craves [his] drug," according to critics. Yet there was more to Webster than greed. No man was ever as great as he looked, some said. Nicknamed "Black Dan," he had a swarthy complexion, black bushy

Showdown in the Senate. On January 26, 1830, Daniel Webster refuted Robert Y. Hayne's idea of nullification. From G.P. Healy's painting in Faneuil Hall, Boston.

eyebrows, deep-set eyes, and a wide, almost fierce mouth. A spellbinder, he made the most of a rich voice that fairly hypnotized listeners. In debate, Webster went after the opponent with "lethal intent," as he called it, aiming to humiliate him while demolishing his argument.[5]

On January 26, 1830, Black Dan gave the speech of a lifetime. The Union was all-important to him— more important even than money. And he meant to do it justice. Beginning slowly, he spoke softly, as if embarrassed to confront Hayne. Yet he was only warming up, like an actor sensing his audience's mood.

Gradually, his voice rose and he struck his favorite pose, his left hand tucked under his coattails, his right hand sweeping the chamber.

Webster said the nullifiers were wrong. Wrong! The Constitution is the supreme law of the land. Why? Because the Union is *not* a compact of sovereign states, but the creation of the American people. "It is the people's Constitution, the people's government, made for the people, made by the people, and answerable to the people." What the Constitution made could only be changed constitutionally, that is, lawfully. Nullification was the opposite of law. It was anarchy, the absence of any rules or authority. It must lead to force—ultimately to that horror of horrors, civil war.[6]

Black Dan's eyes blazed, became "touched with fire," as an onlooker put it. Now the words tumbled from his lips. This was a magical moment for him. Afterward, he said everything he had ever seen, read, and heard floated before him as he gathered energy for the windup. Leaning forward, as if speaking to each member of the audience personally, he ended with words that struck like brilliant sparks. Nullifiers, he said, cried, "Liberty first and Union afterwards." What foolishness! In their "delusion and folly," they did not realize that you could not have one without the other. After a moment to let the idea sink in, he thundered, "Liberty *and* Union, now and forever, one and inseparable!"[7]

No cheers. No applause. The audience sat dumb, as "in a trance, all motion paralyzed." Flustered, Vice President Calhoun slammed down his gavel, crying, "Order! Order!" That snapped the tension. Gradually, the chamber emptied. Next morning, newspaper headlines blared LIBERTY *AND* UNION across the land. In New Salem, on the Illinois frontier, Abraham Lincoln, a few days shy of his twenty-first birthday, read them. He never forgot them; he would later call Webster's speech "the greatest specimen of American oratory."[8]

Did the president support Webster or Hayne? That was a mystery. Everyone knew Jackson favored states' rights, believed, like Thomas Jefferson, the federal government should interfere with the states as little as possible. While he said nothing about nullification publicly, those who thought he favored it were only fooling themselves. Old Hickory belonged to that fast-dying generation that had fought the Revolutionary War. They knew the sacrifices so many patriots had made for victory. They also knew that only "a more perfect union" could protect liberty and independence. So, when Jackson told a White House visitor, "I would die for the Union," he meant it.[9]

Nullifiers decided to trap the president into declaring himself. On April 13, 1830, they would stage a nullification rally disguised as the annual banquet celebrating Thomas Jefferson's birthday. Jackson received an invitation to attend, and speak, at the banquet in a Philadelphia hotel. Sensing what they wanted, the old soldier decided to turn the tables.

Jackson sat on the dais, between Calhoun and Van Buren. The meal over, one guest after another raised his wineglass and toasted states' rights, a code word for nullification. All eyes focused on Jackson, but he just sat there, his face rigid as a mask. Finally, his turn came to speak. The president rose and raised his glass, a signal that he expected everyone to join in his toast, standing. The vice president stood up, slowly. All the while Jackson stared into his eyes—hard. "Our Union. It must be preserved," Jackson said firmly. Although Calhoun's hand shook as he drank the toast, he met the challenge. "The Union," he replied, "next to our liberties most dear." In effect, the vice president had declared war on his chief.[10]

Soon afterward, Jackson broke with Calhoun over nullification and the Eaton affair. Calhoun resigned from the vice presidency in 1832 and returned home, allowing Van Buren to become Jackson's running mate in the upcom-

This bronze statue of Old Hickory stood in Lafayette Square, across Pennsylvania Avenue from the White House, in 1853. Jackson's rearing horse symbolizes that its rider had won battles. The statement on its base comes from his remarks during the annual banquet celebrating Thomas Jefferson's birthday.

ing election. Meanwhile, the South Carolina legislature elected Calhoun to Hayne's seat in the Senate. Having resigned to make room for the champion of nullification, Hayne won the election for governor.

As Americans went to the polls in 1832, the nullification movement gathered steam. Although Congress had lowered the tariff at Jackson's request, South Carolinians were in no mood for compromise. "Nullies"—fanatical nullifiers—demanded a confrontation. Led by Governor Hayne, they called a convention in Charleston. It passed a nullification ordinance, declaring the tariff "null and void." If the federal government tried to collect the tariff in South Carolina, the state would secede. Finally, if the federal government tried to keep it in the Union by force, South Carolina would resist with force.

The president stood firm. He had no choice. Should South Carolina get away with disobeying a federal law, he knew it would spell disaster for the Union. Jackson compared the situation to a bag of grain open at both ends. Pick it up anywhere, and the grain will spill out. "I must tie the bag and save the country," he declared. Jackson hammered home the importance of the nullification issue in a letter to his old friend General John Coffee. "Nullification means insurrection and war," he wrote with passion and conviction. "Can anyone of common sense believe the absurdity that a . . . state has the right to secede and destroy this union and the liberty of our country with it, or nullify the laws of the Union; then indeed is our constitution a rope of sand, under which I would not live. . . . The union must be preserved, and it will now be tested, by the support I get by the people. I will die for the union."[11]

Jackson answered South Carolina's challenge. On December 10, barely two weeks after winning his second term, he issued a "Proclamation to the People of South Carolina." Again, someone else—Secretary of State Edward Livingston—wrote the words, but the ideas were the chief's.

Twice in one paragraph Jackson quoted from the preamble to the Constitution. Its aim was "to form a more perfect Union," a nation of laws binding upon all. "The Constitution is . . . the bond of our Union, our defense in danger, the source of our prosperity and peace. . . . We are ONE PEOPLE. . . . To say that any state may at pleasure secede from the Union is to say that the United States is not a nation. . . . Disunion by armed force is TREASON." Overnight, the proclamation turned enemies into allies. John Quincy Adams, Henry Clay, and Daniel Webster differed with Jackson on most things. On the

Union, however, they stood together.[12]

The Nullies were furious. Jackson might issue proclamations till the crack of doom, but they shouted "we are unconquerable!" Defiant South Carolinians flew the Stars and Stripes upside down, a challenge to fight. To encourage other states to secede, if necessary, they struck medals with a menacing inscription: "John C. Calhoun, First President of the Southern Confederacy." Charleston became an armed camp, as the city fathers stockpiled weapons and munitions. Volunteers marched and drilled, cheered and gave their battle cry. It was a spine-tingling screech given on the run: *Yip-Yip-Yip-e-e-e-e-e-e-e! Yah-ah-ah-Yah-e-e-e-e-e-e-e!* A generation later, as the "Rebel yell," it would echo across Civil War battlefields.[13]

The mighty threesome: Andrew Jackson, Daniel Webster, and Henry Clay in an engraving by John Sartain.

Jackson replied with a carrot and a stick. The carrot was an even lower tariff, offered by Henry Clay, which the president supported. The stick was military force. Jackson ordered federal troops south. Warships were sent to Charleston and the defenses of Fort Sumter in the harbor strengthened.

However, Jackson's personality, his strength of character, outweighed any military steps. Jackson left no doubt he would live up to his nickname. He really was tough as old hickory. Nobody could bully him, because fighting back was a vital part of his upbringing. Nobody could force him to retreat when he thought himself right. Let the Nullies shed one drop of blood in defiance of the laws of the United States, he warned, and he would hang them all, including South Carolina's leading senator and governor. The new governor had his doubts, but Senator Benton set him straight. "I tell you, Hayne," said the Missourian, "when Jackson begins to talk about hanging, they can begin to look for the ropes."[14]

The Force Bill, signed by Jackson on March 2, 1833, gave him the power to enforce the proclamation by military action. At the same time, he signed yet another bill lowering the tariff. These actions persuaded Calhoun that Jackson meant business; perhaps he also imagined a scratchy noose tightening around his neck. Anyhow, he urged the Nullies to back down. On March 15,

1833, they repealed the nullification ordinance. It was Old Hickory's sixty-sixth birthday, but they did not intend it as a gift.

Each side claimed victory. South Carolina had made Congress reduce the hated tariff. Jackson had saved the Union forever, or so people thought. The old soldier knew better. Nullification and secession were still alive—very much so. He predicted that enemies of the Union, all who wanted a Southern confederacy, would reach into their bag of tricks again. That bag held another issue, one far more explosive than the tariff. Next time, he said, it "will be the Negro, or slavery question."[15]

To understand what polite Southerners called their Peculiar Institution, slavery, we must go back a bit. The enslavement of Africans had existed in the New World since Spain introduced it into her colonies in the 1520s. A century later, in 1619, a Dutch warship sold the first African captives in North America at Jamestown, Virginia. From then on, slavery flourished. Every colony had slaves, though the vast majority of slaves lived in the South. In 1700, the colonies had 21,000 unfree black people; there were over ten times that many, 242,000, in 1750. In 1790, the first federal census recorded 698,000 slaves. By 1810, the number had reached 1,191,000.[16]

In this announcement of a sale of slaves, the seller notes that his human "stock" already had smallpox, making them immune to future attacks of the disease and also guaranteeing that they would not spread it to anyone living on the plantation.

TO BE SOLD on board the Ship *Bance-Island*, on tuefday the 6th of *May* next, at *Afhley-Ferry*; a choice cargo of about 250 fine healthy

NEGROES,

juft arrived from the Windward & Rice Coaft. —The utmoft care has already been taken, and fhall be continued, to keep them free from the leaft danger of being infected with the SMALL-POX, no boat having been on board, and all other communication with people from *Charles-Town* prevented.

Auftin, Laurens, & Appleby.

N. B. Full one Half of the above Negroes have had the SMALL-POX in their own Country.

Slavery was justified not only on economic grounds, that slaves' labor produced wealth for their owners, but on racist grounds. According to the racist theory, blacks deserved to be enslaved because they were innately inferior to whites. Blacks were described as dim-witted creatures, little more than beasts in human form. In 1748, David Hume, the great Scottish philosopher, much admired by educated Americans in Jackson's youth, gave a classic statement of white superiority and black inferiority. Although Europeans had not yet studied African history and culture in any meaningful way, Hume felt confident enough to insist that blacks had never created anything of value.

. . . The negroes . . . [are] naturally inferior to the whites. There never was a civilized nation of any other complexion than white, nor even any individual eminent either in action or speculation. No ingenious manufactures amongst them, no arts, no sciences. On the other hand, the most rude and barbarous of the whites, such as the ancient GERMANS . . . have still something eminent about them, in their valor, form of government, or some other particular. . . . There are NEGRO slaves dispersed all over EUROPE, of which none ever discovered [anything useful], tho' low [white] people without education, will start up amongst us and distinguish themselves in every profession. In JAMAICA indeed they talk of one negro man of . . . learning; but 'tis likely he is admired for slender accomplishments, like a parrot who speaks a few words plainly.

Although discredited by modern science, racist ideas were influential on both sides of the Atlantic for centuries. They were held not only by ignorant bigots, but by educators, scientists, and presidents well into the twentieth century. Presidents Theodore Roosevelt and Woodrow Wilson firmly believed in the inferiority of black people.[17]

In America, all slaves were equal in their bondage. The law treated them as chattel, as property, with no say in their own lives. In 1828, the year Jackson won the presidency, a Kentucky court explained the situation with brutal clarity. "A slave by our code," it said, "is not treated as a person but as a *negotium,* a thing, as he stood in the civil code of the Roman Empire." Slaves, according to that court, were merely objects resembling persons. Like objects, they could be bought, sold, traded, given as gifts, left in wills, used to pay debts, rented out, and raffled off. One Southern lady, for example, entertained her guests by raffling "a likely young Virginia Negro Woman, fit for House Business, and her child."[18]

The Revolutionary War raised a serious chal-

Slaves might be sold, rented, given as gifts and, as this handbill says, offered as raffle prizes.

lenge to slavery. As Americans fought for their own freedom, they also began to question the morality of the Peculiar Institution. That questioning began with the Declaration of Independence. Although it does not mention the word "slavery," it declares that "all men are created equal." God has given humanity certain "unalienable rights"—rights nobody can take away. Among these are the right to "life, liberty, and the pursuit of happiness." It followed, therefore, that slavery should be abolished as a violation of human rights.

Abolitionist societies formed in the Northern states, where the economy depended far less on slavery than in the South. In 1777, as the Revolutionary War raged, Vermont abolished slavery, followed in 1781 by Pennsylvania. Massachusetts, Connecticut, New York, and Rhode Island did the same between 1783 and 1786. In 1787, during the Constitutional Convention, Congress issued the Northwest Ordinance, outlawing slavery in the territory north of the Ohio River. By this single act, it restricted slavery to the southern part of the country. Since slavery was less profitable than before the war because of soil exhaustion in many areas, some Southerners freed their slaves or allowed them to buy their freedom with earnings from off-plantation jobs.

Slavery put the Founding Fathers in a bind. Of our first six presidents, four were slaveholders; only the Adamses, John and John Quincy, owned no slaves. George Washington, with 317 slaves, had more human "property" than any other president, followed by Thomas Jefferson, with 267 slaves. All saw the contradiction between their belief in liberty and the reality of slavery. Jefferson, author of the Declaration of Independence, said, "I tremble for my country when I reflect that God is just; that His justice cannot sleep forever." None, however, had the courage to translate his commitment to the idea of "unalienable rights" into government policy.[19]

Part of the reason was personal: they felt they needed unfree labor to support their standard of living. Slaves—unfree people—grew their masters' crops, built their houses, dug their wells, drew their baths, emptied their chamber pots, washed their clothes, fanned them while they slept on hot nights, suckled their babies, and did countless other chores.

Most important, however, the Founders fully realized that the very existence of the United States rested on the enslavement of black people, however paradoxical and uncomfortable that might be. During the Constitutional Convention, some delegates wanted to weaken or even abolish slavery. Yet Georgia and South Carolina declared they needed *more* slaves to work newly opened farmlands. If anything, their delegates demanded that the Constitution strengthen slavery. It must not merely protect existing "property," they said, but allow the free importation of slaves. Just as important, even though slaves wouldn't be given the right to vote, they wanted slaves counted equally with whites in drawing the lines of election districts, increasing slaveholders' power in Congress. If they lost on any of these points, they threatened to leave Philadelphia, wrecking the convention. They even vowed to make an alliance with foreign powers, England and France, to protect slavery.

To save the Constitution and create the Union, the delegates to the convention made three compromises. Under the "three-fifths clause," three slaves counted as five free people in deciding the number of seats a state had in the House of Representatives, which was based on population. This was outrageous, because it added enormously to the oppressors' political power. The Constitution also forbade preventing the return of runaway slaves to their owners, even if they sought refuge in a free state. Lastly, Southerners gained the right to import enslaved Africans until the year 1808. For good measure, the Constitution dropped the word "slave" in favor of a say-nothing term: "Persons held to Service or Labor." The acceptance of slavery, then, was an essential compromise that allowed the United States to form its constitutional foundation. In effect, liberty for white Americans came at the price of bondage for African-Americans.

The importation of slaves, but not the buying and selling of slaves within the United States, ended just as Eli Whitney's cotton gin was remaking the South. Cotton growing became the royal road to riches. Yet raising production demanded more labor, in turn causing slave prices to soar. By 1830, the cost of an adult male field-worker had risen from about $500 to about $1,500. Smugglers made fortunes trading in "black ivory"—slaves smuggled into the country. The Lafitte brothers, Jackson's allies at the battle of New Orleans, made a specialty of hijacking Spanish slave ships bound for South America.

Larger families, rather than illegal imports, accounted for the largest increase in the slave population. Under the laws, slave "marriages" had no more

After the Sale: Slaves Going South from Richmond *is the title of this print of a painting by Eyre Crowe, dating from about 1855.*

legal standing than those of cows or oxen. Nevertheless, masters encouraged slaves to have large families. Normally, they expected a woman to be a mother by age fifteen. If not, they might choose another mate for her, whether she liked it or not. Pregnant women worked less and got more food. Fanny Kemble, the English wife of a Georgia plantation owner, despised slavery for what it did to women, black and white. Black women's lives, she wrote, "are for the most part those of mere animals, their increase is literally animal breeding, to which every encouragement is given, for it adds to the master's livestock and the value of his estate."[20]

White women had a different grievance. Slavery tempted husbands to be unfaithful. Since a female slave "belonged" to her master, as we have seen, she had no right to resist his advances. By law, there was no such thing as a master raping a slave. Thus, thousands of mulattoes were born each year. "Nobody pretends to deny that, throughout the South, a large proportion of the population is the offspring of white men and colored women," Fanny Kemble wrote. "Almost every Southern planter has a family more or less numerous of illegitimate colored children." The law declared that any child born to a slave, whoever its father, was still a slave. Not only did slaveholders sell black children, they often sold their own flesh and blood.[21]

Where did the seventh president stand on slavery? Having grown up with slavery in the Waxhaws, he understood both its economic and social importance. Nearly everyone who enjoyed influence and respect in the South was a slaveholder.

Jackson was a model go-ahead Southerner, rising in the world by means of the law, land, cotton, slaves, war, and politics. He became a slaveholder as a young man, when he had some spare cash, probably from gambling. Recall how, in 1788, the rookie lawyer arrived in Jonesborough with Nancy, a black woman about his own age. Although he had no land, owning her already showed that he had set his sights high. Later, in Nashville, his marriage to Rachel introduced him to a wealthy slaveholding family. During their early days at The Hermitage, he bought a cotton gin; it was the only one in the neighborhood. Besides cleaning the seeds from his own cotton crop, it cleaned other planters' cotton—for a fee.

Historians have pointed out that the master of The Hermitage was more active in the slave trade than most plantation owners. In justifying these activities, Jackson insisted that liberty, for white Americans, included the right to own, buy, and sell African-Americans. He began profiting from slavery early. As a young lawyer, before his marriage to Rachel, he took money for capturing runaway slaves; whether he did this himself or hired professional slave catchers is unclear. In 1790, for example, he received power of attorney—legal authorization—from a Nashville man to track down five slaves. As Jackson's human "property" increased, he used enslaved people in ways other than planting his cotton or serving in his house. One man, Ned, Jackson hired out as a cook, pocketing Ned's earnings. Like other slaveholders, Jackson paid debts with slaves and bet his slaves on horse races. Once he collected money owed him in slaves, then used them to buy a piano for The Hermitage. Jackson had 10 slaves in 1794, 15 in 1798, 44 in 1820, and 95 in 1828. During his two terms as president, he continued to buy slaves for The Hermitage. When he died in 1845, he had 110 slaves. In his will, he left them to Andrew Jr., except two boys he gave to his grandson, Andrew III. To Sarah, his daughter-in-law, he left "the Negro girl Gracy, which I bought for her . . . as her maid and seamstress," along with Gracy's children and "my house-servant Hannah and her two daughters."[22]

What was it like for enslaved people at The Hermitage? Visitors' accounts, all by whites, hardly mention them. From his letters, it seems that Jackson viewed blacks in two ways. A racist, he believed them naturally inferior to whites. When, for example, The Hermitage burned, he blamed the damage on "the cursed blacks," who were "all so stupid & confused" they could do nothing without orders from whites. Most Americans shared his attitude. Racism had no limitations of geography or social class. It formed a basic part of the American outlook in the 1800s, and for a long time afterward. George Washington and Thomas Jefferson also thought blacks inferior to whites.[23]

As on all plantations, Jackson's slaves lived in "the quarters." Everywhere, in the 1700s, these consisted of rows of log cabins with dirt floors, each housing one or two families. By the early 1800s, some planters began to house their slaves in brick cabins. Hermitage slaves, it seems, built homes of bricks they made of clay found on the property. Each had a single four-hundred-square-foot room, a wooden floor, a door, and a single window—not much space for a family.[24]

Archaeologists are adding to our knowledge of slave life at The Hermitage. In the 1990s, these scientists who study the physical remains of past human activities began digging where the slave cabins once stood. They found that Jackson's slaves had a variety of private possessions: tobacco pipes, sewing equipment, bone-handled knives and forks, china dolls, glass beads. Judging from food remains, slaves ate corn bread made of meal, surely provided by the master, and vegetables grown in their own small gardens. Besides the regular issue of salt pork, bones show that slaves ate geese, ducks, chickens, opossums, raccoons, groundhogs, turtles, fish, and shellfish. Hermitage slaves also had weapons: guns, lead, bullet molds. How they got these, or how many they had, is unknown. In any case, Jackson's slaves probably added to their rations by hunting.[25]

One fascinating discovery suggests that at least some Hermitage slaves could read. This is important. What you are doing this very instant, with this book in your hands, was a crime for enslaved Americans. Every Southern state forbade blacks to read and write, or for whites to teach them these skills. Learning to read, a friend told Fanny Kemble, "impairs their value as slaves, for it instantly destroys their contentedness." In other words, reading exposed slaves to "dangerous" ideas—ideas like unalienable human rights. Yet archaeologists have dug up fragments of writing slates and slate pencils at The Hermitage. How did the slaves get these? Who taught them their use? We have a hint, but no proof. A visitor noted that Sarah Jackson wanted to teach slave children to read as a way, she said, of "improving their condition." If so, the president's daughter-in-law had nullified Tennessee law. We do not know what he thought about it, or if he even knew about it.[26]

In Jackson's absence, his wife passed his orders to a hired white overseer. Those orders dealt with every detail of running a plantation, including the treatment of slaves. "I do not wish my hands labored too hard," Jackson wrote Rachel. "I wish them well fed & warmly cloothed [sic]. . . . I do not want them in any way oppressed." Hermitage slaves could expect "good" treatment in return for obedience and hard work. But Jackson ran a business, not a charity. Whatever increased profits was good. Whatever reduced them was bad. Like most slaveholders, he was no kinder than he needed to be.[27]

What little evidence we have suggests that his slaves resented their bondage. Take Alfred, Jackson's favorite. Alfred supervised other slaves, rode his master's horses in races, and cared for Andrew Jr. when he was a child. Born at The Hermitage, Alfred spent his entire life there; he is buried in the garden, across the gravel path from the graves of his master and mistress. His gravestone reads, "Faithful servant of Andrew Jackson."

Having special privileges, unlike those of any other Hermitage slave, did not satisfy Alfred. Roeliff Brinkerhoff, a private tutor to Jackson's grandchildren, reported:

> Alfred was a man of powerful physique, and had the brains and executive powers of a major-general. He was thoroughly reliable, and was fully and deservedly trusted with the management of plantation affairs. He had the easiest and most honorable position possible for a slave, but he was far from being content. He thirsted for freedom. I remember I [once] showed him how freedom had its burdens as well as slavery. . . .

Alfred did not seem disposed to argue the question with me . . . but he quietly looked up into my face and popped this question to me, "How would you like to be a slave?" It is needless to say I backed out as gracefully as I could, but I have never found an answer to the argument embodied in that question.[28]

While Jackson trusted Alfred, he was wary of his other slaves. At The Hermitage, as on every plantation, slaves did "silent sabotage," working as little as they could get away with. Understandably, slaves played sick, wasted time, broke tools, and ran away. "My Negroes shall be treated humanely," Jackson insisted. Yet business was business. To support his lifestyle and pay his debts, he had to get as much work out of each slave as possible. All masters, including "humane" ones, used force to do that.[29]

Whipping was the most common punishment for soldiers, sailors, and slaves. Jackson did not hesitate to order whippings. To him, "slackers" were thieves; they stole their labor from him, which ultimately translated into money taken from his pocket. Similarly, a slave working for someone else, without his permission, was also a thief. For example, Rachel's maid, Betty, washed clothes for white neighbors, earning a few pennies for her work. Furious, Jackson wrote the overseer, "the first cloaths [sic] she attempts to wash for another person but the family, without the express permission of her Mistress, that he is to take her to the public whipping post and give her fifty lashes." Soldiers usually received thirty-nine lashes for a first offense.[30]

Runaways were another matter. Not only did the master lose the slave's dollar value, he lost his or her productivity. By the owners' calculation, every time a slave escaped, it was as if ten acres of prime farmland, or a barn with five cows, went up in smoke. Like George Washington and Thomas Jefferson, Jackson advertised for runaways in Southern newspapers, offering generous rewards for their capture. One advertisement promised fifty dollars for a mulatto man "with a remarkable large foot." The reward would go to anyone who captured him. In addition, Jackson offered "ten dollars extra for every hundred lashes any person will give him, to the amount of three hundred."[31]

Recently, members of The Hermitage Slave Descendants' Organization claimed that family traditions and records show Jackson had a child by his slave known as House Hannah. Such behavior was common in the Old South, as we saw. For example, enemies scolded Thomas Jefferson for having children with a female slave, Sally Hemings, a charge apparently supported by DNA studies. In the election of 1828, opponents issued a pamphlet, "General Jackson's Negro Speculations, and His Traffic in Human Flesh." As stated in the title, they (correctly) accused the candidate of trading in slaves. Having a child by a slave would have been red meat to his foes, yet nobody mentioned it. This does not mean the descendants are wrong. It means we need more evidence, like DNA, before making a final decision.[32]

Andrew Jackson hoped to keep slavery from unraveling the Union by preventing it from becoming a subject of bitter political debate, as the framers of the Constitution had also hoped to do. In this, he had powerful allies. The major political parties, Democrats and Whigs, cooperated in the effort, surrounding the issue with a wall of silence. Apart from the Quakers, a religious body opposed to every form of violence, few Americans wanted to discuss slavery. The Peculiar Institution was all but impossible to mention in public, let alone do anything about.

The 1830s saw the growth of a vigorous movement to reform various aspects of American life. "Demon Rum" impoverished families, causing countless personal tragedies. In this engraving, a young woman empties a bottle of whiskey out the window.

Yet things were changing, largely because of a religious revival that swept the country in the 1820s and 1830s. That revival aimed at bringing Americans closer to God by reforming social evils. Reformers crusaded against gambling and tobacco chewing. To fight whiskey, temperance societies sprang up. Through speeches, newspapers, and pamphlets they urged Americans to give up "Satan's deadly brew." Countless groups formed to demand free public schools, women's rights, humane prisons, and decent treatment of the insane. Slavery, however, was the "sin of sins." More than all other sins combined, it kept America from becoming perfect in God's eyes, reformers said. America must live up to the ideals of the Declaration of Independence. All people,

whatever their color, have the right to "life, liberty, and the pursuit of happiness."

Ideals on their own can go only so far. To become reality, ideals need people of a special sort to inspire and energize others and create change. Abolitionism, the organized movement to abolish slavery, owed its drive to such a person. William Lloyd Garrison was not the first, but he was surely the loudest and most influential, abolitionist of his day. A white man born in 1805, the son of a drunken father who left his family in poverty, Garrison knew oppression firsthand. Deeply religious, on New Year's Day, 1831, he began printing a weekly newspaper, *The Liberator,* in Boston.

The Liberator became the mouthpiece for Northern abolitionists. These were mostly well-off, devout Protestants who felt called by God to rid the world of the sin of slavery. Garrison and his readers attacked slaveholders not as misguided people, but as evil people. The tragedy of slavery, abolitionists said, went beyond the wrongs done to blacks—terrible as these were. The Peculiar Institution degraded those who benefited from it most. It brutalized masters, teaching their children contempt for fellow humans. By extension, it dehumanized anyone who participated in an economy touched by slavery.

Slavery, Garrison insisted, had corrupted America from the outset. The Constitution? He despised its compromises with slavery, burning a copy of it in public. The Union? Garrison hated it. "This Union is a lie," he cried. "The American Union is a sham, an imposture, a covenant with death, an agreement with hell." Let the Union perish in a civil war, if this is what it took to end the sin of sins! Such fierce language had a purpose. Garrison meant it, he said, as a "jarring blast" to awaken the nation to evils it preferred to ignore. He believed that the first to denounce monstrous evils must speak loudly, even violently, grabbing people's attention by shocking their consciences. That he did—and a lot more.[33]

Fear of slave rebellions had gripped the South for decades. In 1801, while Jackson was serving as a Tennessee judge, Gabriel Prosser had planned an uprising in Richmond, Virginia. It failed, and the rebels went to the gallows. In 1822, as the Tennessee legislature nominated Jackson for the presidency, Denmark Vesey planned an uprising in Charleston, South Carolina, only to have the plan leaked to the authorities. The worst slave revolt was in Southampton County, Virginia, during Jackson's first term. In August 1831, Nat Turner, a slave preacher, led his followers on a rampage. All would pay with their lives, but not before killing fifty-seven whites, including women and children.

There is no proof that abolitionists had a hand in the Turner uprising. Nevertheless, Southerners had all the proof *they* needed. To them, the fact that it came just seven months after *The Liberator* appeared was no accident, but revealed a "plot" to massacre white people. What observers called a wave of "terrorism" rolled across the Cotton

The capture of Nat Turner, leader of an 1831 rebellion to free slaves in Virginia. Note Turner's defiant posture. After capture, he and his followers were executed.

Kingdom. Posters offering rewards for abolitionists' heads or ears appeared everywhere. The mail brought at least one abolitionist, Arthur Tappan of New York, a slave's ear. Georgia offered anyone five thousand dollars to kidnap Garrison for trial in a state court.[34]

Countless Northerners would have liked to see Garrison out of the way, too. Although slavery had not existed in the North for years, racism there was as bad as—some free blacks said worse than—in the South. Robert Purvis, a black leader in Philadelphia, declared: "Press, Church, Magistrates, Clergymen and Devils are against us. The measure of our suffering is full. . . . In the feelings, views and acts of this community—in regard to us—I am convinced of our utter and complete nothingness in public estimation."[35]

Segregation was the racist rule in the North. Every state had laws forbidding blacks from mingling with whites in public places: transportation facilities, hotels, theaters. Blacks had to live in black-only neighborhoods, usually the worst in town. If allowed to attend a white church, they must sit in "nigger pews." (Whites used "nigger," from the Spanish *negro*—black—as a degrading insult.) Often, if an employer hired a black, white workers went on strike. Black children attended black-only schools. Black bodies rested in blacks-only cemeteries. Blacks also served as what social scientists call "culture frighteners," demons to scare children into behaving properly. In Jackson's day, white parents warned their children to behave or "the old nigger will carry you off."[36]

Surprisingly, while branding slavery a sin, some abolitionists held racist ideas—proof of how deeply racism affected the American consciousness. Denouncing racism, a black teacher said, "even our professed friends have not yet rid themselves of it." For example, *The Liberator* called dark skin "a perpetual mark of disgrace." Some abolitionists used "nigger" to describe black people, noting their "niggerly odour." Free blacks praised abolitionists' work against slavery, but condemned their prejudices in everyday matters. Abolitionists usually hired blacks only for menial jobs in their businesses, if they hired them at all, and kept them from working for antislavery organizations.[37]

Many white Northerners hated abolitionists. Factory workers accused them of wanting to give their jobs to lower-paid blacks. Merchants resented abolitionists' attacks on their best customers, the slaveholders. Fear sparked violence. In 1835, Boston rioters tied a rope around Garrison's waist. Vowing to hang him, they dragged him through the streets until he was rescued by the mayor. These riots were not outbursts by drunken down-and-outs. Solid citizens organized, led, and formed the mobs. Nearly all observers used the same phrase to describe rioters: "gentlemen of property and standing."[38]

William Lloyd Garrison founded The Liberator, *the leading abolitionist newspaper of his day. An engraving by John Sartain after a painting by M.C. Torrey dated 1835.*

Jackson sympathized with these "gentlemen." The president denounced abolitionism as pure evil, condemning its "unchristian methods." In his annual message for 1835, during his second term of office, he demanded "severe penalties" against abolitionists. In the same message, he praised Northerners' "strong and impressive" reply to abolitionists' "unconstitutional and wicked activities." Rioters, naturally, read this as presidential support, however indirect, of mob violence.[39]

Jackson believed the Constitution had decided the slavery question forever. Under it, freedom for whites included the right to hold blacks in bondage. While abolitionists used moral arguments, the president gave them no credit for morality. How could they be moral when men like Garrison cursed the very thing—the Constitution with all its compromises—that had made the United States possible? Jackson saw the antislavery movement as "the wicked design of demagogues," a plot by rabble-rousers to harm the Southern states. Like South Carolina Nullifiers, abolitionists wished to destroy the Union, Jackson claimed, even at the price of civil war. Civil war would not only end the United States, but also democracy. Afterward, he predicted, the Northern states would form a separate nation and become a plutocracy, a country ruled by the rich. Without popular control, the rich—bankers, manufacturers, merchants, stockbrokers—could do as they pleased. Meanwhile, Southerners would have their own confederacy based on slavery.[40]

The president's warnings did not end the war of words. Abolitionists organized two major groups, the New England Anti-Slavery Society and the American Anti-Slavery Society. Each, in turn, formed hundreds of chapters in the free states, with over 200,000 members throughout the North.[41]

Besides holding election-campaign-style rallies, abolitionists used the products of the industrial revolution to spread their message. Steam-powered printing presses churned out their posters, handbills, pamphlets, and newspapers. Railroads, steamboats, and the postal system made it easy to circulate them. In 1835, abolitionists distributed over a million publications in all parts of the country, including the South. In June alone, they mailed 175,000 pamphlets from the New York City post office. These went to opinion makers like ministers, schoolteachers, and members of state legislatures. Volunteers handed them out at street corners and left them everywhere from saloons to courtrooms.

The "great postal campaign" of 1835 raised a vital question. What (if any) are the limits of free speech in a democracy? Although the First Amendment to the Constitution guarantees this right, it says nothing about any limits to this right. Are there any? Can citizens always say what they please, wherever they please, under all conditions?

Southerners had an easy answer: Nobody could read anything that might inspire another Nat Turner–style revolt. Anyone caught with abolitionist writings got a coat of boiling tar and feathers. In Charleston, citizens raided the post office, stole sacks of abolitionist pamphlets, and burned them. Soon the matter went "upstairs"—to Kitchen Cabinet member Amos Kendall. Recently appointed postmaster general, Kendall knew his boss called those who circulated abolitionist literature "monsters." So, without hesitating, he allowed postmasters to remove such writings from the southbound mails.

Jackson opposed Kendall's action as giving in to "the spirit of mob-rule." Instead, he proposed a law banning abolitionists from sending what he called "incendiary publications" through the mails. Senator Calhoun and his congressional allies objected; they wanted the states, not the federal government, to decide what to ban from the mails. In the end, Jackson had it both ways. By the Post Office Act of 1836, Congress forbade postmasters from interfering with mail deliveries. However, when Southern postmasters refused to deliver abolitionist mail, the authorities pretended not to notice.[42]

Abolitionists changed their tactics, focusing on a narrower issue, slavery in Washington, D.C. While dedicated to human dignity and freedom, the capital was also a center of the slave trade in the United States. Wherever visitors turned, they saw advertisements like this: "FOR SALE, A NEGRO WOMAN, with one or more children, to suit the purchaser." The windows of the Capitol overlooked the infamous Georgia Pen, a cluster of barred shacks crowded with slaves.[43]

Under the First Amendment, the American people have the right "to petition the government for the redress of grievances." A simple affair, each petition was short, with a title describing its contents and a request for Congress to remedy the grievance. By gathering petitions to end slavery in Washington, abolitionists exercised a fundamental civil right in a democracy.

The campaign began in December 1835. Since Congress lacked the time to discuss all petitions, it "tabled" most, that is, received them without comment and did not discuss them; yet the number grew steadily. In the year 1837–1838, an incredible 130,200 antislavery petitions flooded Congress. Desperate, the House passed a "gag rule," shutting off discussion of the petitions. As of January 1840, it refused even to receive petitions. The House would renew the gag five times, each time with heavy Southern support. Ordinary whites,

Slaves on the way to auction within sight of the U.S. Capitol. In Jackson's day, Washington, D.C., was a leading center of the slave trade.

who loved liberty but cared little for blacks, nevertheless saw this as a threat to free speech. For if Congress could gag debate on slavery, what would prevent it from doing the same with any subject it disliked? John Quincy Adams knew the answer.

Losing the presidency had left him angry and depressed, feeling his life as a public servant was at an end. That changed in 1830, when Plymouth, Massachusetts, elected him to the House of Representatives. Adams did not see this as a step down but as an honor, a chance to continue serving the country he loved. The hardest-working member of the House, he opposed the gag more fiercely than anyone. These were his finest hours.

While Adams made the free-speech cause his own, his reasons for doing so are not simple. He was a racist. As with countless others of his time, including Thomas Jefferson, he feared "amalgamation," interracial marriage. "Black and white blood cannot be intermingled in marriage without a gross outrage upon the laws of nature," he wrote, calling persons of mixed race "half-breed" and "mongrel." Personally, Adams despised slavery as "that curse of God." Yet, as president, he had kept quiet about it in public, because it was the law of the land; afterward, he ignored invitations to join abolitionist societies. Now he stubbornly refused to support calls for ending slavery in the capital. As did Jackson, he knew the Constitution protected slavery, it did not end it. Like it or not, that was that.[44]

The former president, then, saw the petitions as a free-speech issue, but not an antislavery issue. He supported the right to petition Congress to end slavery, but not actual legislative measures to end slavery. Adams presented batches of petitions to the House, often fifty at a time. To get it to focus on the free-speech issue alone, he often brought business to a standstill with sly legal arguments. Dubbed "Old Man Eloquent," Adams challenged foes to debate complicated issues like liberty and the nature of the human race. As he droned on, faces reddened in anger. Shouting matches erupted. Insults flew across the chamber. "Out of order! Out of order!" the speaker shouted, pounding his gavel for silence. Sour-faced as ever, Adams would not be silent. Even when his mail brought death threats, he attacked the gag rule. Southern congressmen threatened civil war—again.[45]

Adams's tactics did not endear him to the man in the White House. "De-

mented," "the most reckless and depraved man living," Old Hickory splut-
tered. As ever, he feared for the Union. To his mind, Adams was playing with
fire. For only a lunatic, or a traitor, would turn the gag rule into a possible
cause for the country's breakup. The Northern states, fearing Southern
"tyranny," finally forced their representatives to come down in favor of free
speech. In December 1844, eight years after Jackson left office, the House
ended the gag forever. It was a great personal victory for Old Man Eloquent.
In his 1956 book, *Profiles in Courage,* John F. Kennedy described the former
president's fight against the gag rule as "the brightest chapter of his history."[46]

Yet another problem, Texas, threatened the Union during Jackson's presidency. Although Mexico owned Texas, Mexico itself was owned by Spain and
lacked the power and the population to develop such a vast area. So, in 1821,
after winning its independence from Spain, Mexico offered Americans tracts
of free land in return for settling in Texas and becoming Mexican citizens. The
newcomers were called "Anglos," for Anglo-Saxons, after the Germanic pio-
neers who settled England in ancient times.

Land-hungry Anglos came by the thousands. Some were shady characters
with prices on their heads; others were adventurers who felt out of place in
American society. The majority, however, were plain folks from the Southern
states. Many brought slaves with them to work the cotton plantations they
would carve out of Texas's rich coastal lands. In doing so, these Anglos defied
Mexican law, which banned slavery.

Life was good in Texas. Within a few years, nearly thirty-five thousand settlers were living there. Now outnumbered ten to one, native Mexicans came
to feel like strangers in their own land. Worse, they distrusted the newcomers' intentions. Although settlers swore allegiance to Mexico, deep down they
were still Americans, and the Mexicans sensed that. Indeed, some spoke
openly about breaking away and bringing Texas into the Union. Seeing trouble ahead, President John Quincy Adams offered to buy Texas from Spain for
$1 million. Mexico refused. In 1829, Old Hickory offered $5 million, but
again Mexico turned him down.

Soon afterward, General Antonio López de Santa Anna seized power in
Mexico City. To control the Anglos living in Texas, he raised taxes and ended

immigration. Settlers began to speak angrily of "tyranny" and "taxation without representation." Early in 1836, they declared their independence and unfurled their Lone Star flag, a gold star on a blue background.

Santa Anna invaded Texas with a 6,000-man army. Moving swiftly, he trapped 187 Texans in the Alamo mission at San Antonio. The dictator warned that he would show no mercy unless the defenders surrendered immediately. They replied with gunshots. On March 6, after a thirteen-day siege, Mexican army bands blared the *deguello*—literally "the throat cutting," a signal that they would take no prisoners. The Alamo's defenders died fighting, a "victory" that cost Santa Anna 1,550 men—eight attackers for each defender. Two weeks later, at Goliad, he had 350 Texans shot, despite having promised them mercy if they surrendered.

Meanwhile, Sam Houston formed a small army to resist the Mexican advance. Sam was Jackson's friend, practically his second son, since his service in the Creek War. Jackson had supported him for governor of Tennessee and was saddened when his marriage fell apart. Brokenhearted, Sam had gone to live with the Cherokee. Chief Oolooteka took him into his family, naming him the Raven. Other Cherokee called him Big Drunk because of his fondness for whiskey. Hoping to pull his life together, he joined the settlers' rush to Texas. A natural leader, he quickly won a large following among the Anglos.

Jackson watched events closely. The Alamo and Goliad shocked him. At night, he read reports and traced the movements of the Texas army on a map with a bony finger. Finally, it halted at a spot along the San Jacinto River, near Galveston Bay. "Here's the place," said the old soldier. "If Sam Houston is worth one *bawbee* [halfpenny], he will make a stand here, and give them a fight."[47]

So he did. On April 21, 1836, Houston caught the Mexican army during its afternoon siesta. Shouting "Remember the Alamo!" the Texans tore into the camp with rifles and hunting knives. In just eighteen minutes, they slaughtered 630 Mexicans, losing nine of their own men. Soon after, Texas got its independence from Mexico and asked to join the Union.

Old Hickory had always favored annexation. Making Texas a state, he believed, would greatly strengthen the United States by preventing possible foreign enemies from gaining a foothold on the coast of the Gulf of Mexico.

Expanding slavery, it seems, did not influence his thinking. Yet others saw things differently.[48]

Benjamin Lundy, an ally of Garrison's, had opposed slavery all his adult life. A Quaker, Lundy issued a pamphlet titled "The War in Texas" in 1836. In it, he accused slaveholders of a plot to steal Texas from Mexico to expand "the SYSTEM OF SLAVERY [and] to open a vast and profitable SLAVE-MARKET therein." Overnight, annexation became an explosive political issue.[49]

While no historian has shown that a plot to expand slavery into Texas existed, Lundy still had a point. Today we grow cotton with chemical fertilizers, which did not exist back then. Cotton lands wore out quickly, making it necessary for slavery to expand into new areas or die. Thus, in the long run, the Cotton Kingdom's future lay in the vast spaces of the West, beyond the Mississippi River.

For planters, Texas was God's country. "Come to Texas," one wrote his nephew. "Get as many young Negro women as you can. . . . It is the best country for an increase that I have ever saw in my life. I have been hear six years and I have had fifteen Negro children born and the last years more young Negro women commenced breeding which added seven born last year and five of them is living and doing well." More slave children meant more workers, more cotton, and more profits—and a demand for more slaves.[50]

Printed while the struggle against the gag rule raged, a copy of Lundy's pamphlet found its way to John Quincy Adams. It instantly changed his thinking about Texas. Having offered to buy it as president, he now opposed taking it for nothing. Old Hickory fumed. "This wretched old man," this hypocrite, was deliberately spreading lies about annexation, he said. Yet Jackson did not want Texas to become another hot issue, like nullification and abolition. Rather than endanger the Union, he decided not to press for annexation. In 1837, on the day his second term ended, he recognized Texas not as a state, but as an independent country.[51]

A Virginia politician, John Randolph, once compared Jackson to a "sticking plaster," what we would call a Band-Aid. "While he sticks," said Randolph, "the Union will last." Still, nothing is forever. Jackson was a person of his own time, as we are of ours.[52]

As for preserving the Union, Old Hickory was both a success and a failure.

Although he stopped the Nullifiers, he failed to prevent slavery from becoming a subject of bitter political debate. He could only delay, not avert, the calamity that overtook the United States twenty-three years after he left the White House. The abolitionists steadily grew stronger. Battles raged in Congress over extending slavery to territories such as Kansas and Nebraska. Secession talk grew louder. Secessionists grew bolder.

In 1860, the storm broke. On November 6, the American people elected for president the candidate of a new, vigorous Republican Party. Abraham Lincoln hated slavery, but he also disliked abolitionists. He called them fanatics who would destroy the Union, "even burn the last copy of the Bible, rather than slavery should continue a single hour." Yet he strenuously opposed the expansion of slavery, a vital issue in the Cotton Kingdom. Lincoln's victory persuaded South Carolina, followed by ten other Southern states, to secede. As Jackson had feared, they formed a separate nation, the Confederate States of America. Its president was Jefferson Davis, an admirer of the Nullifier-in-chief and called "the Calhoun of Mississippi."[53]

With civil war looming, friends of the Union remembered the seventh president. "Oh, for an hour of Old Hickory Jackson!" they cried. Others went hoarse shouting, "God and Old Hickory are with us!" The old man—what a fellow! Union loyalists said. He would already have hung the traitors, as he once threatened to hang the Nullifiers.[54]

Lincoln looked to Jackson, too. Crowds gathered along the route of the train that bore him to Washington from his home in Springfield, Illinois. Cries of "Save the Union, Abe!" rose above the click-clacking of its iron wheels. He modeled his inaugural address on Jackson's proclamation to South Carolina. In it he warned that, should secession lead to bloodshed, the Confederacy would bear the guilt. Then Chief Justice Roger B. Taney administered the oath of office.[55]

As the Civil War exploded across the land, Old Hickory's kin sided with the Confederacy. His grandson, Andrew III, left The Hermitage with three cousins, the sons of Sarah Jackson's widowed sister, to join the Confederate army. Only Andrew III, an artillery officer in a Tennessee unit, returned. We can only imagine what his namesake would have thought of this combination of family tragedy and tragedy for the country he loved.

VIII

THE CHILDREN OF THE SOIL

We were at Washington at the time [1830] that the measure for chasing the last of several tribes of Indians from their forest homes was . . . finally decided upon by the President. If the American character may be judged by their conduct in this matter, they are most lamentably deficient in every feeling of honor and integrity. . . . It is impossible for any mind of common honesty not to be revolted by the contradictions of their principles and practice. . . . You will see them one hour lecturing . . . on the indefeasible rights of man, and the next driving from their homes the children of the soil, whom they have bound themselves to protect by the most solemn treaties.

— FRANCES TROLLOPE, *DOMESTIC MANNERS OF THE AMERICANS*, 1832

Cherokee people used to call him Jacksa Chula Harjo, "Jackson Old and Fierce." Experience had taught them to see him as a ruthless enemy, determined to take their lands. More than anyone, Old Hickory was responsible for uprooting the Cherokee from their homes in Georgia and Tennessee and packing them off to a strange land far to the west, beyond the Mississippi River. The Cherokee gave a name to the road he made them travel. In their language it was *Nuna-da-ut-sun'y*—"The Trail Where They Cried." Yet the Cherokee were not alone in making this journey. Thanks to the fierce old man, other tribes had equally sad trials, each following its own unique Trail of Tears.

The numbers tell the story. While Jackson forced Indians to give up millions of acres in the War of 1812 and its aftermath, tribes east of the Mississippi River were still not land-poor. Sometimes, as did the Cherokees and Creeks, tribes still held vast tracts 350 miles by 100 miles. From 1789, at the start of government under the Constitution, until 1838, the year after Jackson left the White House, some eighty-one thousand Native Americans had moved west. During the eight years of his presidency, he was responsible for removing more than half, some forty-six thousand people. About twenty thousand stayed behind, confined to small, impoverished reservations, islands in a sea of white settlements.[1]

For generations, American history teachers overlooked this tragedy. That was because most had not learned about it when *they* went to school; until recently, few textbooks mentioned the Trail of Tears. It is an embarrassing subject, involving bribery, trickery, lies, and force by the U.S. government. Only in the last decades of the twentieth century did Native American experiences begin to get the attention they deserve. If we have learned anything from the civil rights movement, it is that all Americans must have a place in the story of their country. For there can never be a genuine American history, and thus a true appreciation of who we are, without an understanding of how—and by what means—we arrived at where we are.

Jacksa Chula Harjo was not the first president to favor Indian removal. The reason others supported it lay at the heart of American life. An ever-increasing white population demanded ever more land for homes, farms, and natural resources. Land—that was the beginning of how many Americans sought to "rise." Roads, canals, steamboats, and finally railroads helped open the country's interior to settlement. No natural barrier was allowed to stop the settlers' westward march. Each year, thousands crossed rugged mountain ranges, forded swift rivers, and chopped their way through dense forests. In time, they would cross the Great Plains, which teemed with buffalo, and the Rocky Mountains, to reach the shore of the Pacific Ocean.

"New" lands for whites, however, were ancient homelands to Native Americans. Throughout history, and right into our own times, when different peoples have wanted the same land, each claimed to have the "better right" to it. Native Americans claimed they had always occupied their lands, that the lands were theirs from the beginning of the world. Their homelands were sacred ground, made holy by the graves of their ancestors. These were, to Indians, part of their flesh and blood. "We love our land; it is our mother," said a council of Creeks. Speaking of Florida, a Seminole chief told John Quincy Adams, "Here our navel strings were first cut and the blood from them sank into the earth, and made the country dear to us."[2]

Whites saw things differently. Success in life, whites believed, was a sign of God's favor, measured in terms of property, above all land. Land ownership, they claimed, depended upon "best use." God had told mankind, "Be fruitful, and multiply, and replenish the earth, and subdue it." People earn rights to the land, said James Madison, by "incorporating their labor . . . with the soil." Thus, claimed whites, the farmer's labor, expressed in houses, barns, wells, and fences, gave him the better right. Whites, a "superior race," could use the land to its fullest extent, they said. Indians could not. Compared to whites, Indians were primitive "children of nature" who did not know their own best interests. Whether they liked it or not, whites must guide them as strict parents, insisting Indians call the president the "white chief," the "Great Father," or "Great White Father."[3]

The "Great Father" and his children. Although Jackson claimed to know what was best for Native Americans, he brought them more misery than any person in the history of the United States.

How to get "red children" to give up their land peacefully? During the Revolutionary War, nearly every Eastern tribe sided with England. Afterward, the country still faced many large, warlike tribes, particularly along its frontiers. George Washington, that veteran Indian fighter, decided to make treaties with the tribes, a practice that continued into the 1820s. Treaties enabled the federal government to buy land with trade goods and annuities, yearly money payments. Moreover, the government promised to treat the tribes as sovereign "nations" in their remaining territory. Like any nation, tribes could run their affairs in their own way, without white interference. If white settlers intruded, the government pledged to remove the settlers, by force if necessary.[4]

Thomas Jefferson was the first president to call for Indian removal. He did not consider Native Americans inferior to whites. Like whites in past ages, Jefferson thought Indians could become "civilized." Left in their homelands, however, he believed that they had no chance of surviving white diseases, whiskey, and violence. Removal would save Indian culture and Indian lives, he argued. It would also open more land to settlers, a goal dear to the heart of all presidents. The Louisiana Purchase of 1803 seemed to offer a sanctuary. Government maps labeled part of it "Indian Territory." Later, the territory's Indian name would combine two Choctaw words: *houma* (red) and *okla* (people). Oklahoma is the "Red People's Land."[5]

Jefferson hoped to persuade Eastern tribes to move to the Indian Territory. He also decided that America must acquire Native American ancestral lands. If persuasion failed, he was prepared to use other means. For example, trading posts should encourage chiefs to get into debt; government agents could then make them sign away tribal lands to cancel their debts. Moreover, the third president saw treaties as temporary measures to calm Indians with "sincere assurances of friendship," thus gaining their land without having to fight them for it. In a letter to an aide, he warned against revealing the government's long-term objective. "For their interests and their tranquility it is best they should see only the present age of their history," he wrote. In plain English, do not let the Indians know what we have in store for them, what our long-range goals are. Sadly, so much of the U.S. government's policy toward Native Americans has been based on fraud; indeed, it is said that, of the more than three hundred treaties the government made with Native Americans since George Washington's time, it broke every one of them. Keep in mind, we are explaining history to learn how and why things happened, but not to justify them.[6]

Presidents Madison, Monroe, and John Quincy Adams favored Indian removal, too, but did not push for it in Congress. However, white Americans' demands for removal grew louder throughout the 1820s. Citing government treaties, Indian nations were able to claim immunity from state laws, a claim resented by state legislators. White voters became downright angry. Southern tribes were doing exactly what white leaders since Jefferson said they *should*

President Thomas Jefferson favored opening new lands to white settlers at the expense of the native peoples. A painting by Rembrandt Peale from the White House Collection.

do—adopt white ways. This was especially true of the "Five Civilized Tribes," as whites called the Cherokee, Creek, Choctaw, Chickasaw, and Seminole. These had private family farms, herds of cattle, and cotton plantations worked by slaves. Thus, "red children" were playing the whites' game, and winning! If things continued this way, Native Americans believed, they would keep their lands forever. Most Southerners, however, wanted them removed—and the sooner the better.

So did Andrew Jackson. The Choctaw used to say their troubles began in 1829, the year "the Devil became President of the United States." Jackson, they believed, was evil and meant to do them harm. Given their experiences, they had ample reason for thinking so. Yet, conflicting ideas about Indians drove the president. As a young man, he had hated them. As a soldier, he had fought both beside them and against them. In doing so, he came to know Indians better than most Americans of his day, admiring their courage and considering one, Lyncoya, a son. However, he wanted the best for *his* America—white America. In the past, Indians had sided with foreign enemies. As president, he vowed they would never be strong enough to do so again. Nor would he allow them to stand in the way of "progress."[7]

The nation, Jackson insisted, needed Congress to pass an Indian removal act to legalize what he thought was inevitable, law or no law. For the Indians' own good, he believed, they could not be left in place, living peacefully among whites. A growing white population demanded Indian lands; that was a fact. Experience also taught that whites would not stop trying to take these lands whatever the law might say. For Jackson, it was unthinkable that the government would use force against American citizens, and voters, to protect Indian lands. Moreover, like Jefferson, he believed that leaving Indians among whites subjected them to all the whites' evil influences. The best thing, Jackson believed, was for Indians to have their own country, far away from whites, where they might preserve their way of life.

Jackson explained his ideas about removal in his first message to Congress, December 8, 1829:

> The people of . . . every state . . . submit to you the interesting question, whether something cannot be done, consistently with the rights of the States, to preserve this much injured race? As a means of effecting

this end, I suggest . . . setting apart an ample district west of the Mississippi, and without the limits of any State or Territory, now formed, to be guaranteed to the Indian tribes, so long as they shall occupy it. . . . There they may be secured in the governments of their own choice, subject to no other control from the United States than such as may be necessary to preserve peace on the frontier, and between the several tribes. . . . This emigration should be voluntary. . . . But they should be distinctly informed that, if they remain within the limits of the States, they must be subject to their laws.[8]

In short, forget all previous treaties! State laws rank higher than treaties the federal government made with Indians. Tribes are not sovereign, not independent nations within states. Indians living in a state must abide by its laws. If they object, they must move away and live under a form of government they choose. Nobody can force them to go, but if they refuse, Washington supports the states' right to bring them under its laws, if necessary by force.

This was not merely talk. Unlike past presidents, Jackson used all his influence to get action. Thus, by February 1830, congressional leaders had fashioned an Indian Removal Bill similar to his message. The bill raised several questions. Could the government ignore solemn treaties? Was removal just? Might one people order another people to live in a certain place in a certain way? Reformers answered *no* to each question. Calling themselves "Friends of the Indian," they mounted protests throughout the Northern states. Anticipating the abolitionists' petitions to end slavery in Washington, D.C., they sent Congress hundreds of petitions against the proposed law.

Both houses debated the bill. The high point, however, came in the Senate, where Theodore Freilinghuysen of New Jersey led the foes of removal. A devout man, known as the "Christian statesman," he spoke for three days. Who, the senator asked, would be so cruel as to send helpless Indians to the wastelands of the West? Surely no decent person, especially since long possession and treaties gave Indians the better right to the land. More important, he denounced the bill as a violation of human rights.

In the judgment of natural and unchangeable truth and justice, I ask, who is the injured, and who is the aggressor? . . . Do the obligations of justice change with the color of the skin? Is it one of the prerogatives of the white man, that he may disregard the dictates of moral principles, when an Indian shall be concerned? . . . Our fathers . . . successfully and triumphantly contended for the very rights and privileges that our neighbors now implore us to protect and preserve to them. . . . *We, whom God has exalted to the very summit of prosperity, whose brief career forms the brightest page in history, [are] about to turn traitors to our principles and . . . become the oppressors of the feeble. . . . The question has ceased to be: What are our duties? An enquiry much more embarrassing is forced upon us: How shall we, most plausibly, break our faith?*[9]

Tennessee frontiersman and politician Davy Crockett denounced Old Hickory, his former commander, for persecuting the Southern tribes. He would later die in the Alamo, fighting for Texas independence.

Freilinghuysen's speech had a strong impact. William Lloyd Garrison praised the senator's courage. Thomas McKenney, the very able superintendent of the Bureau of Indian Affairs created in 1824 to oversee relations between the government and the tribes, called the removal bill "a mockery." Jackson fired him. Congressman Davy Crockett of Tennessee denounced his former commander for betraying the trust Indians had placed in the United States when they signed treaties with it. Crockett declared that, even if voting against the bill cost him his political career, he would do so gladly. He did, and Old Hickory never forgave him. Defeated in the next election, he went to Texas—and died in the Alamo. The bill passed both houses of Congress on May 24, 1830. Four days later, the president signed it into law.[10]

The Indian Removal Act removed no Indians. It merely allowed the federal government to send them to Oklahoma if they agreed to go, and to pay their moving expenses. But the tribes wanted to stay where they were. That should have ended the matter, but Jacksa Chula Harjo decided otherwise. The Indians' wishes were not something to be considered or discussed. Whatever the Indians wanted meant nothing to Jackson, if it was not what he wanted, too. "The President views the Indians as children of the Government," an aide explained. "He sees what is best for them." One of Jackson's greatest strengths, his willpower, would now lead to tragedy.[11]

To get their tribes' consent for removal, the president gave them the full treatment; we may call it the "Jackson squeeze." He put the squeeze on each tribe by sending special agents with a message from the Great Father. The message reminded them that they were not sovereign; they must obey state law or leave. If not, in Jackson's menacing words, "you must disappear and be forgotten."[12]

To keep up the pressure, he encouraged the states—as if they needed encouragement—to pass laws assailing every aspect of Indian life. Legislatures abolished tribal courts on tribal lands, replacing them with state courts to enforce state laws. Anyone caught trying to enforce tribal law paid a stiff fine for the first offense and went to jail for the second. Although Indians could not vote, they had to pay state taxes and serve in the state militia, even fight against other Indians if called upon. When white intruders seized Indian property, the army stood by, doing nothing. When Indians begged for protection, as promised in treaties, Jackson claimed he had no right to interfere with state laws. This was nonsense. Southerners well knew Old Hickory would hang anyone who dared to enforce state nullification laws. Yet the president was nullifying national laws—treaties.

"Confidential agents," both whites and mixed bloods, worked secretly. On the president's orders, they bribed some chiefs to persuade their people to sign removal agreements. Agents allowed other chiefs to stay behind, on large private reservations, if they got fellow tribesmen to leave.

Jackson's squeeze worked. Slowly, the tribes yielded, tricked into leaving their lands or forced out when government agents allowed whites to loot farms or drive their owners away at gunpoint. Disarmed long ago, they had few guns to oppose the looters even had they wished to try. Faced with overwhelming force if it opposed the "White Father's"—Jackson's—wishes, each tribe took its separate path westward, its own Trail of Tears. In September 1830, the Choctaw set out from Mississippi. Hired to provide them with food, white contractors took the government's money but never delivered all they promised. Hunger, disease, and exhaustion killed hundreds of Choctaws. "Death is hourly among us," an army major wrote. "The road is filled with the sick. Fortunately they are a people that will walk to the last, or I know not how we could get on."[13]

The last Creeks, once considered by whites the scourge of the Southern frontier, left Alabama early in 1836. To speed their removal, white land speculators started a rumor that the Creeks were preparing for war. When some hotheads urged resistance, they played into the speculators' hands. In the panic that followed, federal troops were rushed to Alabama. To crush any hope of resistance, 1,600 Creek men were handcuffed and chained together. While their families rode in army wagons, the men were driven westward on foot. One, Neamathla, though eighty-four years old, was handcuffed and driven along with the rest. That was too much for the *Montgomery Advertiser*. This newspaper favored removal, but demanded that it be done humanely— as if there has ever been *anything* humane about a mass expulsion. "To see a remnant of the once-mighty people fettered and chained together forced to depart from the land of their fathers into a country unknown to them is . . . sufficient to move the stoutest heart," the editor wrote. Yet most Alabamians, apparently, cared little about the miseries inflicted upon an "inferior" race.[14]

The Indian Removal Act applied to all Indians east of the Mississippi, not just the Five Civilized Tribes. Native Americans from the vast country south of the Great Lakes went to Oklahoma, too. The Chippewa, Ottawa, and Potawatomi left Michigan and Wisconsin. The Miami and Kickapoo moved from Indiana. From Ohio came the Wyandot, Delaware, and Shawnee, Tecumseh's people—to mention but a few.

In resisting removal, the Sauk and Fox of Illinois paid dearly. What whites called the Black Hawk War was really a senseless slaughter of people who had been driven to despair. Chief Black Hawk claimed he had no idea, when he "touched the goose quill to the treaty" and crossed the Mississippi to hunt, that he had given away his country. When the tribe tried to reclaim its lands in the spring of 1832, panic swept the state.

Army troops rushed to the scene, backed by hastily formed militia companies, one led by Abraham Lincoln. His company saw no action; the only casualties Lincoln reported were five farmers with bloody circles on top of their heads, where their scalps had been. Under mounting pressure, Black Hawk fled with his people into southern Wisconsin, only to fall into a trap on the bank of the Bad Axe River. Now without hope, they begged to surrender. The troops, however, were out for blood. As the steamboat *Warrior* hammered them with its cannon, the infantry charged. At least five hundred Indians lost their lives. Afterward, whites scalped the dead, raped Indian women, and shot babies. "Kill the nits and you'll have no lice," a militiaman shouted.[15]

Taken prisoner, Black Hawk faced his captors. For eloquence, his words to the Americans rank with the Declaration of Independence and Daniel Webster's defense of the Union. Although defeated, the chief had not lost his dignity.

An Indian who is as bad as a white man could not live in our nation; he would be put to death and eaten by the wolves. The white men . . . carry false looks and deal in false actions; they smile in the face of the Indian to cheat him, they shake his hand to gain his confidence, to make him drunk, to deceive him. . . . Black Hawk is a true Indian, and disdains to cry like a woman. He feels for his wife, his children and his friends. But he does not care for himself. He cares for his nation, and the Indians. . . . Black Hawk has done nothing of which an Indian need feel ashamed. He has fought the battles of his country against the white man, who came year after year to cheat his people and take away their lands. You know the cause of our making war. It is known to all white men. They ought to be ashamed of it. The white men despise the Indians and drive them from their homes. But the Indians are not deceitful. . . . Black Hawk is satisfied. He will go to the world of the spirits contented. He has done his duty.

Later, Black Hawk met the president in Baltimore. Jackson scolded him for fighting, warning him never to raise the hatchet again—or else. Jacksa Chula Harjo did not mention the atrocities committed by whites.[16]

Black Hawk's people were not alone in fighting removal. In May 1832, fifteen Seminole chiefs signed a removal agreement and a paper federal agents did not translate for them. The agents said the paper was just a formality; they should pay no attention to it. That was a lie. The paper was a report praising the new land as beautiful and fertile. When Seminole scouts went to see for themselves, they found the part of Oklahoma assigned to them barren and dusty, a far cry from their rich, moist, semitropical country. It was too late to change their minds, agents said. Their chiefs had signed, and that was that. Meanwhile, land-hungry whites swarmed into Florida. Guns went off on both sides.

A young chief named Osceola, the son of a Scottish trader and an Indian mother, led the Seminole. When Osceola spoke against removal, the government agent, General Wiley Thompson, invited him to talk things over at headquarters. Instead of talking, however, Thompson arrested Osceola; the chief's wife, the daughter of a runaway slave and an Indian, Thompson sold into slavery. Many more slaves had fled to Florida since the expansion of the Cotton Kingdom into neighboring states. The U.S. government, to its shame, helped slave catchers recover their "property"—that is, anyone they decided to call a runaway. Osceola gained his release with a promise of good behavior. Soon afterward, in December 1835, he personally killed Thompson, beheading his body. Osceola's warriors riddled the general's 110-man escort with bullets and arrows. So began the Second Seminole War.

One of the finest artists of his day, George Catlin painted this portrait of the Seminole leader Osceola from life. Osceola led his people's resistance to the land grab of the United States government in the 1830s.

President Jackson sent more troops to Florida. Outnumbered, bands of Seminole retreated to the Everglades, endless marshes bristling with razor grass interlaced by narrow, winding streams. Osceola refused to fight large-scale battles, like the British at New Orleans. Using the Everglades as a base, he waged guerrilla warfare, striking where least expected. Moving cautiously, under cover of darkness, his war parties ambushed army patrols and raided settlements as far away as Georgia. Most war parties consisted of Seminoles and former slaves, who knew what to expect if captured by Americans. If they met strong resistance, or if soldiers gave chase, they fled to their villages deep in the unmapped marshes.

The Second Seminole War dragged on after Jackson left office in 1836 at the end of his second term, then for another five years under President Martin Van Buren. Generals came and went, none able to win it. Frustrated, officers violated the laws of warfare—laws they had sworn to uphold. According to these, safe-conduct passes and truce flags are sacred. Such laws, apparently, did not apply to Native American "savages."

In October 1837, Osceola accepted General Thomas S. Jesup's offer of peace talks, along with a safe-conduct pass. Upon his arrival at the American camp, the general arrested him. Held in a dungeon in a military prison, a dark and unhealthy place, Osceola died two months later. An army surgeon, Dr. Frederick Weedon, beheaded the body and boiled the flesh off the skull. Whenever his little sons misbehaved, the doctor hung the chief's skull on their bedpost to scare the badness out of them. Grisly and shameful though the doctor's action was, it is a good example of how racism can warp a person's, or a society's, moral sense. Weedon, remember, was a doctor, one pledged to help *all* human beings in distress, perhaps the highest form of respect people can show toward one another. By dehumanizing the "other," however, he had turned a fellow human being into a specimen for study, like a rock, or into an instrument of terror.[17]

Shortly before leaving office, Jackson ordered his generals to change their tactics. They had to find where the "Indian women were collected," seize them, destroy their villages, and burn their crops, much in the way George Washington had fought the Iroquois in the American Revolution. The Seminoles' strong family bonds would put the warriors on the defensive, allowing the army to end the war with "one blow," Jackson thought. Under Van Buren, officers gave black captives offers they dared not refuse: guide us in the Everglades or die. More, a thousand Creek, Shawnee,

A black Seminole fighter. Some escaped slaves from Georgia and Alabama fled to Florida, intermarrying with the Seminole and setting up communities of their own.

Delaware, Kickapoo, Choctaw, and Sauk and Fox trackers arrived from Oklahoma to join the hunt. They came for money and promises of better treatment for their families. From Cuba, the army imported vicious dogs trained to track runaway slaves.[18]

Nevertheless, the army wallowed in a quagmire, a swamp of a war with no end in sight. As in a later quagmire, Vietnam, soldiers hated the place. Even the strongest wilted in Florida's heat and humidity. Clothing and shoes became moldy, quickly falling apart. Mosquito bites and skin diseases tortured the troops. Alligators, rattlesnakes, and yellow fever killed them. One fellow put it like this: "If I were given the choice of emigrating to Florida or Hell, Sir, why then, Sir, I should choose Hell." The war continued.[19]

Yet it could not go on forever. Gradually, the Seminole lost hope. Battered and exhausted, always on the run, always hungry, they gave up the fight in 1842. Some three thousand men, women, and children began their Trail of Tears aboard ships bound for New Orleans. From there, they walked to the dusty lands of Oklahoma.

To remove the Seminole, the United States spent $20 million and used over 30,000 troops, including nearly the entire army and half the Marine Corps. Of these, some 1,500 died in action, of disease, or from animal attacks. Put another way, it cost about $6,500 to remove each Seminole. It also cost the life of one soldier for each two Seminoles removed. Fewer than a thousand Seminoles stayed behind, concealed in the Everglades. These never signed an agreement with the United States, considering themselves members of the free Seminole Nation. As citizens of a "foreign" country, many young Seminole men refused to serve in the military during the Second World War.[20]

The Cherokee of Georgia, once dreaded fighters, resisted the removal non-violently. Among Native Americans, none showed more willingness, or had more success, in adopting white ways than they. For years, missionaries had taught them the Christian religion, the English language, and white farming methods. However, what really set the Cherokee apart from other tribes was their faith in white-style education. Cherokee people noticed that education, apparently, gave whites marvelous powers. The key to those powers, it seemed, lay in the written word. Writing and reading allowed whites to transmit ideas over vast distances, share knowledge quickly, and keep detailed records forever. No Indians could do that—yet.

A Native American genius accomplished one of history's most amazing leaps forward as far as written language is concerned. His name was Sequoyah, or "pig's foot," which he may have been given on account of a birth defect. Sequoyah was a mixed-race Cherokee whom a white farmer taught to write his name with a quill pen. That experience convinced him that, to survive, his people must become literate. Sequoyah began working on his "Talking Leaves," a method of writing down the Cherokee language, perhaps the most complicated of all Indian languages. Neighbors, however, thought him a witch and burned his house.

A true genius, Sequoyah devised a series of symbols to allow the Cherokee to become the first Native American people to read and write their own language.

Success came in 1821, after twelve years of work. Sequoyah devised a phonetic system, that is, one in which a set of written symbols represents the sounds of speech in a given language. The Talking Leaves used eighty-five symbols—regular English letters, English letters reversed, shapes of Sequoyah's own design. In effect, Sequoyah had devised a Cherokee alphabet that would accommodate the whole Cherokee language.

His symbols worked beautifully. Sequoyah's six-year-old daughter, Ayoka, learned to read and write her native language in two weeks—a lot faster than today's students learn to do the same in English. The Cherokee genius had created a peaceful revolution. Within three years, nearly his entire nation could read and write its own language. Cherokee of all ages read their tribal newspaper, the *Cherokee Phoenix,* wrote letters, and sent them to one another through the U.S. mail. Best of all, Sequoyah's system exploded the myth of Indian inferiority. Native Americans were not children, but as intelligent as any white person.[21]

Literacy sped up changes that had already been under way for a generation. Protected by treaties with the federal government, the Cherokee had created a police force, judges, and courts. Tribal councils outlawed gambling and

A page from the Cherokee Phoenix for July 9, 1829, the first newspaper published in a Native American language.

whiskey. In 1827, the nation adopted a constitution modeled on that of the United States, with an elected legislature or General Council, a president or Principal Chief, and a Supreme Court. All males over eighteen could vote, except "those of African descent." Further, the constitution declared the Cherokee Nation "sovereign and independent," nullifying Georgia law in its territory.[22]

The Cherokee lived better than many whites. Prosperous families owned two-story brick houses, model farms, and thriving cotton plantations. In 1826, the year before adopting their constitution, the Cherokee made a census of their wealth. They had 22,000 cattle, 7,600 horses, 46,000 pigs, 2,500 sheep, 2,488 spinning wheels, 172 wagons, 2,942 plows, 8 sawmills, 63 blacksmith shops, 18 schools, 8 cotton gins, and 1,277 enslaved black people. The Cherokee adopted whites' racist beliefs, declaring interracial marriage illegal. Like fellow Georgians, they despised abolitionists. During the Civil War, they would support the Confederacy against the Union.[23]

Yet each advance also increased the Cherokee's danger. Poor whites, called "white trash" even by slaves, envied their prosperity. Ambitious whites thought them too successful. If other Indians were to follow their example, before long each state would contain several strong, independent Indian nations. And what then?

Georgia decided to crack down on the Cherokee living within its borders. In 1827, the state legislature asked Adams's government to remove the Cherokee immediately. Next year, the discovery of gold on Cherokee lands brought louder calls for removal. As a first step, in 1829 the Georgia legislature declared the Cherokee government illegal and its laws without effect. Jacksa Chula Harjo's arrival in the White House in 1829, followed by the Indian Removal Act, sealed their fate.

What should or could the Cherokee do? To move and lose their homeland was unthinkable for them. Fighting like Black Hawk and Osceola's people was impossible, too; the new way of life had made most forget the old warrior ways. So the Cherokee did a very American thing—they hired a team of top-notch lawyers. The lawyers brought their case before the U.S. Supreme Court. In 1832, it ruled in the Indians' favor. Writing for the majority in *Worcester v. Georgia,* Chief Justice Marshall called treaties, including Indian treaties, "the supreme law of the land." It followed, therefore, that Georgia's actions "are repugnant to the Constitution, laws, and treaties of the United States." Since Georgia had no right to impose its laws on the Cherokee, the court ordered the legislature to respect their treaty rights.[24]

This decision was everything the Cherokee had hoped for, but it accomplished little. Georgia had not defended itself before the court, had not even sent an observer to the hearings. Georgia simply ignored the order, refusing to accept the court's right to rule on a purely "state" matter. In this, Georgia had many supporters in Washington. For his part, Old Hickory already hated John Marshall for doing something no Supreme Court justice had ever done before. Justices are supposed to be above politics, but Marshall had openly supported John Quincy Adams in the 1828 presidential race. Now, since the court had not said Jackson must enforce its order against Georgia, the president did nothing.[25]

John Marshall, chief justice of the U.S. Supreme Court, regarded treaties made with Native Americans "the supreme law of the land." Portrait by Chester Harding from the Boston Athenaeum.

Jackson's refusal to act signaled that the state could do as it pleased with the Cherokee. Within weeks of the court's decision, Georgia shut down the *Cherokee Phoenix,* closed Cherokee schools, and seized hundreds of Cherokee farms. These it offered in a lottery open only to whites, who gleefully sang the hit song of the day:

> All I want in this creation
> Is a pretty little girl and a big plantation
> Way down yonder in the Cherokee nation.[26]

Land grabbers swarmed like locusts. "We are not safe in our homes," John Ridge, a Cherokee leader, wrote Jackson. "Our people are assailed day and night by the rabble. . . .

This barbarous treatment is not confined to the men, but the women are stripped also, and whipped without law or mercy. Send regular troops to protect us from these lawless assaults." Women stripped and whipped! Jackson, who boasted that he never made war on women, would have been outraged had *white* women been so abused. Yet these were Cherokee women. Old Hickory did not act. The Cherokee, he insisted, must obey state law or leave.[27]

Some decided they had had enough. Led by John Ridge, they urged the nation to make the best deal possible and go to Oklahoma. "Friends of the Indian," including Senator Freilinghuysen, agreed; the Cherokee must give in or face worse hardships. Most Cherokee, however, sided with Principal Chief John Ross. The son of a Scottish father and a mixed-blood mother, Ross had fought beside Jackson at the Battle of Horseshoe Bend. Wealthy in respect and slaves—he held twenty black people in bondage—Ross urged peaceful resistance. Remember, federal law is on our side, he said. The U.S. Supreme Court says so. Under the Indian Removal Act, nobody can make us move without our consent.[28]

Chief John Ross opposed U.S. government plans to move the Cherokee from their lands in Georgia to Indian Territory, the future state of Oklahoma.

Jacksa Chula Harjo would do whatever it took to get their consent. In December 1835, he ordered the Cherokee to a conference at New Echota, the tribal capital in northwestern Georgia. Of the Cherokee Nation's 15,560 people, about 500 came to the conference. Neither John Ross, nor any other official, appeared. Nevertheless, the president's agents browbeat and bribed a tiny group of unelected Cherokee into signing a removal agreement. Soon afterward, more than 14,000 Cherokee signed a petition calling the agreement a fraud. Jackson ignored them, claiming it expressed the will of the Cherokee people. John Quincy Adams knew better. Old Man Eloquent denounced the agreement in the House, saying, "It brings with it eternal disgrace upon this country."[29]

Since most Cherokee refused to leave Georgia, federal authorities set May 1838 as the deadline for their "voluntary" departure. Although Jackson had retired to The Hermitage by then, Van Buren carried out his policies to the letter. Thus, both share the blame for the unfolding tragedy.

Van Buren wanted action. "Get the Indians out of Georgia, sir!" he told army chief Winfield Scott, a veteran of the War of 1812. The general devised a three-part plan. First, he built stockades, log-walled enclosures to hold the Cherokee. Second, he organized units to round them up and take them to the stockades. Finally, his plan called for the prisoners to walk to the Mississippi, cross it by steamboat, and walk the rest of the way to Oklahoma—a distance of eight hundred miles in all. Scott urged the Cherokee to avoid violence. "I am an old warrior, and have been present at many a scene of slaughter," he said, "but spare me . . . the horror of witnessing the destruction of the Cherokees." Scott ordered his men to be firm but kind.[30]

General Winfield Scott, a veteran of the War of 1812, carried out President Martin Van Buren's order to expel the Cherokee from their lands in Georgia.

On May 23, cavalry patrols quietly blocked every road to prevent escape. Meanwhile, as Cherokee prepared for the day's work, foot soldiers surprised them at home and in their fields. Regular army men for the most part obeyed Scott's orders. The poorly disciplined militia did not. A Georgian who later served as a colonel in the Confederate army said of the roundup: "I fought through the Civil War and have seen men shot to pieces by the thousands, but the Cherokee removal was the cruelest work I ever knew." The Civil War pitted soldiers against soldiers, not against unresisting civilians.[31]

The Reverend Evan Jones described the roundup in detail:

Multitudes were allowed no time to take anything with them except the clothes they had on. . . . Females who have been [used] to comforts and comparative affluence are driven on foot before the bayonets of brutal men. . . . The poor captive, in a state of distressing agitation, his weeping wife almost frantic with terror, surrounded by a group of crying, terrified children . . . is in a poor condition to make a good disposition of his property, and in most cases is stripped of the whole in one blow. Many of the Cherokees who a few days ago were in comfortable circumstances are now victims of abject poverty. . . . It is the work of war in time of peace.

Hunger and disease stalked the stockades, taking their daily toll of victims. They had already lost everything they had worked for; now despair made others lose the will to live. "They are dying like flies," white observers reported.[32]

The westward walk began in June. This proved a false start, because record heat and drought made it necessary to postpone the journey until fall. Early in October, thirteen large groups of Cherokee took their first steps along *Nunada-ut-sun'y*. It was literally the Trail Where They Cried. A survivor recalled: "People feel bad when they leave old nation. Women cry and make sad wails. Children cry and many men cry, and all look sad like when friends die."[33]

Fall gave way to winter, the coldest in memory. Frost bit into exposed skin. Snow and freezing rain slowed the columns to a crawl. Hunger gnawed at empty bellies. Pneumonia killed without mercy. An unidentified "Native of Maine" watched a group, three miles of misery in length, pass:

The sick and feeble were carried in wagons, about as comfortable for traveling as a New England ox cart with a covering over it. A great many ride on horseback and multitudes go on foot. Even aged females, appar-

This engraving is a copy of Robert Lindneux's 1840 painting The Cherokee Trail of Tears. *Although the federal government did not intend to harm those it expelled, the practical result of its arrogance and poor planning cost thousands of innocents their lives.*

ently nearly ready to drop into the grave, were traveling with heavy burdens attached to the back on the sometimes frozen ground . . . with no covering for the feet except what nature had given them. . . . We learned from the inhabitants on the road where the Indians passed that they had buried fourteen or fifteen at every stopping place, and they make a journey of ten miles a day only on an average. . . . The Indians as a whole carry in their countenances everything but the appearance of happiness. . . . Most of them seemed intelligent and refined. . . . When I passed the last detachment of those suffering exiles and thought that my . . . countrymen had thus expelled them from their native soil and their . . . loved homes, I turned from the sight with feelings which language cannot express and wept like childhood then.[34]

The last group, led by John Ross, reached Fort Gibson, Oklahoma, in March 1839. His wife, Quatie, lay buried beside the trail, a victim of pneumonia.

Afterward, Van Buren praised the government's "wise, humane" removal policy. That policy, he said, had "the happiest effects" in sending thousands of "friends" west of the Mississippi. The president neglected to mention that the government's wisdom and humanity had claimed 4,500 lives, that is, more than one out of every four Cherokee. Some whites, who thought the government's actions unjust, shielded several hundred stay-behinds in Georgia, claiming them as visiting relatives, although with darker skins than they.[35]

Indian removal was the ugliest stain on Jackson's career, possibly the worst thing he ever did. Yet he never saw it that way. Nothing he said or wrote shows he intended the horrors of the Trail of Tears. Nor did he ever claim that the only good Indian was a dead Indian. He would make "hard war" on Indians when he thought it necessary, but he had no intention of committing genocide, annihilating them as a people. Nevertheless, he wanted to remove them, for, he claimed, their own and the American nation's good.

While Jackson imagined Native Americans as children, he understood white Americans, especially frontier people, too. Like himself, they were bold and generous, but also land-hungry, violent, and racist. Indians stood in the way of their "go-ahead" drive, their longing to get ahead by owning land.

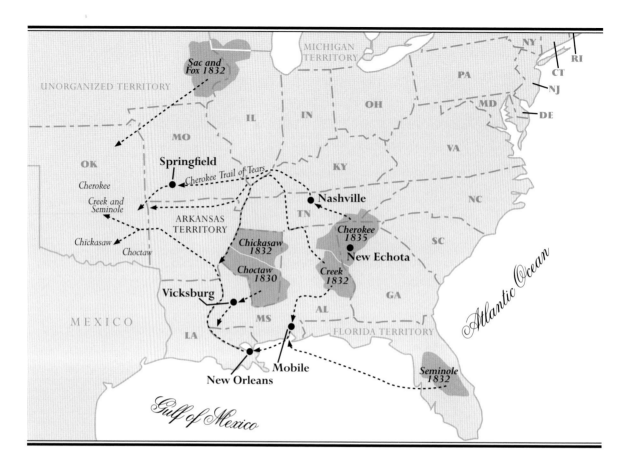

The Removal of the Southern Tribes

Gustaf Unonius, a Swedish immigrant, explained their mind-set in his autobiography, *A Pioneer in Northwest America:*

> The frontiers are often settled by a peculiar kind of people who nourish inwardly a mortal hatred of the red men. They . . . have two kinds of conscience, one for whites, another for Indians. They are people whose behavior in their relations with their own race, whose kindness . . . would entitle them to respect and esteem in any ordered community. For them, however, the red man's rights and privileges, his possessions, and his life weigh little in the scales, and they consider any injustice towards the Indians justifiable and permissible. Brave, seasoned and enterprising, faithful, honest, benevolent, and hospitable toward the white stranger, they lack in their hearts all kindly feeling, all compassion for nature's children.[36]

Given these attitudes, Jackson never doubted that he saved the tribes from destruction by forcing them westward. Thus, for the seventh president, removal was the lesser evil; he called it a "just and humane policy toward the Indians." Once relocated, he said in a letter to John Coffee, the tribes would grow "to be our equals in privileges, civil and religious." Trying to hold on to their lands, however, "must necessarily entail destruction upon their race."[37]

Sadly, the best intentions may end in tragedy. People of different backgrounds see the world differently. Justice and the so-called lesser evil to one people may be pure wickedness to another. The Cherokee had not waged war upon the United States since the 1790s. Those driven westward fifty years later were innocents, every one of them. They simply wanted to live on a small portion of their traditional lands, on terms recognized by treaties with the United States—treaties upheld by the Supreme Court. Not for a moment could the stubborn old man bring himself to see things through any eyes but his own. Worse, Jackson's eagerness to solve the Indian "problem" blinded him to the harm his policy did to helpless people—really victims. Surely this was his greatest failure as a man and a leader.

IX

AN OLD, OLD MAN

A natural king with a raven wing;
Cold no more, weary no more—
Old, old, old, old Andrew Jackson.
—VACHEL LINDSAY,
"GOING TO THE STARS," 1926

Old Hickory toward the end of his life. In constant pain and lonely for his wife, the former president had no fear of death.

Jackson was glad to see his presidency ending. He had achieved most of what he had set out to do. True, Texas was still outside the Union, but he had left the Bank of the United States powerless, about to close its doors forever. Nullification and secession lay defeated—for the time being. Native Americans were leaving their ancestral lands in the East, clearing the way for white settlers, black slaves, and King Cotton. Democrats controlled both houses of Congress.

The president felt old, very old, and very tired. Eight years in the White House had drained his strength. Frequent bouts of illness had confined him to bed for weeks on end. It was time to go. Let a younger man fill his boots—if he could. "My only ambition," Jackson wrote a friend, "is to get to the Hermitage as soon as the interest of my country and the will of the people will permit me, and there to set my house in order and go to sleep along side of my dear departed wife."[1]

So he was thrilled when Martin Van Buren won the election of 1836. Good news continued to raise his spirits, as when Thomas Hart Benton showed himself a true friend. Benton knew the Senate's censure for his removing federal deposits from the bank still gnawed at Jackson. On January 16, 1837, he persuaded the Senate to change its mind. Not only did it withdraw the censure, it *expunged* it—inked it over in the official journal with heavy black lines. In gratitude, Old Hickory gave a lavish dinner for his supporters and their wives. Too weak to sit at the table, he offered Benton the seat of honor, then returned to his bedroom.[2]

As the time for leaving drew near, farewell gifts poured into the White House. Each day brought its share of tobacco pipes, hickory canes, and knick-knacks bearing his likeness. Jackson admired the carriage made of timbers from the U.S.S. *Constitution,* "Old Ironsides," America's most famous warship. A huge Cheddar cheese, four feet across by two feet thick, also arrived, the gift of a loyal Democrat. Jackson saved the 1,400-pound gift for his last official reception on George Washington's birthday, February 22. Everyone from Supreme Court justices to stable boys jammed the East Room to wish him well—and eat cheese. Oh, what a glorious day for cheese! Carpets grew slippery with cheese. Pockets filled with wedges of cheese. "All you heard was cheese; all you smelled was cheese," a guest reported.[3]

March 4, inauguration day, dawned clear and mild. Although Martin Van Buren was about to become president, it was really Andrew Jackson's day. The two men sat close together as the *Constitution* carriage left the White House driveway. Cheering crowds lined Pennsylvania Avenue. At the approach of the gleaming carriage, its sides painted with scenes of naval battles, people fell silent. Men removed their hats as it rolled toward the Capitol. All eyes were on the frail figure in the backseat.

Justice Roger B. Taney administered the oath of office to Van Buren on a platform built on the East Portico. Afterward, Jackson slowly started down the Capitol steps, toward the waiting carriage. He walked alone. Halfway down, he stopped, perhaps to steady himself with his cane. As he did, the crowd roared. The old man bowed. The crowd erupted in window-rattling cheers. Tom Benton, deeply moved, nearly wept. Those cheers, he recalled, came from the people's heart. "It was affection, gratitude, and admiration . . . breaking from [their] bosoms. . . . I was looking from a side window and felt an emotion which had never passed through me before."[4]

Van Buren invited him to rest a few days in the White House, but Jackson wanted to leave without delay. On March 5, he met political allies to say good-bye. Some were curious. Could he have done anything differently? Yes, he said. He was sorry for not having shot Henry Clay and hanged John C. Calhoun. Next day, he left Washington for the last time. As before, crowds lined his route, this time to the railroad station. Arriving, Jackson stood on the train's rear platform, holding his tall hat in his hand. People grew quiet. Finally, the engineer tooted his whistle and iron wheels began turning amid clouds of steam. The train left the station, everyone watching it until there was nothing more to see. As the crowd broke up, a man observed it was "as if a bright star had gone out of the sky."[5]

Westward, ever westward. Going from train to steamboat, from steamboat to coach, Jackson headed home to Tennessee. Not since George Washington left office had the people greeted a homeward-bound president so warmly. Wherever he stopped, cheering, flag-waving crowds welcomed him. Mothers handed him children to cuddle and kiss. "His name is Andrew Jackson," more than one proud parent called out. Like a proud grandfather, the old man beamed with pleasure.[6]

On March 23, he reached Nashville. The place went wild. A tiny village, Lebanon, lay down the road a bit. Every villager turned out to meet him. War veterans lined the road, a crowd of young men and boys behind them. After a speech by a judge, Jackson turned to the crowd. Just then, a boy stepped forward. "General," he said in his squeaky voice, "the children of your old soldiers and friends welcome you home, and we're ready to serve under your banner." At these words, Jackson's body shook with emotion. "I could have stood all but this, it is too much, too much!" he replied, tears streaming down his cheeks. The villagers never forgot that day. "I may live a hundred years," said one, "but no future can erase that scene from my memory."[7]

The driver snapped his whip, and the coach lurched forward. Moments later, it rolled into The Hermitage driveway. Andrew Jr., Sarah, and their children met him at the front door.

Home at last, Jackson settled into his familiar routines. Waking before dawn, he ate a light breakfast and, weather permitting, inspected the plantation. He made his rounds on his favorite mount, slow, gentle Sam Patch; he ached too much to ride spirited horses. Granddaughter Rachel, his "little pet," usually came along. When she was very small, she rode in front of him, grasping the pommel of the saddle with both hands; later, she rode behind, holding on to Grandpa's waist. Years later, as an adult, she described how the slaves would "give three loud cheers for 'old master.'" Did they love him, or was there a hidden reason for cheering? We must remember that, upon a master's death, slaves were often sold, and families broken up, to settle debts. Perhaps, through such demonstrations of love and loyalty, they tried to curry favor with the heirs to keep their families intact? Perhaps they really loved Jackson? We will never know.[8]

Afternoons found Jackson with visitors, mostly aspiring politicians come for advice and to cut hickory walking sticks, which Democrats regarded as good-luck charms. Besides the *Constitution* carriage and the pen used to expunge the Senate censure, he had countless mementos to show them. Among these were Indian peace pipes, gold medals and silver cups awarded to him at various times, and George Washington's pistols. Nothing, however, gave him more pleasure than showing off his favorite pistol, the one he used on Charles Dickinson in 1806. "That is the pistol with which I killed Mr. Dickinson," he would say with delight.[9]

Each day, as the sun dipped low in the west, he took a walk, usually holding little Rachel by the hand. When his steps turned to the garden path, as they always did, she knew to let go and leave Grandpa alone. Jackson would stand beside his wife's grave, head bowed and silent. One day, a young man came from Nashville to collect a bill. Since it was getting late, Jackson asked him to walk with him in the garden. As they neared Rachel's grave, he said, "My son, there lies the best woman that ever lived." Later, when he was too sick to walk, servants carried him to the graveside in a chair.[10]

Returning to the mansion, the old man had supper. For an hour or two, he read newspapers, to which he was addicted, and answered his mail. Letters poured in from all parts of the country. Most came from people he never met, much as a rock star's fan mail does today. Jackson was a celebrity. People wanted to feel close to him by owning something of his, like locks of his hair, precious keepsakes in the nineteenth century. To satisfy the demand, whenever he had a haircut, he saved the trimmings in a bag. About nine o'clock, a house slave, George, helped him undress and get into bed. Finally, little Rachel climbed a three-step ladder, leaned over, and kissed Grandpa's cheek. "Bless my baby," he would say, returning the kiss. "Bless my little Rachel. Goodnight."[11]

Jackson left office only days before the Panic of 1837 began. Later, some historians would blame the disaster on his victory over the bank. With its hold on the state banks broken, they argue, state bank directors felt free to print as many banknotes as they pleased. Suddenly, credit became easier to get. Easier credit made land sales, cotton production and manufacturing output soar, since there was great demand. However, as prices soared, too, in response to demand, people rushed to exchange banknotes for specie. But since banks lacked the specie reserves to cover all their notes, they closed their doors, sending the economy into a sharp downturn. Other historians accept this explanation, but they say it does not go far enough. The crisis, they explain, began not in America, but in Europe. An economic crisis there soon lowered demand for all American goods, triggering the Panic of 1837. Jackson's bank policy only made matters worse.

Everyone agrees on the effect of the panic. Millions in paper money became all but worthless. With credit cut off, businessmen could not buy raw

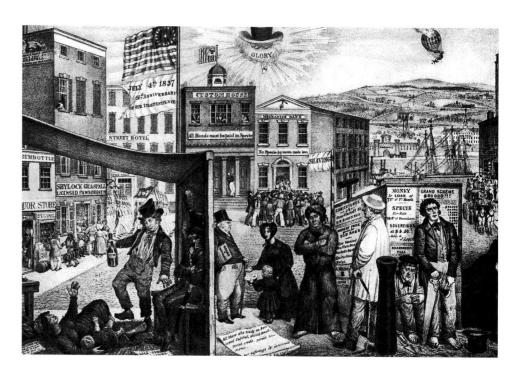

Edward W. Clay titled his view of America in 1840 The Times. *A severe economic downturn had struck the nation, as evident from the beggars, the unemployed, and closed businesses shown in the picture.*

materials or pay wages. Unemployment spread. Work on canals stopped. Railroad tracks ended in empty fields. Hungry mobs attacked city grocery shops and flour mills. A powerful cartoon, titled "The Times," depicts wretched women and children begging or sleeping in the streets. "The merchants going to the devil *en masse,*" a wealthy New Yorker, George Templeton Strong, wrote in his diary. "Workmen thrown out of employ by the hundred daily. Business at a stand . . . [People] begin to talk ominously about rebellion."[12]

Jackson felt the pinch, too. The slump in cotton prices cost him a fortune. Desperate to pay his creditors, he mortgaged The Hermitage and sold nearly a thousand acres of farmland in western Tennessee. Despite his money troubles and illnesses, he still kept up with politics. Democrats regarded him as their elder statesman, a wise man whose advice they trusted. As the election of 1840 drew near, he campaigned in Tennessee for Van Buren, who was running for a second term. Nevertheless, the Little Magician had big problems. Calling him "Martin Van Ruin," the Whig opposition blamed him for the panic.

The Whigs nominated General William Henry Harrison of Ohio for president. Famous as a frontier soldier, in November 1811 he had won a major battle against the Shawnee at the Tippecanoe River in Indiana Territory. Harrison understood that, with state laws now allowing most white men to vote, he must appeal to as many of them as possible.

Like their rivals, the Whigs fought a "hurrah" campaign. They held torchlight parades, handed out food and drinks, and even called themselves "Democratic" to get votes away from Van Buren. A wealthy man, Harrison lived in a stately mansion he called the "Log Cabin," because such a cabin had once stood on the spot. Whig publicists ignored this, portraying their candidate as a humble "man of the people." They flooded the country with pictures and stories about the hero, and rousing campaign songs like "Harrison's Log Cabin March." By contrast, they depicted Van Buren as a dandy who drank French wines from crystal goblets. And

"Harrison's Log Cabin March," a song that portrayed the wealthy William Henry Harrison as a simple "man of the people," during the presidential campaign of 1840.

William Henry Harrison defeated Martin Van Buren in the election of 1840. Succumbing to pneumonia soon afterward, he was the first president to die in office.

it worked. The voters gave Harrison 234 electoral votes to Van Buren's 60. Not only did the New Yorker lose his home state, he lost Jackson's stronghold, Tennessee, by twelve thousand votes. "Corruption, bribery and fraud has been extended over the whole Union," Old Hickory groaned, as if the Democrats were pure as fresh snow.[13]

Harrison did not enjoy his victory for long. On April 4, 1841, he succumbed to pneumonia, becoming the first president to die in office. Vice President John Tyler, a former U.S. senator from Virginia, took over. Tyler never lived down his nickname, "His Accidency," for the way he became president. No one had ever risen to the highest office in the land over his predecessor's death.

Tyler was a one-issue president—he wanted to annex Texas to the Union. However, in 1843 the Senate rejected its bid to become the twenty-eighth state. Disappointed, Tyler and his secretary of state, John C. Calhoun, devised a plot to scare the nation into accepting annexation. Britain, they claimed, hoped to prevent the United States from becoming a world power. To do that, they said, Britain would halt America's westward expansion by recognizing Texas as an independent country and then give it military protection. Using Texas as a base, Britain might also encourage slave rebellions throughout the Cotton Kingdom.

Britain had no such plan. The very idea of plunging the chief source of its cotton into a bloody revolution was ridiculous. Sam Houston knew the truth, but he played along to win Jackson's support for annexation. Although retired, Jackson still had considerable influence with Democratic politicians and voters. If the United States could not annex Texas, Houston warned, Texas must seek support from another friendly power. Houston visited The Hermitage several times to drive this point home. During one visit, he and his friend discussed annexation over roasted bear meat.[14]

We recall that while Jackson had hoped to annex Texas, he refused to press the issue, fearing a crisis over slavery. Houston's arguments persuaded him to change his mind. Always willing to think the worst of Britain, he suspected it had never given up hopes of destroying American independence. Now he began a letter-writing campaign to convince opponents to change their minds, too. The United States needs Texas! "With such a barrier on our west we are invincible," he wrote. "The whole European world could not, in combination against us, make any impression on our Union."[15]

Meanwhile, Tyler quarreled with Daniel Webster, Henry Clay, and other Whig leaders over the economy. The dispute grew so bitter that the party expelled him, nominating Clay as its presidential candidate for 1844. Tyler, no quitter, hoped to win reelection by running an independent campaign. Terrified that Tyler might split the Democratic vote, Jackson persuaded him to quit the race, then threw his support to a fellow Tennessean, James K. Polk. A former governor, Polk took pride in his nickname "Young Hickory," from his determination to expand the nation's boundaries.

Jackson saw Clay's opposition to annexation as the key to a Democratic victory. "Lash Clay on Texas," he urged Polk. Polk did, becoming at age forty-nine the youngest man yet to win the presidency. Polk's victory allowed Tyler to go all out for Texas in the time remaining to him. On March 1, 1845, three days before he left office, Congress admitted Texas to the Union as a slave state. Under Polk, Texas statehood would become a full-blown crisis with Mexico, which had never granted Texas its independence. The following year, the crisis exploded into the Mexican War.[16]

By then, however, Andrew Jackson was no more.

On May 26, Sam Houston set out with his young boy, Sam Jr., to thank Jackson in person for his efforts on behalf of Texas. Without their realizing it, their journey became a race against time.

The old man's health had been failing for

Jackson supported a fellow Tennessean, James K. Polk, in the presidential election of 1844. Under Polk, Congress admitted Texas to the Union as a slave state.

over a year. He had become blind in his right eye; vision in his left eye was also failing. Day and night, spasms of coughing racked his frail body. Earaches tormented him. Breathing became an ordeal as tuberculosis destroyed one lung and attacked the other. Each hemorrhage left him weaker than the one before. Jackson treated the hemorrhages, as usual, by bleeding himself. Yet he still smoked his pipe, chewed tobacco, and drank black coffee. His doctors warned against the use of these things by one so frail. Although physicians would not understand the scientific reasons for another century, they knew from experience that heavy tobacco use and coffee drinking undermined health. Jackson, however, ignored their advice. Strangely, for such an intelligent man, he did not see—or refused to see—any connection between his habits and his illnesses.

Old, old Andrew Jackson, as seen in a photo by Daniel Adams taken a few months before his death.

Finally, Jackson developed dropsy, a disease that causes the body to retain fluids. Slowly, he began to swell. "I am a blubber of water," he wrote his nephew, Andrew Jackson Donelson. "I am . . . swollen from the toes to the crown of my head, and in bandages to my hips. Have had a bowel complaint . . . with a constant nausea in my stomach. How far my god may think proper to bear me up under my weight of affliction, he only knows." When Dan Adams came from Nashville to make a daguerreotype, an early kind of photograph, he found his subject in agony. The photo did not please Old Hickory. "Humph!" he growled. "Looks like a monkey!"[17]

Word of Jackson's condition spread, bringing hordes of visitors to The Hermitage. Most came to pay their last respects. Others pestered him for job recommendations in the Polk administration. Usually, he turned them down politely. But not always. Once he growled, "I am dying as fast as I can, and they all know it, but they will keep swarming about me in crowds, seeking for office—intriguing for office."[18]

On June 8, 1845, Old Hickory died peacefully at six o'clock in the evening, surrounded by his grieving family. He was seventy-eight years old.

Within the hour, a carriage halted outside the door of The Hermitage. Sam Houston stepped down, holding his son by the hand, and went upstairs. When he saw the tall figure outlined by the blanket, so still, so silent, the Texan fell to his knees, sobbing.

Finally, he stood up and drew Sam Jr. to the bedside. "My son," he said, "try to remember that you have looked in the face of Andrew Jackson."[19]

Two days later, they buried him in the garden, beside his Rachel.

The Death of Genl. Andrew Jackson, *a lithograph
by Nathaniel Currier dated 1845.*

NOTES

PROLOGUE
UP FROM THE PEBBLES

1. James Parton, *The Life of Andrew Jackson,* 3 vols. (Boston: Houghton Mifflin, 1888), I, 108–109.
2. Allan Nevins, ed., *The Diary of Philip Hone, 1828–1851* (New York: Dodd, Mead, 1927), 732; Robert V. Remini, *Andrew Jackson and the Course of American Democracy, 1833–1845* (Baltimore: The Johns Hopkins University Press, 1984), 447.
3. *Cincinnati Daily Gazette,* August 22, 1834.
4. Remini, *Andrew Jackson and the Course of American Democracy,* 412.
5. Ibid., 345–346.
6. Marquis James, *The Life of Andrew Jackson* (Indianapolis: Bobbs-Merrill, 1938), 720.
7. Remini, *Andrew Jackson and the Course of American Democracy,* 412.
8. James MacGregor Burns, *Roosevelt, The Lion and the Fox, 1882–1940* (New York: Harcourt, Brace & World, 1956), 208; Arthur M. Schlesinger, Jr., *The Age of Roosevelt: The Politics of Upheaval* (Boston: Houghton Mifflin, 1960), 503, 673; David McCullough, *Truman* (New York: Simon & Schuster, 1992), 606.
9. Margaret Truman, ed., *Where the Buck Stops: The Personal and Private Writings of Harry S. Truman* (New York: Warner Books, 1999), 274.

I A RAW LAD

1. Michael Paul Rogin, *Fathers and Children: Andrew Jackson and the Subjugation of the American Indian* (New York: Alfred A. Knopf, 1975), 40.
2. Patrick Griffin, *The People with No Name: Ireland's Ulster Scots, America's Scots Irish, and the Creation of a British Atlantic World,* *1689–1764* (Princeton: Princeton University Press, 2001), 95.
3. Gottlieb Mittelberger, *Journey to Pennsylvania,* trans. Oscar Handlin and John Clive (Cambridge, Mass.: Harvard University Press, 1960), 12–16.
4. Hendrik Booraem, *The Making of Andrew Jackson* (Dallas: Taylor Trade Publishing, 2001), 9.
5. Parton, *The Life of Andrew Jackson,* I, 59; David Hackett Fischer, *Albion's Seed: Four British Folkways in America* (New York: Oxford University Press, 1989), 676. I owe much of the material in this section to Dr. Fischer's wonderful book. In it, the historian traces how immigrants brought various aspects of the culture of the British Isles to America, where they continued to influence their behavior in new surroundings.
6. Ibid., 629; James G. Leyburn, *The Scots-Irish: A Social History* (Chapel Hill: University of South Carolina Press, 1962), 38.
7. Fischer, *Albion's Seed,* 650.
8. Griffin, *The People with No Name,* 96; R. C. Simmons, *The American Colonies: From Settlement to Independence* (New York: David McKay, 1967), 182.
9. Booraem, *The Making of Andrew Jackson,* 5.
10. Harry L. Watson, *An Independent People: The Way We Lived in North Carolina, 1770–1820* (Chapel Hill: University of North Carolina Press, 1982), 5; Gordon G. Whitney, *From Coastal Wilderness to Fruited Plain: A History of Environmental Change in Temperate North America, 1500 to the Present* (Cambridge: Cambridge University Press, 1994), 53.
11. John James Audubon, *Writings and Drawings* (New York: The Library of America, 1999), 263.
12. Fischer, *Albion's Seed,* 641, 652.
13. Ibid., 660–661.
14. Ibid., 665.
15. Ibid., 375.
16. Page Smith, *The Shaping of America* (New York: McGraw-Hill, 1980), 177.
17. Lee Kennett and James LaVerne Anderson, *The Gun in America: The Origins of a National Dilemma* (Westport, Conn.: Greenwood Press, 1975), 62; Parton, *The Life of Andrew Jackson,* I, 111.
18. Fischer, *Albion's Seed,* 687, 689; Burstein, The Passions of Andrew Jackson, 38.
19. Elliott J. Gorn, " 'Gouge and Bite, Pull Hair and Scratch': The Social Significance of Fighting in the Southern Backcountry," *American Historical Review* (February 1985): 25.
20. Fischer, *Albion's Seed,* 730–731.
21. Charles Miller, *Early English Travelers in North America: Eyewitness Reports from the First Visitors to the New World* (Dover, N.H.: Alan Sutton, 1994), 83; Whitney, *From Coastal Wilderness to Fruited Plain,* 134; Richard Drinnon, *Facing West: Indian Fighting and Empire Building* (New York: Schocken Books, 1990), 100.
22. Frances Trollope, *Domestic Manners of the Americans* (St. James, N.Y.: Brandywine Press, 1993), 11.
23. Fischer, *Albion's Seed,* 711–713.
24. Smith, *Shaping of America,* 178.
25. Parton, *The Life of Andrew Jackson,* I, 60; Booraem, *The Making of Andrew Jackson,* 29.
26. Marquis James, *Andrew Jackson: The Border Captain* (New York: The Literary Guild, 1933), 15; Edward Pessen, *Jacksonian America: Society, Personality, and Politics* (Chicago: University of Illinois Press, 1985), 181.
27. Parton, *The Life of Andrew Jackson,* I, 64.
28. Robert V. Remini, *Andrew Jackson and the Course of American Empire, 1767–1821* (New York: Harper & Row, 1977), 13;

Parton, *The Life of Andrew Jackson,* I, 111; Booraem, *The Making of Andrew Jackson,* 40–41.

29. Remini, *Andrew Jackson and His Indian Wars* (New York: Viking, 2001), 15; Remini, *Andrew Jackson and the Course of American Empire,* 8; Parton, *The Life of Andrew Jackson,* I, 64, 68.

30. Parton, *The Life of Andrew Jackson,* I, 64, 112.

31. Augustus C. Buell, *History of Andrew Jackson,* 2 vols. (New York: Charles Scribner's Sons, 1904), II, 411.

32. Ibid., II, 411.

33. Parton, *The Life of Andrew Jackson,* I, 113; Remini, *Andrew Jackson and the Course of American Empire,* 7.

34. Joseph J. Ellis, *Founding Brothers: The Revolutionary Generation* (New York: Alfred A. Knopf, 2001), 10.

35. James, *Andrew Jackson: The Border Captain,* 358.

36. Burke Davis, *Old Hickory: A Life of Andrew Jackson* (New York: The Dial Press, 1977), 4.

37. Remini, *Andrew Jackson and the Course of American Empire,* 15, 19.

38. Remini, *Andrew Jackson and His Indian Wars,* 17.

39. Davis, *Old Hickory,* 7; Parton, *The Life of Andrew Jackson,* I, 68.

40. James, *Andrew Jackson: The Border Captain,* 26; Booraem, *The Making of Andrew Jackson,* 90, 93.

41. Booraem, *The Making of Andrew Jackson,* 49.

42. Parton, *The Life of Andrew Jackson,* I, 89.

43. Remini, *Andrew Jackson and the Course of American Empire,* I, 22.

44. Davis, *Old Hickory,* 6; Buell, *History of Andrew Jackson,* I, 52–53.

45. Davis, *Old Hickory,* 7.

▮▮ MAKING HIS OWN WAY

1. Davis, *Old Hickory,* 252.

2. Booraem, *The Making of Andrew Jackson,* 118–119.

3. Stephen B. Oates, *The Ruling Race: A History of American Slaveholders* (New York: Alfred A. Knopf, 1982), 123.

4. Ibid., 10, 43.

5. Parton, *The Life of Andrew Jackson,* I, 98.

6. Robert E. Riegel, *Young America, 1830–1840* (Norman: University of Oklahoma Press, 1949), 232–235.

7. Parton, *The Life of Andrew Jackson,* I, 104–105, 108.

8. Booraem, *The Making of Andrew Jackson,* 187.

9. Buell, *History of Andrew Jackson,* I, 69.

10. Parton, *The Life of Andrew Jackson,* I, 123.

11. Francis Jennings, *The Invasion of America: Indians, Colonialism, and the Cant of Conquest* (New York: W. W. Norton, 1976), 165.

12. Richard Drinnon, *Facing West: Indian Hating and Empire Building* (New York: Schocken Books, 1990), 43; Jennings, *The Invasion of America,* 150.

13. Jennings, *The Invasion of America,* 151–152; James Axtell, "The White Indian of Colonial America," *William & Mary Quarterly* 32 (1975): 55–88.

14. Jennings, *The Invasion of America,* 164; Norman Gelb, *Less Than Glory* (New York: G. P. Putnam's Sons, 1984), 196.

15. Tucker, *Tecumseh,* 88.

16. Parton, *The Life of Andrew Jackson,* I, 139.

17. Remini, *Andrew Jackson and His Indian Wars,* 14–15.

18. Booraem, *The Making of Andrew Jackson,* 194.

19. Davis, *Old Hickory,* 17.

20. James, *Andrew Jackson: The Border Captain,* 55.

21. Remini, *Andrew Jackson and the Course of American Empire,* 44.

22. Parton, *The Life of Andrew Jackson,* I, 165–166.

23. Ibid., 151.

24. Marshall B. Davidson, *Life in America,* 2 vols. (Boston: Houghton Mifflin, 1951), II, 241; Edith Coombs, ed., *America Visited* (New York: Book League of America, n.d.), 343.

25. James, *Andrew Jackson: The Border Captain,* 70.

26. Ibid., 70, 74. Andrew Burstein, a recent Jackson biographer, argues that the couple did not marry in Natchez. Instead, he believes, they went there intending to provoke Robards into suing for divorce. This may be true, but it cannot be proven

from existing documents. What we *do* know is that Jackson's friends, especially John Overton, agreed that he had made an honest mistake. Also, if Jackson intended to force Robards's hand, he hurt Rachel deeply. Yet, if we read his character correctly, that was something he seemed incapable of doing. See Andrew Burstein, *The Passions of Andrew Jackson* (New York: Alfred A. Knopf, 2003), 28–33.

27. Remini, *Andrew Jackson and the Course of American Empire,* 67.

28. Ibid., 67.

29. Robert V. Remini, *Andrew Jackson and the Course of American Freedom, 1822–1832* (New York: Harper & Row, 1981), 9.

30. Parton, *Life of Andrew Jackson,* I, 158.

31. Ibid., I, 158–159.

32. James, *Andrew Jackson: The Border Captain,* 94.

33. Stanley F. Horn, *The Hermitage: Home of Old Hickory* (Nashville: Ladies' Hermitage Association, 1950), 6.

34. Parton, *The Life of Andrew Jackson,* I, 249–250.

35. Ibid., 196. A queue was a long braid of hair, or pigtail, that men wore hanging down the back of the neck.

36. Rogin, *Fathers and Children,* 132; James, *Andrew Jackson: The Border Captain,* 74.

37. James, *Andrew Jackson: The Border Captain,* 86–87.

38. Ibid., 88.

39. Parton, *The Life of Andrew Jackson,* I, 219.

40. James, *Andrew Jackson: The Border Captain,* 94.

41. Parton, *The Life of Andrew Jackson,* I, 228–229.

42. Davis, *Old Hickory,* 35.

43. Parton, *The Life of Andrew Jackson,* I, 164.

44. Jack K. Williams, *Dueling in the Old South* (College Station: Texas A&M University Press, 1980), 26, 76.

45. John Spencer Bassett, *The Life of Andrew Jackson* (New York: Macmillan, 1928), 729–730; Remini, *Andrew Jackson and the Course of American Freedom,* 5.

46. Remini, *Andrew Jackson and the Course of American Empire,* 39.

47. Ibid., 122.

48. Parton, *The Life of Andrew Jackson,* I, 235.

49. Horn, *The Hermitage,* 17.

50. James, *The Life of Andrew Jackson,* 371.

51. Parton, *The Life of Andrew Jackson,* I, 253.

52. Remini, *Andrew Jackson and the Course of American Democracy,* 435.

53. Remini, *Andrew Jackson and the Course of American Empire,* 7.

54. Burstein, *The Passions of Andrew Jackson,* 161–162.

55. Horn, *The Hermitage,* 1, 99; Burstein, *The Passions of Andrew Jackson,* 160.

56. Parton, *The Life of Andrew Jackson,* III, 162.

57. Remini, *Andrew Jackson and the Course of American Empire,* 69.

58. Parton, *The Life of Andrew Jackson,* I, 295–306, still has the best description of the duel. I have used it freely in my description of this affair.

59. Davis, *Old Hickory,* 49.

60. Thomas Hart Benton, *Thirty Years' View: A History of the Working of the American Government for Thirty Years, 1820–1850* (New York: D. Appleton, 1854), 737.

61. Davis, *Old Hickory,* 63.

62. Horn, *The Hermitage,* 102.

▌▌▌ "IMMORTAL JACKSON"

1. Davis, *Old Hickory,* 47.

2. Paul Johnson, *A History of the American People,* 217.

3. Remini, *Andrew Jackson and the Course of American Empire,* 169.

4. James, *Andrew Jackson: The Border Captain,* 151–152.

5. Remini, *Andrew Jackson and the Course of American Empire,* 232–233.

6. James, *Andrew Jackson: The Border Captain,* 155–156.

7. Remini, *Andrew Jackson and the Course of American Empire,* 179.

8. Parton, *The Life of Andrew Jackson,* I, 382.

9. Ibid., 382.

10. Remini, *Andrew Jackson and the Course of American Empire,* 181; Parton, *The Life of Andrew Jackson,* I, 386–387.

11. Glen Tucker, *Tecumseh: The Vision of Glory* (New York: Russell & Russell, 1973), 200–201, 209, 210, 215.

12. Remini, *Andrew Jackson and His Indian Wars,* 5.

13. Robert V. Remini, *The Battle of New Orleans* (New York: Viking, 1999), 10.

14. Rogin, *Fathers and Children,* 148.

15. James, *Andrew Jackson: The Border Captain,* 163.

16. Frederick M. Binder, *The Color Problem in Early National America as Viewed by John Adams, Jefferson and Jackson* (Mouton: The Hague, 1968), 138.

17. William C. Davis, *Three Roads to the Alamo: The Lives and Fortunes of David Crockett, James Bowie, and William Barret Travis* (New York: HarperCollins, 1998), 29.

18. Gloria Jahoda, *The Trail of Tears: The American Indian Removals, 1813–1855* (London: Book Club Associates, 1976), 6.

19. Parton, *The Life of Andrew Jackson,* I, 439; Remini, *Andrew Jackson and the Course of American Empire,* 194; Remini, *Andrew Jackson and His Indian Wars,* 64; Horn, *The Hermitage,* 122.

20. Parton, *The Life of Andrew Jackson,* I, 446.

21. Ibid., III, 633.

22. Ibid., I, 507–508.

23. Davis, *Old Hickory,* 89; Remini, *Andrew Jackson and the Course of American Empire,* 212.

24. James, *Andrew Jackson: The Border Captain,* 179–180.

25. Marquis James, *Raven: A Biography of Sam Houston* (New York: Blue Ribbon Books, 1929), 32–33.

26. Ibid., 33; Remini, *Andrew Jackson and His Indian Wars,* 78–79.

27. Parton, *The Life of Andrew Jackson,* I, 532–534.

28. Rogin, *Fathers and Children,* 131.

29. Remini, *Andrew Jackson and His Indian Wars,* 89.

30. Remini, *Andrew Jackson and His Indian Wars,* 89; Remini, *Andrew Jackson and the Course of American Empire,* 231.

31. Remini, *Battle of New Orleans,* 6.

32. James, *Andrew Jackson: The Border Captain,* 208.

33. Parton, *The Life of Andrew Jackson,* I, 577.

34. James, *Andrew Jackson: The Border Captain,* 194.

35. Remini, *The Battle of New Orleans,* 22; James, *Andrew Jackson: The Border Captain,* 212.

36. Robin Reilly, *The British at the Gates: The New Orleans Campaign in the War of 1812*

(New York: G. P. Putnam's Sons, 1974), 219; Robert Leckie, *From Sea to Shining Sea: From the War of 1812 to the Mexican War, the Saga of America's Expansion* (New York: HarperPerennial, 1993), 379.

37. Davis, *Old Hickory,* 107; James, *Andrew Jackson: The Border Captain,* 216; Parton, *The Life of Andrew Jackson,* II, 30.

38. Parton, *The Life of Andrew Jackson,* II, 31; James, *Andrew Jackson: The Border Captain,* 216.

39. Parton, *The Life of Andrew Jackson,* II, 76; James, *Andrew Jackson: The Border Captain,* 227.

40. Binder, *The Color Problem in Early National America,* 127, 128; Davis, *Old Hickory,* 109.

41. James, *Andrew Jackson: The Border Captain,* 206, 285; Remini, *The Battle of New Orleans,* 48.

42. Parton, *The Life of Andrew Jackson,* II, 66.

43. Ibid., II, 70.

44. Ibid., II, 73.

45. Ibid., II, 77.

46. Remini, *The Battle of New Orleans* (New York: Viking, 1999), 73.

47. Parton, *The Life of Andrew Jackson,* II, 103.

48. Davis, *Old Hickory,* 123.

49. Ibid., 124.

50. Remini, *The Battle of New Orleans,* 89.

51. Parton, *The Life of Andrew Jackson,* II, 158.

52. Ibid., II, 138.

53. Ibid., II, 126–127.

54. Davis, *Old Hickory,* 134.

55. Parton, *The Life of Andrew Jackson,* II, 179.

56. Ibid., II, 189; James, *Andrew Jackson: The Border Captain,* 261.

57. Ibid., 263.

58. Parton, *The Life of Andrew Jackson,* II, 192.

59. Ibid., II, 141.

60. Davis, *Old Hickory,* 140.

61. Ibid., 141.

62. Ibid., II, 196–197.

63. Ibid., II, 208; Remini, *The Battle of New Orleans,* 167–168.

64. Parton, *The Life of Andrew Jackson,* II, 244.

65. Nolte, *The Memoirs of Vincent Nolte,* 238; Parton, *The Life of Andrew Jackson,* II, 324.

66. James, *Andrew Jackson: The Border Captain,* 284.

67. Allan Nevins, ed., *The Diary of John Quincy Adams, 1794–1845* (New York: Charles Scribner's Sons, 1951), 151.

68. Parton, *The Life of Andrew Jackson,* II, 331.

IV ON THE BRINK OF FATE

1. Remini, *Andrew Jackson and the Course of American Empire,* 313.

2. Ibid., 302–305.

3. Paul Johnson, *The Birth of the Modern: World Society 1815–1830* (New York: HarperCollins, 1991), 226.

4. Remini, *Andrew Jackson and the Course of American Empire,* 344; Parton, *The Life of Andrew Jackson,* II, 402.

5. Parton, *The Life of Andrew Jackson,* II, 406.

6. Remini, *Andrew Jackson and His Indian Wars,* 130–131.

7. Ibid., 132–133.

8. Remini, *Andrew Jackson and the Course of American Empire,* 346; Parton, *The Life of Andrew Jackson,* II, 430–431.

9. Parton, *The Life of Andrew Jackson,* II, 434.

10. Margaret L. Coit, *John C. Calhoun* (Boston: Houghton Mifflin, 1950), 124.

11. Parton, *Andrew Jackson,* I, 441.

12. Parton, *The Life of Andrew Jackson,* II, 441.

13. Remini, *Andrew Jackson and His Indian Wars,* 150; Drinnon, *Facing West,* 106.

14. Drinnon, *Facing West,* 108.

15. Remini, *Andrew Jackson and His Indian Wars,* 156–157.

16. Ibid., 364.

17. George Dangerfield, *The Era of Good Feelings* (New York: Harcourt, Brace, 1952), 49; James, *Andrew Jackson: The Border Captain,* 315.

18. Remini, *Andrew Jackson and His Indian Wars,* 157; Davis, *Old Hickory,* 169–170; Remini, *Andrew Jackson and the Course of American Empire,* 371–372.

19. Nevins, *The Diary of John Quincy Adams,* 196; Remini, *Andrew Jackson and the Course of American Empire,* 368.

20. James, *Andrew Jackson: The Border Captain,* 316; Samuel Flagg Bemis,

John Quincy Adams and the Foundations of American Foreign Policy (New York: Alfred A. Knopf, 1949), 315–316; Burstein, *The Passions of Andrew Jackson,* 132.

21. James, *Andrew Jackson: The Border Captain,* 319–320; Bemis, *John Quincy Adams and the Foundations of American Foreign Policy,* 323–325.

22. Bemis, *John Quincy Adams and the Foundations of American Foreign Policy,* 327.

23. Ibid., 339.

24. James, *Andrew Jackson: The Border Captain,* 327.

25. Parton, *The Life of Andrew Jackson,* II, 657–658.

26. Remini, *Andrew Jackson and the Course of American Empire,* 9; James, *The Life of Andrew Jackson,* 463.

27. Ibid., 334.

28. Pessen, *Jacksonian America,* 50.

29. Frederick Marryat, *A Diary in America* (New York: Alfred A. Knopf, 1962), 273–274; Carl N. Degler, *At Odds: Women and the Family from the Revolution to the Present* (New York: Oxford University Press, 1980), 26, 27.

30. Davidson, *Life in America,* II, 198.

31. Rogin, *Fathers and Children,* 175–176; Anthony F. C. Wallace, *The Long Trail: Andrew Jackson and the Indians* (New York: Hill and Wang, 1993), 54.

32. Pessen, *Jacksonian America,* 110. A cotton bale weighed fifty pounds.

33. Captain Basil Hall, *Travels in North America in the Years 1827 and 1828,* in Allan Nevins, ed., *American Social History as Recorded by British Travellers* (New York: Henry Holt, 1923), 139–158.

34. Riegel, *Young America,* 151.

35. Charles Dickens, *American Notes* (Books, Inc.: New York, n.d.), 116, 140.

36. Daniel J. Boorstein, *The Americans: The National Experience* (New York: Random House, 1965), 101.

37. Kirkpatrick Sale, *The Fire of His Genius: Robert Fulton and the American Dream* (New York: The Free Press, 2001), 194.

38. George Rogers Taylor, *The Transportation Revolution, 1815–1860* (New York: Rinehart, 1958), 79.

39. Davy Crockett, *The Autobiography of Davy Crockett* (New York: Charles Scribner's Sons, 1923), 154.

40. Marryat, *A Diary in America,* 366.

41. Rogin, *Fathers and Children,* 282.

42. Frances Trollope, *Domestic Manners of the Americans,* 60–61.

43. Marryat, *A Diary in America,* 371.

44. Edward Pessen, ed., *Jacksonian Panorama* (Indianapolis: Bobbs-Merrill, 1976), 4, 6.

45. Russell Blaine Nye, *Society and Culture in America, 1830–1860* (New York: Harper Torchbooks, 1974), 18.

46. Marryat, *A Diary in America,* 260–265.

47. Boorstein, *The Americans: The National Experience,* 286–288; Marryat, *A Diary in America,* 458; Miller, *Early Travelers in North America,* 41.

48. Boorstein, *The Americans: The National Experience,* 286–288; Marryat, *A Diary in America,* 268; Miller, *Early Travelers in North America,* 34.

49. Page Smith, *The Nation Comes of Age* (New York: McGraw-Hill, 1980), 250.

50. Pessen, *Jacksonian Panorama,* 38.

51. W. J. Rorabaugh, *The Alcoholic Nation: An American Tradition* (New York: Oxford University Press, 1979), 95–98.

52. Ibid., 8.

53. Marryat, *A Diary in America,* 389–390; Rorabaugh, *The Alcoholic Nation,* 118.

54. New York had 124,000 people; Philadelphia, 113,000; Baltimore, 63,000; Boston, 43,000; New Orleans, 27,000; Charleston, 24,000. Taylor, *The Transportation Revolution,* 7.

55. Nevins, *The Diary of Philip Hone,* 45.

56. Pessen, *Jacksonian America,* 65; Nevins, *The Diary of Philip Hone,* 74.

57. Michael Slater, ed., *Dickens on America and the Americans* (Austin: University of Texas Press, 1978), 80.

58. Davidson, *Life in America,* II, 130.

59. Riegel, *Young America,* 36; Smith, *The Nation Comes of Age,* 746.

60. Ibid., 258.

61. Coit, *John C. Calhoun,* 204.

V THE GREAT RACE

1. James, *Andrew Jackson: The Border Captain,* 359.

2. Parton, *The Life of Andrew Jackson,* II, 12.

3. Remini, *Andrew Jackson and the Course of American Freedom,* 15, 17.

4. Alexander Hamilton, *Writings* (New York: The Library of America, 2001), 164.

5. Arthur M. Schlesinger, *The Age of Jackson* (Boston: Little, Brown, 1950), 310.

6. Remini, *Andrew Jackson and the Course of American Democracy,* 340.

7. Robert V. Remini, *The Legacy of Andrew Jackson: Essays on Democracy, Indian Removal, and Slavery* (Baton Rouge: Louisiana State University Press, 1988), 24; Remini, *Andrew Jackson and the Course of American Democracy,* 337–340.

8. Remini, *Andrew Jackson and the Course of American Freedom,* 37.

9. James, *The Life of Andrew Jackson,* 338; Parton, *The Life of Andrew Jackson,* III, 101.

10. Alistair Cooke, *Alistair Cooke's America* (New York: Alfred A. Knopf, 1973), 153.

11. Johnson, *The Birth of the Modern,* 938–939.

12. Coit, *John C. Calhoun,* 271; Rorabaugh, *The Alcoholic Nation,* 102.

13. Miller, *Early Travelers in North America,* 46; Marryat, *A Diary in America,* 154.

14. Dickens, *American Notes,* 109.

15. James, *The Life of Andrew Jackson,* 353, 383; Remini, *Andrew Jackson and the Course of American Freedom,* 60.

16. Davis, *Old Hickory,* 194.

17. James, *The Life of Andrew Jackson,* 392, 393.

18. Burstein, *The Passions of Andrew Jackson,* 156.

19. Bemis, *John Quincy Adams and the Union,* 6.

20. Robert V. Remini, *Henry Clay: Statesman of the Union* (New York: W. W. Norton, 199), 266; Parton, *The Life of Andrew Jackson,* III, 68.

21. Parton, *The Life of Andrew Jackson,* III, 72, 74.

22. Ibid., III, 72; Remini, *The Legacy of Andrew Jackson,* 83.

23. Dangerfield, *The Era of Good Feelings,* 7; Davis, *Old Hickory,* 181.

24. Johnson, *The Birth of the Modern,* 388; Bemis, *John Quincy Adams and the Union,* 121.

25. James, *The Life of Andrew Jackson,* 447; Remini, *Andrew Jackson and the Course of American Freedom,* 111.

26. Ibid., 110.

27. John F. Marszalek, *The Petticoat Affair: Manners, Mutiny, and Sex in Andrew Jackson's White House* (New York: The Free Press, 1997), 59.

28. Parton, *The Life of Andrew Jackson,* III, 136. See also Robert V. Remini, *Martin Van Buren and the Making of the Democratic Party* (New York: Columbia University Press), 1959.

29. Samuel Eliot Morison, *The Oxford History of the American People* (New York: Oxford University Press, 1965), 421.

30. Harriet Martineau, *Society in America,* 3 vols. (London: Saunders & Otley, 1837), III, 166.

31. Remini, *Henry Clay,* 325.

32. Parton, *The Life of Andrew Jackson,* III, 141.

33. James, *The Life of Andrew Jackson,* 464.

34. Ibid., 467.

35. Carl Sandburg, *Abraham Lincoln: The Prairie Years,* 2 vols. (New York: Harcourt, Brace, 1926), I, 93.

36. A total of 1,155,340 white males voted in 1828, over 800,000 more than in 1824. Jackson got 647,276 votes to Adams's 508,064.

37. Parton, *The Life of Andrew Jackson,* II, 153; Remini, *Andrew Jackson and the Course of American Freedom,* 149.

38. Remini, *Andrew Jackson and the Course of American Democracy,* 150.

39. James, *The Life of Andrew Jackson,* 480.

40. Parton, *The Life of Andrew Jackson,* III, 161.

41. Ibid., III, 158.

42. James, *The Life of Andrew Jackson,* 483.

VI THAT MOST AMERICAN OF AMERICANS

1. James, *The Life of Andrew Jackson,* 483.

2. Trollope, *Domestic Manners of the Americans,* 83.

3. Margaret B. Smith, *The First Forty Years of Washington Society,* ed. Gaillard Hunt (New York: Charles Scribner's Sons, 1906), 293.

4. Remini, *Andrew Jackson and the Course of American Freedom,* 178; Davis, *Old Hickory,* 241.

5. Smith, *The First Forty Years of Washington Society,* 295.

6. Parton, *The Life of Andrew Jackson,* III, 170; Schlesinger, *The Age of Jackson,* 6.

7. Davis, *Old Hickory,* 325.

8. Remini, *Andrew Jackson and the Course of American Freedom,* 105; James, *The Life of Andrew Jackson,* 343; Miller, *Early Travelers in North America,* 114.

9. Remini, *Andrew Jackson and the Course of American Freedom,* 2.

10. Parton, *The Life of Andrew Jackson,* III, 63–64.

11. Remini, *Andrew Jackson and the Course of American Democracy,* 399.

12. Davis, *Old Hickory,* 259; Marszalek, *The Petticoat Affair,* 120.

13. Parton, *The Life of Andrew Jackson,* III, 179.

14. Ibid., III, 605.

15. Remini, *Andrew Jackson and the Course of American Democracy,* 345–346.

16. Coit, *John C. Calhoun,* 271; Remini, *Andrew Jackson and the Course of American Democracy,* 147–148.

17. Parton, *The Life of Andrew Jackson,* III, 602.

18. Remini, *Andrew Jackson and the Course of American Democracy,* 397.

19. Davis, *Old Hickory,* 345; Stephen M. Archer, *Junius Brutus Booth* (Carbondale: Southern Illinois University Press, 1992), 135.

20. Benton, *Thirty Years' View,* 521.

21. Ibid., 521–524; Martin Van Buren, *Autobiography* (New York: Chelsea House, 1983), 353.

22. Remini, *Andrew Jackson and the Course of American Democracy,* 401; Margaret L. Coit, *Andrew Jackson* (Boston: Houghton Mifflin, 1965), 122–123.

23. James, *The Life of Andrew Jackson,* 591.

24. Remini, *Andrew Jackson and the Course of American Democracy,* 188.

25. Remini, *Andrew Jackson and the Course of American Freedom,* 185, 190; Davis, *Old Hickory,* 246.

26. Davis, *Old Hickory,* 246.

27. Ibid., 246.

28. James, *The Life of Andrew Jackson,* 503; Smith, *The Nation Comes of Age,* 183.

29. Remini, *Andrew Jackson and the Course of American Freedom,* 199.

30. William Safire, *Safire's Political Dictionary* (New York: Ballantine Books, 1978), 517–519.

31. Marszalek, *The Petticoat Affair,* 48.

32. Ibid., 240; Remini, *Andrew Jackson and the Course of American Freedom,* 162.

33. Marszalek, *The Petticoat Affair,* 53; Coit, *John C. Calhoun,* 199.

34. Ibid., 143.

35. Coit, *John C. Calhoun,* 199–200.

36. Marszalek, *The Petticoat Affair,* 171–173.

37. Ibid., 124.

38. Blair edited the Washington *Globe,* Green the *United States Telegraph,* and Hill the *New Hampshire Patriot.*

39. Safire, *Safire's Political Dictionary,* 357–358.

40. The first Bank of the United States went out of business after its charter expired in 1811.

41. Coit, *John C. Calhoun,* 261.

42. Davis, *Old Hickory,* 264; Remini, *Andrew Jackson and the Course of American Democracy,* 345; Rogin, *Fathers and Children,* 287, 292; Coit, *John C. Calhoun,* 260.

43. Davis, *Old Hickory,* 304.

44. Remini, *Andrew Jackson and the Course of American Freedom,* 368–369.

45. Safire, *Safire's Political Dictionary,* 396–397; Kenneth Davis, *FDR: The Beckoning of Destiny, 1882–1928* (New York: G. P. Putnam's Sons, 1972), 712.

46. Remini, *Andrew Jackson and the Course of American Freedom,* 366. As we will see in the next chapter, Van Buren became Jackson's running mate when Calhoun resigned the vice presidency.

47. Davis, *Old Hickory,* 310.

48. A third candidate, William Wirt, a former attorney general, took seven electoral votes. Wirt ran on the ticket of the Anti-Masonic Party, which opposed the Freemasons, a secret society whose members pledged to aid one another.

49. Nevins, *The Diary of Philip Hone,* 96–97.

50. Nevins, *The Diary of John Quincy Adams,* 439.

51. Jackson later appointed Roger B. Taney to the Supreme Court. In 1857, he wrote the justices' decision in the case of Dred Scott, a slave who had lived with his master in free territory. Upon returning to Missouri, Scott sued for his freedom, claiming that his time on free soil made him a free man. The justices ruled that enslaved people had never been citizens of the United States and therefore had no rights under its laws.

52. Davis, *Old Hickory,* 335–336.

53. Remini, *Andrew Jackson and the Course of American Freedom,* 369–370, 374–375; Davis, *Old Hickory,* 315.

VII THE SUPREME LAW: PRESERVING THE UNION

1. Parton, *The Life of Andrew Jackson,* III, 442–443.

2. Coit, *John C. Calhoun,* 277; Coombs, *America Visited,* 218.

3. Robert V. Remini, *Daniel Webster: The Man and His Time* (New York: W. W. Norton, 1997), 325.

4. Coit, *John C. Calhoun,* 209–210; Remini, *Daniel Webster,* 324.

5. Pessen, *Jacksonian America,* 172; Remini, *Daniel Webster,* 318.

6. Remini, *Daniel Webster,* 328.

7. Coit, *John C. Calhoun,* 211; Remini, *Daniel Webster,* 328–329.

8. Remini, *Daniel Webster,* 329; William H. Herndon, *Herndon's Life of Lincoln* (Cleveland: The World Publishing Company, 1965), 386.

9. Bemis, *John Quincy Adams and the Union,* 262.

10. James, *The Life of Andrew Jackson,* 539.

11. Parton, *The Life of Andrew Jackson,* III, 462; Bassett, *The Life of Andrew Jackson,* 569–570.

12. James D. Richardson, ed., *A Compilation of the Messages and Papers of the Presidents,* 11 vols (Washington, D.C.: Government Printing Office, 1910), II, 1203–1219.

13. Glyndon G. Van Deusen, *The Jacksonian Era, 1828–1848* (New York: Harper Torchbooks, 1959), 73; Remini, *Andrew Jackson and the Course of American Freedom,* III, 459, 472.

14. James, *The Life of Andrew Jackson,* 604.

15. Remini, *Andrew Jackson and the Course of American Democracy,* 43.

16. Peter Kolchin, *American Slavery, 1619–1877* (New York: Hill & Wang, 1993), 93.

17. Winthrop D. Jordan, *White Over Black: American Attitudes Toward the Negro, 1550–1812* (Chapel Hill: University of North Carolina Press, 1968), 253.

18. Johnson, *The Birth of the Modern,* 312; James Oakes, *The Ruling Race: A History of American Slaveholders* (New York: Alfred A. Knopf, 1982), 26–27.

19. Thomas Jefferson, *Writings* (New York: The Library of America, 1984), 289.

20. Frances Anne Kemble, *Journal of a Residence on a Georgian Plantation in 1838–1839* (New York: Alfred A. Knopf, 1961), 157.

21. Ibid., 9–10.

22. James, *The Life of Andrew Jackson,* 737; Oakes, *The Ruling Race,* 63; Brian William Thomas, "Community Among Enslaved Africans on The Hermitage Plantation, 1820s–1850s" (Ph.D. diss., State University of New York at Binghamton, 1995), 230; Horn, *The Hermitage,* 210.

23. Remini, *Andrew Jackson and the Course of American Democracy,* 185; Binder, *The Color Problem in Early National America,* 122–123; Rogin, *Fathers and Children,* 56; Remini, *The Legacy of Andrew Jackson,* 90.

24. Larry McKee, "'The Earth Is Their Witness': Archaeology is shedding new light on the secret lives of American slaves," in *The Sciences* (March/April 1995): 38.

25. Larry McKee, "Bread in Captivity: Did American slaves have a higher standard of living than previously thought?" *Earthwatch* (March/April 1996): 8–10; McKee, "The Earth Is Their Witness," 36–41.

26. Kemble, *Journal of a Residence on a Georgian Plantation,* 5; Thomas, "Community Among Enslaved Africans on The Hermitage Plantation," 128–129.

27. Remini, *Andrew Jackson and the Course of American Democracy,* 66.

28. Thomas, "Community Among En-slaved Africans on The Hermitage Plantation," 176–177.

29. Remini, *Andrew Jackson and the Course of American Empire,* 133.

30. Thomas, "Community Among En-slaved Africans on The Hermitage Plantation," 69.

31. Smith, *The Shaping of America,* 760.

32. Thomas Goldsmith, "Black woman says Andrew Jackson is her ancestor," July 9, 2000, www.tennessean.com.

33. Ralph Korngold, *Two Friends of Man: The Story of William Lloyd Garrison and Wendell Phillips and Their Relationship with Abraham Lincoln* (Boston: Little, Brown, 1950), 50.

34. Smith, *The Nation Comes of Age,* 604.

35. Leon F. Litwack, *North of Slavery: The Negro in the Free States, 1790–1860* (Chicago: University of Chicago Press, 1961), 102.

36. Pessen, *Jacksonian America,* 44; Litwack, *North of Slavery,* 98.

37. Litwack, *North of Slavery,* 224–229; Eugene H. Berwanger, "Negro Phobia in Northern Proslavery and Antislavery Thought," *Phylon* 33 (Fall 1972): 266–275.

38. Leonard A. Richards, *"Gentlemen of Property and Standing": Anti-Abolition Mobs in Jacksonian America* (New York: Oxford University Press, 1970), 82–88.

39. Remini, *Legacy,* 100; Richardson, *A Compilation of the Messages and Papers of the Presidents,* III, 175.

40. Remini, *The Legacy of Andrew Jackson,* 89–108.

41. Bemis, *John Quincy Adams and the Union,* 333.

42. Binder, *The Color Problem in Early National America,* 131–132; Remini, *Andrew Jackson and the Course of American Democracy,* 262.

43. Riegel, *Young America,* 101.

44. William Jerry MacLean, "Othello Scorned: The Racial Thought of John Quincy Adams," *Journal of the Early Republic* 4 (Summer 1984): 149, 151, 157, 158; Bemis, *John Quincy Adams and the Union,* 327.

45. Remini, *The Legacy of Andrew Jackson,* 104–105; Riegel, *Young America,* 299;

Bemis, *John Quincy Adams and the Union,* 348.

46. Remini, *Andrew Jackson and the Course of American Democracy,* 440–441.

47. Parton, *The Life of Andrew Jackson,* III, 605.

48. Remini, *Andrew Jackson and the Course of American Democracy,* 359; Binder, *The Color Problem in Early National America,* 135.

49. Riegel, *Young America,* 76.

50. Oakes, *The Ruling Race,* 74.

51. Remini, *The Legacy of Andrew Jackson,* 106.

52. Davis, *Old Hickory,* 365.

53. Roy P. Basler, ed., *The Collected Works of Abraham Lincoln,* 9 vols. (New Brunswick, N.J.: Rutgers University Press, 1953–1955), II, 130; William C. Davis, *Jefferson Davis: The Man and His Hour* (New York: HarperCollins, 1991), 114. The Confederacy included: Alabama, Arkansas, Florida, Georgia, Louisiana, Mississippi, North Carolina, South Carolina, Tennessee, Texas, Virginia.

54. James, *The Raven,* 406; James, *The Life of Andrew Jackson,* 618.

55. Victor Searcher, *Lincoln's Journey to Greatness* (Philadelphia: John C. Winston, 1960), 11.

VIII THE CHILDREN OF THE SOIL

1. Dale Van Every, *Disinherited: The Lost Birthright of the American Indian* (New York: William Morrow, 1966), 27; Remini, *Andrew Jackson and His Indian Wars,* 277–278.

2. Rogin, *Fathers and Children,* 209.

3. Genesis, 1:28; Rogin, *Fathers and Children,* 114, 117.

4. Francis Paul Prucha, *The Great Father: The United States Government and the American Indian* (Lincoln: University of Nebraska Press, 1984), 35–60.

5. Prucha, *The Great Father,* 135–138.

6. Jefferson, *Writings,* 1118, 1120; Drinnon, *Facing West,* 87.

7. Jahoda, *The Trail of Tears,* 39.

8. Wallace, *The Long Trail,* 121–122.

9. Van Every, *Disinherited,* 116.

10. Jahoda, *The Trail of Tears,* 43–44; Mark Derr, *The Frontiersman: The Real Life and the*

Many Legends of Davy Crockett (New York: William Morrow, 1993), 175.

11. Rogin, *Fathers and Children,* 225.

12. Remini, *Andrew Jackson and the Course of American Freedom,* 270.

13. Jahoda, *The Trail of Tears,* 87.

14. Ibid., 153–155.

15. Ibid., 137.

16. Ibid., 139–140. Cecil Eby tells the whole sad story in *That Disgraceful Affair: The Black Hawk War* (New York: W. W. Norton, 1973).

17. Jahoda, *The Trail of Tears,* 269.

18. Remini, *Andrew Jackson and the Course of American Democracy,* 308; Grant Foreman, *Indian Removal: The Emigration of the Five Civilized Tribes of Indians* (Norman: University of Oklahoma Press, 1956), 240; Jahoda, *The Trail of Tears,* 270–271.

19. Jahoda, *The Trail of Tears,* 244.

20. Riegel, *Young America,* 62; John Tebbel, *The Compact History of the Indian Wars* (New York: Hawthorn Books, 1966), 142.

21. Van Every, *Disinherited,* 58–61.

22. Ibid., 66–68; Henry T. Malone, *Cherokees of the Old South: A People in Transition* (Athens, Ga.: University of Georgia Press, 1956), 74–90; Wallace, *The Long Trail,* 62.

23. Van Every, *Disinherited,* 45; Oakes, *The Ruling Race,* 46, 47; Scott L. Malcomson, *One Drop of Blood: The American Misadventure of Race* (New York: Farrar Straus Giroux, 2000), 92.

24. Van Every, *Disinherited,* 144.

25. Ibid., 147; Remini, *Andrew Jackson and the Course of American Freedom,* 276–277.

26. Jahoda, *The Trail of Tears,* 224.

27. Van Every, *Disinherited,* 224.

28. Remini, *The Legacy of Andrew Jackson,* 72.

29. Remini, *Andrew Jackson and the Course of American Democracy,* 301; Jahoda, *The Trail of Tears,* 224.

30. Ibid., 229–230.

31. Van Every, *Disinherited,* 242–243.

32. Jahoda, *The Trail of Tears,* 232–234.

33. Ibid., 236.

34. Foreman, *Indian Removal,* 304–306.

35. Rogin, *Fathers and Children,* 247; Van Every, *Disinherited,* 249; Jahoda, *The Trail of Tears,* 235.

36. Smith, *America Comes of Age*, 108.
37. Remini, *Andrew Jackson and the Course of American Freedom*, 221.

IX AN OLD, OLD MAN

1. Remini, *Andrew Jackson and the Course of American Freedom*, 375.
2. Parton, *The Life of Andrew Jackson*, III, 618–619.
3. Remini, *Andrew Jackson and the Course of American Democracy*, 393–394.
4. Benton, *Thirty Years' View*, 735.
5. James, *The Life of Andrew Jackson*, 724.

6. Remini, *Andrew Jackson and the Course of American Democracy*, 425.
7. Parton, *The Life of Andrew Jackson*, III, 629.
8. Remini, *Andrew Jackson and the Course of American Democracy*, 432.
9. Parton, *The Life of Andrew Jackson*, III, 636–637.
10. Horn, *The Hermitage*, 154.
11. Remini, *Andrew Jackson and the Course of American Democracy*, 433.
12. Allan Nevins and Milton H. Thomas, eds., *The Diary of George Templeton Strong: Young Man in New York, 1835–1875*, 4 vols. (New York: Macmillan, 1952), I, 55–65.

13. Remini, *Andrew Jackson and the Course of American Democracy*, 470.
14. Horn, *The Hermitage*, 200–201.
15. Parton, *The Life of Andrew Jackson*, III, 658.
16. James, *The Life of Andrew Jackson*, 775.
17. Remini, *Andrew Jackson and the Course of American Democracy*, 519; Davis, *Old Hickory*, 283; Burstein, *The Passions of Andrew Jackson*, 215–216.
18. Parton, *The Life of Andrew Jackson*, III, 371.
19. James, *The Raven*, 357.

ADDITIONAL READING

Alistair Cooke's America. New York: Alfred A. Knopf, 1973.

Axtell, James. "The White Indians of Colonial America," *William & Mary Quarterly* 32, 1975.

Barber, James G. *Old Hickory: A Life Sketch of Andrew Jackson.* Washington, D.C.: National Portrait Gallery, 1990.

Bassett, John Spencer, ed., *The Correspondence of Andrew Jackson.* 6 vols. Washington: Government Printing Office, 1926–1933.

———. *The Life of Andrew Jackson.* New York: Macmillan, 1928.

Bemis, Samuel Flagg. *John Quincy Adams and the Foundations of American Foreign Policy.* New York: Alfred A. Knopf, 1949.

———. *John Quincy Adams and the Union.* New York: Alfred A. Knopf, 1956.

Benton, Thomas Hart. *Thirty Years' View: A History of the Working of the American Government for Thirty Years, 1820–1850.* New York: D. Appleton & Company, 1854.

Bergman, Virginia. *The Florida Wars.* Hamden, CT: Archon Books, 1979.

Berwanger, Eugene H. "Negro Phobia in Northern Proslavery and Antislavery Thought," *Phylon* 33 (Fall 1972): 266–275.

Binder, Frederick M. *The Color Problem in Early National America as Viewed by John Adams, Jefferson and Jackson.* Mouton: The Hague, 1968.

Booraem, Hendrik. *Young Hickory: The Making of Andrew Jackson.* Dallas: Taylor Trade Publishing, 2001.

Boorstin, Daniel J. *The Americans: The National Experience.* New York: Random House, 1965.

Buell, Augustus C. *History of Andrew Jackson.* 2 vols. New York: Charles Scribner's Sons, 1904.

Burstein, Andrew. *The Passions of Andrew Jackson.* New York: Alfred A. Knopf, 2003.

Cain, William E., ed. *William Lloyd Garrison and the Fight Against Slavery: Selections from* The Liberator. New York: Bedford Books, 1994.

Coit, Margaret L. *Andrew Jackson.* Boston: Houghton Mifflin, 1965.

———. *John C. Calhoun.* Boston: Houghton Mifflin, 1950.

Cole, Donald B. *The Presidency of Andrew Jackson.* Lawrence: University Press of Kansas, 1993.

Coombs, Edith, ed. *America Visited.* New York: Book League of America, nd.

Crété, Liliane. *Daily Life in Louisiana, 1815–1830.* Baton Rouge: Louisiana State University Press, 1978.

Crockett, Davy. *The Autobiography of Davy Crockett.* New York: Charles Scribner's Sons, 1923.

Curtis, James C. *Andrew Jackson and the Search for Vindication.* New York: Longman, 1975.

Dangerfield, George. *The Awakening of American Nationalism, 1815–1828.* New York: Harper & Row, 1965.

———. *The Era of Good Feelings.* New York: Harcourt, Brace, 1952.

Davis, Burke. *Old Hickory: A Life of Andrew Jackson.* New York: The Dial Press, 1977.

Davis, William C. *Three Roads to the Alamo: The Lives and Fortunes of David Crockett, James Bowie, and William Barret Travis.* New York: HarperCollins, 1998.

Degler, Carl N. *At Odds: Women and the Family from the Revolution to the Present.* New York: Oxford University Press, 1980.

Derr, Mark. *The Frontiersman: The Real Life and the Many Legends of Davy Crockett.* New York: William Morrow, 1993.

Dickens, Charles. *American Notes.* Books, Inc.: New York, n.d. A reprint of a book first published in London in 1842.

Drinnon, Richard. *Facing West: Indian Hating and Empire Building.* New York: Schocken Books, 1990.

Eby, Cecil. *That Disgraceful Affair: The Black Hawk War.* New York: W. W. Norton, 1973.

Ehle, John. *Trail of Tears: The Rise and Fall of the Cherokee Nation.* New York: Doubleday, 1988.

Filler, Louis. *Crusade Against Slavery: Friends, Foes, and Reforms, 1820–1860.* Algonac, Michigan: Reference Publications, 1986.

Fischer, David Hackett. *Albion's Seed: Four British Folkways in America.* New York: Oxford University Press, 1989.

Foreman, Grant. *Indian Removal: The Emigration of the Five Civilized Tribes of Indians.* Norman: University of Oklahoma Press, 1956.

———. *Sequoyah.* Norman: University of Oklahoma Press, 1938.

Franklin, John Hope. *From Slavery to Freedom: A History of American Negroes.* New York: Alfred A. Knopf, 1960.

——— and Loren Schweninger. *Runaway Slaves: Rebels on the Plantation.* New York: Oxford University Press, 1999.

Freeling, William W. *Prelude to Civil War: The Nullification Controversy in South Carolina, 1816–1836.* New York: Harper & Row, 1965.

Gelb, Norman. *Less Than Glory.* New York: G. P. Putnam's Sons, 1984.

Gossett, Thomas F. *Race: The History of an Idea in America.* New York: Schocken Books, 1965.

Griffin, Patrick. *The People with No Name: Ireland's Ulster Scots, America's Scots Irish, and the Creation of a British Atlantic World, 1689–1764.* Princeton: Princeton University Press, 2001.

Grummond, Jane Lucas de. *The Baratarians and the Battle of New Orleans.* Baton Rouge: Louisiana State University Press, 1961.

Halbert, Henry Sale, and Timothy Horton Ball. *The Creek War of 1813–1814.* University, Ala.: University of Alabama Press, 1969 [1895].

Hall, Captain Basil. *Travels in North America in the Years 1827 and 1828.* In Nevins, *American Social History,* 139–158.

Hecht, Marie B. *John Quincy Adams: A Personal History of an Independent Man.* New York: Macmillan, 1972.

Hickey, David R. *The War of 1812.* Urbana: University of Illinois Press, 1989.

Hofstadter, Richard. *The American Political Tradition and the Men Who Made It.* New York: Alfred A. Knopf, 1948.

Horn, Stanley F. *The Hermitage: Home of Old Hickory.* Nashville: Ladies' Hermitage Association, 1950.

Jahoda, Gloria. *The Trail of Tears: The American Indian Removals, 1813–1855.* London: Book Club Associates, 1976.

James, Marquis. *Andrew Jackson: The Border Captain.* New York: The Bobbs-Merrill Company, 1933. This volume, published separately, is the first part of James's masterpiece, *The Life of Andrew Jackson.*

———. *The Life of Andrew Jackson.* 2 vols. Indianapolis: Bobbs-Merrill, 1938.

———. *The Raven: A Biography of Sam Houston.* New York: Blue Ribbon Books, 1929.

Jennings, Francis. *The Invasion of America: Indians, Colonialism, and the Cant of Conquest.* New York: W. W. Norton, 1976.

Johnson, Paul. *A History of the American People.* London: Weidenfeld & Nicolson, 1997.

———. *The Birth of the Modern: World Society 1815–1830.* New York: HarperCollins, 1991.

Jordan, Winthrop D. *White Over Black: American Attitudes Toward the Negro, 1550–1812.* Chapel Hill: University of North Carolina Press, 1968.

Kemble, Frances Anne. *Journal of a Residence on a Georgian Plantation in 1838–1839.* New York: Alfred A. Knopf, 1961.

Kolchin, Peter. *American Slavery, 1619–1877.* New York: Hill & Wang, 1993.

Korngold, Ralph. *Two Friends of Man: The Story of William Lloyd Garrison and Wendell Phillips and Their Relationship with Abraham Lincoln.* Boston: Little, Brown and Company, 1950.

Leckie, Robert. *From Sea to Shining Sea: From the War of 1812 to the Mexican War, the Saga of America's Expansion.* New York: HarperPerennial, 1993.

Leyburn, James G. *The Scotch-Irish: A Social History.* Chapel Hill: University of North Carolina Press, 1962.

Litwack, Leon F. *North of Slavery: The Negro in the Free States, 1790–1860.* Chicago: University of Chicago Press, 1961.

MacLean, William Jerry. "Othello Scorned: The Racial Thought of John Quincy Adams." *Journal of the Early Republic* 4 (Summer 1984): 143–160.

Mahon, John K. *The History of the Seminole War.* Gainesville: University of Florida Press, 1967.

Malcomson, Scott L. *One Drop of Blood: The American Misadventure of Race.* New York: Farrar Straus Giroux, 2000.

Malone, Henry T. *Cherokees of the Old South: A People in Transition.* Athens, Ga.: University of Georgia Press, 1956.

Marryat, Frederick. *A Diary in America.* New York: Alfred A. Knopf, 1962. Originally published in 1839.

Marszalek, John F. *The Petticoat Affair: Manners, Mutiny, and Sex in Andrew Jackson's White House.* New York: The Free Press, 1997.

Martineau, Harriet. *Society in America.* 3 vols. London: Saunders & Otley, 1837.

Mayer, Henry. *All on Fire: William Lloyd Garrison and the Abolition of Slavery.* New York: St. Martin's Press, 1998.

McCullough, David. *John Adams.* New York: Simon & Schuster, 2001.

McKee, Larry. "Bread in Captivity: Did American slaves have a higher standard of living than previously thought?" *Earthwatch* (March/April 1996): 8–10.

———— "The Earth Is Their Witness: Archaeology is shedding new light on the secret lives of American slaves," *The Science.* (March/April 1995): 36–41.

McReynolds, Edwin C. *The Seminoles.* Norman University of Oklahoma Press, 1957.

Miller, Charles, *Early Travelers in North America: Eyewitness Reports from the First Visitors to the New World.* Dover, N.H.: Alan Sutton, 1994.

Miller, William Lee. *Arguing About Slavery: The Great Battle in the United States Congress.* New York: Alfred A. Knopf, 1996.

Mittelberger, Gottlieb. *Journey to Pennsylvania.* Translated by Oscar Handlin and John Clive. Cambridge, Mass.: Harvard University Press, 1960.

Mooney, James. *Historical Sketch of the Cherokee.* Chicago: Aldine Publishing Company, 1975.

Morison, Samuel Eliot. *The Oxford History of the American People.* New York: Oxford University Press, 1965.

Nagel, Paul C. *John Quincy Adams: A Public Life, a Private Life.* New York: Alfred A. Knopf, 1997.

Nevins, Allan, ed. *American Social History as Recorded by British Travellers.* New York: Henry Holt, 1923.

———— and Milton H. Thomas, eds. *The Diary of George Templeton Strong: Young Man in New York, 1835–1875.* 4 vols. New York: Macmillan, 1952.

————. *The Diary of John Quincy Adams, 1794–1845.* New York: Charles Scribner's Sons, 1951.

————. *The Diary of Philip Hone, 1828–1851.* New York: Dodd, Mead and Company, 1927.

Nolte, Vincent. *The Memoirs of Vincent Nolte . . . or 50 years in Both Hemispheres.* New York: G. Howard Watt, 1934.

Nye, Russell Blaine. *Society and Culture in America, 1830–1860.* New York: Harper Torchbooks, 1974.

Oakes, James. *The Ruling Race: A History of American Slaveholders.* New York: Alfred A. Knopf, 1982.

Oates, Stephen B. *The Fires of Jubilee: Nat Turner's Fierce Rebellion.* New York: HarperPerennial, 1975.

Pacher, Marc, ed. *Abroad in America: Visitors to the New Nation, 1776–1914.* Reading, Mass.: Addison-Wesley, 1976.

Parton, James. *The Life of Andrew Jackson.* 3 vols. Boston: Houghton Mifflin, 1888.

Perdue, Theda, and Michael D. Green. *The Cherokee Removal: A Brief History with Documents.* New York: St. Martin's Press, 1995.

Pessen, Edward. *Jacksonian America: Society, Personality, and Politics.* Chicago: University of Illinois Press, 1985.

————, ed. *Jacksonian Panorama.* Indianapolis: Bobbs-Merrill, 1976.

Prucha, Francis Paul. *The Great Father: The United States Government and the American Indian.* Lincoln: University of Nebraska Press, 1984.

Reilly, Robin. *The British at the Gates: The New Orleans Campaign in the War of 1812.* New York: G. P. Putnam's Sons, 1974.

Remini, Robert V. *Andrew Jackson.* New York: Twayne Publishers, 1966.

————. *Andrew Jackson and the Course of American Democracy, 1833–1845.* Baltimore: The Johns Hopkins University Press, 1984.

————. *Andrew Jackson and the Course of American Empire, 1767–1821.* New York: Harper & Row, 1977.

————. *Andrew Jackson and the Course of American Freedom, 1822–1832.* New York: Harper & Row, 1981.

————. *Andrew Jackson and His Indian Wars.* New York: Viking, 2001.

————. *The Battle of New Orleans.* New York: Viking, 1999.

————. *Daniel Webster: The Man and His Time.* New York: W. W. Norton, 1997.

————. *Henry Clay: Statesman of the Union.* New York: W. W. Norton, 1991.

————. *John Quincy Adams.* New York: Times Books, 2002.

————. *The Legacy of Andrew Jackson: Essays on Democracy, Indian Removal, and Slavery.* Baton Rouge: Louisiana State University Press, 1988.

————. *Martin Van Buren and the Making of the Democratic Party.* New York: Columbia University Press, 1959.

Richards, Leonard A. *"Gentlemen of Property and Standing": Anti-Abolition Mobs in Jacksonian America.* New York: Oxford University Press, 1970.

Richardson, James D., ed. *A Compilation of the Messages and Papers of the Presidents.* 11 vols. Washington, D.C.: Government Printing Office, 1910.

Riegel, Robert E. *Young America, 1830–1840.* Norman: University of Oklahoma Press, 1949.

Rogin, Michael Paul. *Fathers and Children: Andrew Jackson and the Subjugation of the American Indian.* New York: Alfred A. Knopf, 1975.

Rorabaugh, W. J. *The Alcoholic Nation: An American Tradition.* New York: Oxford University Press, 1979.

Sale, Kirkpatrick. *The Fire of His Genius: Robert Fulton and the American Dream.* New York: The Free Press, 2001.

Schlesinger, Arthur M., Jr. *The Age of Jackson.* Boston: Little, Brown and Company, 1950.

Sellers, Charles, ed. *Andrew Jackson: A Profile.* New York: Hill and Wang, 1971.

————, ed. *Andrew Jackson: Nullification and the State-Rights Tradition.* Chicago: Rand McNally, 1963.

————. *The Market Revolution: Jacksonian America, 1815–1846.* New York: Oxford University Press, 1997.

Shackford, James A. *David Crockett: The Man and the Legend.* Chapel Hill: University of North Carolina Press, 1956.

Slater, Michael, ed. *Dickens on America and the Americans.* Austin: University of Texas Press, 1978.

Smith, Margaret B. *The First Forty Years of Washington Society.* Edited by Gaillard Hunt. New York: Charles Scribner's Sons, 1906.

Smith, Page. *The Nation Comes of Age.* New York: McGraw-Hill, 1981.

———. *The Shaping of America.* New York: McGraw-Hill, 1980.

Sugden, John. *Tecumseh: A Life.* New York: Henry Holt, 1998.

Taylor, George Rogers. *The Transportation Revolution, 1815–1860.* New York: Rinehart, 1958.

Tebbel, John. *The Compact History of the Indian Wars.* New York: Hawthorn Books, 1966.

Thomas, Brian William. "Community Among Enslaved Africans on the Hermitage Plantation, 1820s–1850s." Ph.D. diss., State University of New York at Binghamton, 1995.

———. "Power and Community: The Archaeology of Slavery at the Hermitage Plantation," *American Antiquity* 63, no. 4 (1998): 531–551.

Trollope, Frances. *Domestic Manners of the Americans.* St. James, N.Y.: Brandywine Press, 1993.

Tucker, Glen. *Tecumseh: The Vision of Glory.* New York: Russell & Russell, 1973.

Van Buren, Martin. *Autobiography.* New York: Chelsea House, 1983.

Van Deusen, Glyndon G. *The Jacksonian Era, 1828–1848.* New York: Harper Torchbooks, 1959.

Van Every, Dale. *Disinherited: The Lost Birthright of the American Indian.* New York: William Morrow, 1966.

Vogel, Virgil J. *This Country Was Ours: A Documentary History of the American Indian.* New York: Harper & Row, 1972.

Wallace, Anthony F. C. *The Long Trail: Andrew Jackson and the Indians.* New York: Hill and Wang, 1993.

Ward, John William. *Andrew Jackson: Symbol for an Age.* New York: Oxford University Press, 1955.

Watson, Harry L. *Andrew Jackson vs. Henry Clay: Democracy and Development in Antebellum America.* New York: Bedford/St. Martin's, 1998.

———. *An Independent People: The Way We Lived in North Carolina, 1770–1820.* Chapel Hill: University of North Carolina Press, 1982.

Whitney, Gordon G. *From Coastal Wilderness to Fruited Plain: A History of Environmental Change in Temperate North America, 1500 to the Present.* Cambridge, England: Cambridge University Press, 1994.

Williams, Jack K. *Dueling in the Old South.* College Station: Texas A&M University Press, 1980.

Williams, John Hoyt. *Sam Houston: A Biography of the Father of Texas.* New York: Simon & Schuster, 1993.

Woodward, Grace Steel. *The Cherokees.* Norman: University of Oklahoma Press, 1963.

INDEX

Page numbers in *italics* refer to illustrations.